War No More

War No More

Eliminating Conflict
in the Nuclear Age

Robert Hinde and Joseph Rotblat

Foreword by Robert S. McNamara

Pluto  Press

LONDON • STERLING, VIRGINIA

First published 2003 by Pluto Press
345 Archway Road, London N6 5AA
and 22883 Quicksilver Drive, Sterling, VA 20166-2012, USA

www.plutobooks.com

British Library Cataloguing in Publication Data
A catalogue record for this book is available from
the British Library

ISBN 0 7453 2192 5 hardback
ISBN 0 7453 2191 7 paperback

Library of Congress Cataloging in Publication Data
Hinde, Robert A.
    War no more : eliminating conflict in the nuclear age / Robert
Hinde and Joseph Rotblat ; foreword by Robert S. McNamara.
        p. cm.
    ISBN 0–7453–2192–5 (hbk.) — ISBN 0–7453–2191–7 (pbk.)
    1. War. 2. War—Prevention. I. Rotblat, Joseph, 1908– II. Title.

    U21.2.H545 2003
    355.02—dc21
                                                        2003013377

10   9   8   7   6   5   4   3   2   1

Designed and produced for Pluto Press by
Chase Publishing Services, Fortescue, Sidmouth, EX10 9QG, England
Typeset from disk by Stanford DTP Services, Towcester, England
Printed and bound in the European Union by
Antony Rowe Ltd, Chippenham and Eastbourne, England

Contents

III What Should Be Done to Eliminate War?

Acknowledgements

Our intention to write this book arose from an International Pugwash Conference on 'Eliminating the Causes of War', held at Cambridge University in August 2000.

We felt that the message from the conference should be disseminated more widely. We are grateful to all who gave papers at the Cambridge Conference for allowing us to use their material, but they bear no responsibility for the way in which we have done so. We are also grateful to the discussants in the Working Groups. We have, of course, made use of many sources in the literature.

At all stages in preparing this book we have been especially indebted to Dr Tom Milne. Not only did he make stimulating suggestions and constructive criticisms on our drafts, but he played a critical role in preparing the manuscript and assembling the figures and tables. We are also grateful to General Sir Hugh Beach, to Commodore J.W.H. Harris and to Mr R.A. Evans for reading and criticizing parts of the manuscript.

Robert Hinde
Joseph Rotblat

Foreword

My earliest memory as a child is of a city exploding with joy. The city was San Francisco. The date November 11, 1918 – Armistice Day. I was two years old. The city was celebrating not only the end of World War I, but the belief, held so strongly by President Wilson, and by many other Americans, that the United States and its allies had won a war to end all wars.

They were wrong, of course. The twentieth century was on its way to becoming the bloodiest in all of human history: during it, 160 million people were killed in conflicts – within nations and between nations – across the globe. Were similar conflicts to take place in the twenty-first century, when population will have risen three-fold and when wars are likely to be fought with weapons of mass destruction, fatalities would be substantially higher.

Is that what we want in the first century of the new millennium? I hope not.

If not, the time to initiate action to prevent that tragedy is now.

We should begin by establishing a realistic appraisal of the problem. It is readily apparent, very complex and very dangerous.

The Carnegie Commission chaired by the former US Secretary of State, Cyrus Vance and Dr David Hamburg, Chairman of the Carnegie Corporation, stated it very clearly when it said:

> Peace ... will require ... greater understanding and respect for differences within and across national boundaries. We humans do not have the luxury any longer of indulging our prejudices and ethnocentrism. They are anachronisms of our ancient past. The worldwide historical record is full of hateful and destructive behaviour based on religious, racial, political, ideological, and other distinctions – holy wars of one sort or another. Will such behaviour in the next century be expressed with weapons of mass destruction? If we cannot learn to accommodate each other respectfully in the twenty-first century, we could destroy each other at such a rate that humanity will have little to cherish.

It is that problem which this book addresses and, for that reason, it should be read not just by policy-makers, but by citizens of every

x War No More

country in the world. The authors are concerned primarily not with spelling out the consequences of war, but with how war can be abolished – or, at a minimum, how the risk of war can be reduced. No war has a simple cause, and the book identifies some of the multiple factors that interact to precipitate a state of war. These range from the personalities of leaders to the political system itself, so it is necessary to consider many levels of complexity. And once one understands the causes, we must ask how can war be avoided and, in an imperfect world, how can its effects be ameliorated when it does occur? The authors point to many paths that must be followed, and though none is likely to be sufficient on its own, they emphasize that recognition of the authority of the United Nations must be paramount.

These are issues that everyone should attempt to understand. It is not good enough to leave it to the politicians. The politicians are in reality servants of the people, not their masters. I welcome the opportunity to commend this book to individuals everywhere.

Robert S. McNamara
20 May 2003

Introduction

This book is written to convince you, the reader, that if our civilization – indeed, the human species – is to survive in this nuclear age, war of all types will have to be abolished and peaceful means found to solve disputes.

Over the centuries it has been the common view that war is an acceptable way of settling conflicts of interest. That is not to say that it has always been seen as the most desirable way, but as one readily to be undertaken. The principle has been, if you cannot get what you want by negotiation, then try force provided you stand a good chance of winning.

It is easy to feel that that will always be the case. Violent confrontations have been with us throughout human evolution. The history we have been taught has been punctuated by famous battles and humiliating defeats, by glorified victories and wholesale massacres. Wars have shaped political maps: they have been instrumental in creating new states and destroying old ones. But what has always been does not have to remain the case. Rather there are a number of reasons for thinking that war is no longer an acceptable way of solving disputes.

In the first place, war has always been horrible and future wars are likely to be even more so. Yet it is strangely possible not to perceive its horrors. The casualty figures of thousands or millions of dead and wounded convey little impression of the blood and guts of suffering, of naked fear gnawing at the entrails, of the waste of human endeavour. The figures tell us nothing of the suffering of many of the military survivors who have impoverished health for the rest of their lives, or who suffer from what used to be called 'shell-shock', later 'lack of moral fibre', and now more euphemistically 'post traumatic stress disorder'. And war is not limited to the military. In recent decades civilian casualties have been greater, even many times greater, than those of the military – no individual is safe. The figures tell us nothing of the long-drawn-out agony of the bereaved, or of the homelessness and hopelessness of the refugees. The material consequences are felt for years by the survivors – the destruction of their way of life, the need to start again and build up their lives anew.

And now the possible consequences of going to war are infinitely worse than they have ever been in the past. The invention of weapons of mass destruction – chemical weapons, new forms of biological weapons, and above all nuclear weapons – means that war could be even more devastating than it has been in the past.

Pause for a minute and try to imagine what it would be like if some of these things that you read about in the papers or see on the television happened to you. Not only the fear that you would feel if you had to face flame throwers or nuclear shells, but the prospect of having your loved ones killed or maimed in war. What if they were to disappear and you were never to know what happened to them? What if your home were destroyed, if you were forced to wander, begging for medical help or food, for the very necessities of life?

Second, whereas in the past combatants could go to war thinking that it would be an isolated affair, no business of anyone else, that is no longer the case. Modern technology has brought the remotest parts of the earth much closer together than they have ever been before. Financial interdependencies have brought some states into close relations with others, but have also created rivalries. And global communications have made people more conscious of similarities and differences in their outlooks, leading to feelings of brotherhood amongst some, and antagonism amongst others. Thus war anywhere is likely to have widespread repercussions.

Third, wars are increasingly occurring within and not between states, meaning that conflict is almost bound to entail massive civilian involvement. There are a variety of reasons for this. After several centuries of conflicts over territory and colonial conquests, most state boundaries, at least within Europe, have become settled. But during the Cold War the two sides supported opposing factions in many countries, and the conflicts started then gained a momentum of their own. In addition, the end of the Cold War led to a resurgence of ethnic and religious identity in many parts of the world. The United Nations has been restricted by its Charter from taking effective action about disputes within states, and a new approach is clearly needed.

Fourth, modern war, even and perhaps especially intra-state war, inevitably means refugees, the displacement of populations, and the disruption of food supplies. At this time there are many millions of displaced persons and refugees, people who have lost their homes and their way of life. They may be seeking to cross state boundaries into a country where they are not welcome. Massive international relief can sometimes ameliorate the situation in the short term, but the lives of the refugees are permanently disrupted.

Fifth, another reason why we must question the view that war is an acceptable way to solve conflicts concerns the waste of resources involved. Modern war is incredibly expensive. Cruise missiles, many hundreds of which were used in Iraq, cost a million dollars apiece. The US defence budget for 2003–04 was $382 billion before the war started, or over $1,300 per head of the population, and actual expenditure may have been much higher. This is money that could have been spent to improve the life both of US citizens and of those living elsewhere in the world. And the consequences of war are present even before hostilities start, for war requires leaders to extract from the country's resources those that will be consumed by war – resources that could be used to improve health, education and living conditions are squandered on the potential for destruction. The dissipation of resources in preparation for war has a very considerable effect on the way people live in the comfortable West: in parts of the Third World they have been devastating, and have led to widespread deprivation and starvation. The interests of different countries are now so intimately intertwined that even the preparations for war may have global repercussions.

Above all, nearly every instance of war is morally wrong. Just because it causes so much suffering to innocent people, just because it has so many adverse consequences on human well-being, just because it involves doing to others what we should not like to have done to us, it is simply not an acceptable way to behave. It may be, in rare cases, that it is necessary in self-defence, or that it is the only way to prevent a greater evil, but even then it is politically illegitimate unless it has the approval of the United Nations.

For these reasons, we insist that war must be abolished. The two of us are fully aware that the concept of a war-free world is for most people a fanciful idea, a far-fetched, unrealizable vision. But we are also cognizant of the fact that we live in a dynamic world, and that the application of new technologies that have so profoundly affected us in every walk of life call for a revision of some cherished traditions and the abandonment of long-held beliefs.

Scepticism about abolishing war is not surprising considering that violent confrontations have been with us throughout human evolution. It has even been suggested that war is in our genes. That is what has been said, and said too often, but there is no scientific evidence that war is necessarily part of our behaviour. Given certain circumstances humans can behave in the most incredibly brutal ways to our fellow beings. Individuals can kill each other, one group can eliminate another. But we also have the capacity for kindness, for being helpful to others, for being cooperative. Indeed, humans could never have lived in groups were that not the case. Social life is only possible because of our capacity for cooperation.

Our newspapers report murders and mayhem, rapes and torture because they are relatively unusual: the great majority of us do not experience them in our daily lives. But the newspapers do not report the countless acts of kindness that most of us encounter every day. The balance between the capacity for selfish assertiveness and that for cooperation and kindness is often a fine one, and depends on the history of the society and the lifetime experiences of the individual.

Early in human history groups of people competed with other groups for the necessities of life, and sometimes competition led to conflict and war. But these conditions no longer prevail: there is no longer any need for people to kill one another for survival. If, and we agree it is a big 'if', properly managed and equitably distributed, there could be enough food and other life necessities for everybody, even with the huge increase in world population that is occurring.

But the old habits have prevailed and other reasons than survival have been brought to the fore for waging war. The old habits prevailed even under the guise of preventing war. For thousands of years civilized society has been governed by the Roman dictum: *'Si vis pacem para bellum'*. (If you want peace prepare for war.)

Preparation for war means the existence of armed forces ready to go into battle at short notice; it means the possession of weapons of some sort with which to harm the opponents. In Rwanda, pangas were mostly sufficient, but usually the weapons must be much more sophisticated than that.

Not only is the possession of weapons a *sine qua non* for engaging in war activities, but the existence of military arsenals may provide the impetus for starting war. The development of new instruments of combat, giving a state a decisive military superiority, may induce it to initiate a war before a perceived enemy acquires the new technology. The fact is that throughout the centuries, preparation for war, in order to secure peace, has usually brought not peace but war.

Over the centuries, the nature, scale and ferocity of wars have been changing. The advances in science and technology have decidedly changed our day-to-day life for the better; they have given us the possibility to talk with one another across the globe, to meet others from distant continents, to understand one another, to help one another, but they have also brought greater efficiency in warfare.

They are broadening ever more the areas afflicted by war activities, and reducing the cost of killing, whether civilian or military.

The ultimate advance in efficient warfare was achieved with the development of nuclear weapons, with their unprecedented potential for causing death and injury not only to the combatants but to the population anywhere on the globe. At one stage during the Cold War, the arsenals of the then superpowers, the United States and the Soviet Union, had a cumulative destructive power equivalent to 20,000 megatons of TNT (the total of all explosives in all wars before the nuclear age was less than 5 megatons). If detonated, this would have been enough to destroy not only the whole of our civilization but possibly the whole of the human species and many animal species. It is indeed the chief characteristic of the nuclear age that for the first time in history humankind has acquired the technical means to bring its own species to an end in a single act.

We are told that nuclear arsenals, albeit of a smaller size, are necessary to maintain peace. The old Roman dictum has been changed to 'Si vis pacem para arma' (If you want peace stay armed to the teeth), but this time, a failure of this policy could mean the end of humanity.

An agreement to eliminate all existing nuclear arsenals, highly desirable though this would be in removing the immediate danger, would not be sufficient to secure the future of humankind. Nuclear weapons cannot be disinvented. If, in the future, we take the wrong road and a conflict occurs between the great powers of the day, it would not take long to rebuild nuclear arsenals, and we would be back to the Cold War situation – and that might lead to a devastating nuclear exchange. This is the reason why, for world security in the long term, we have to take the big step: elimination of war itself. We have to do it however difficult this may be; there is no other choice. In this nuclear age we simply cannot afford to have war, any war, because even a limited armed conflict could escalate into a nuclear holocaust.

In order to bring the institution of war to an end we need to understand it better. What are the factors that contribute to the outbreak of war? Why are people willing to go to war? What can be done to prevent war? These are the subjects of this book.

Robert Hinde
Joseph Rotblat

Cambridge and London
June 2003

I
Of War and Its Weapons

1   The Diversity of Wars

What is war? By common definition, wars involve violence. Conflicts, disputes, differences of opinion, negotiations and so on are not wars until violence erupts. Conflicts of interest between states and between groups within states are frequent. They may involve resources, boundaries, security, class differences, ideological differences, individual ambitions, and many other factors. Social incompatibilities of one sort or another are ubiquitous, but not all lead to violence. Some political scientists maintain that, given the diversity of modern societies and their situations, conflicts of interest are inevitable, but violence is not. A dispute over resources, rights, borders, religion, or what have you, may be a necessary condition for a violent conflict to occur, but is rarely sufficient. Indeed, as we shall emphasize in a number of contexts, it is seldom possible to point to any one factor as a sufficient cause of any particular war: violence occurs when a number come together.

Wars are diverse, and we could launch into a long discussion about what should and what should not be called a war. It is questionable whether, when President G.W. Bush declared 'war' against a largely unidentified group of terrorists, it should really have qualified as such. The border dispute between Nigeria and Cameroon has resulted in a considerable number of casualties, but does it qualify as war? And what about Northern Ireland, where there were no independent authorities with their own armies and running their own areas of country, but a steady toll of casualties? Some wars are rarely reported in the West, like the long-drawn-out attempts by the Burmese (now Myanamarese) government to subdue the Karen.

Some authorities have taken the criterion of 1,000 battle fatalities a year as a threshold after which a dispute is properly labelled as war. Others prefer 25 casualties a year and a cumulative total of 1,000. But such criteria would be useless for many purposes for their use would mean postponing the decision as to whether an outbreak of violence constituted a war until it was too late to stop the escalation to violence, and until much suffering had already been caused. And do civilian casualties count as battle fatalities? If they do not, a very distorted picture could arise. For instance the Vietnam War (1965–73) is estimated to have involved about a million military combat deaths,

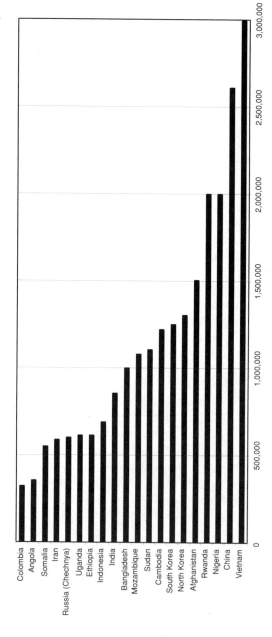

Figure 1 War-related deaths, 1945–2000

Source: *The Illustrated Book of World Rankings: Fifth Edition*, G.T. Kurian ed. (Armonk, NY: M.E. Sharpe, February 2001).

but three times as many deaths in all (Figure 1). For Cambodia the figures are of the order of 160,000 military deaths and 1,200,000 deaths in total.

In any case, in recent decades wars have often been preceded or accompanied by covert operations, arms supplies and even assassinations, carried out by countries that had no public role in the emerging conflict. For instance, the CIA operated for the USA behind the scenes in Chile, Nicaragua, Salvador and Angola, and gave aid to the Mujahideen when the Soviet Union invaded Afghanistan.

In some such cases the distinction between terrorism and international war becomes far from clear. Thus actions in 2002 described by Israel as involving the suppression of Palestinian terrorism were themselves described as terrorism by others. In El Salvador the USA organized a mercenary army whose aim was to subdue the civilian population – a civilian population which, according to Archbishop Oscar Romero, was 'fighting to defend their most fundamental human rights'. The Archbishop was later assassinated by elements of the USA-backed security forces. Again, should the Israeli bombing of Tunis in 1985, or the bombing of Tripoli by the USA a year later, be seen as acts of war or as international terrorism? Actions traced to Lebanese citizens, like the hijacking of an airliner in Karachi, and massacres in Rome and Vienna, seem comparable to these actions by Israel and the USA, but were labelled as terrorism. And more recently the 11 September 2001 terrorist attacks on New York and Washington have been taken as justifying a declaration of war by President G.W. Bush – a declaration which aptly described the military action, though the prisoners who were subsequently taken were not treated as prisoners-of-war according to international standards.

For such reasons, it is rarely profitable to attempt to put precise limits on such a heterogeneous category. We do better to recognize that wars are diverse, and that they differ along many dimensions that are not just matters of scale. For instance, if the dispute is international, taking place between states, the means for its resolution are likely to be quite different from those necessary if it involves conflicting groups within a state. In the past most wars were international, but at present wars between states are far less frequent than intra-state wars. Among the few exceptions in the second half of the twentieth century have been the Iran–Iraq War, the Gulf wars, the conflicts between Israel and the Arab states, India and Pakistan, and within Africa.

Some of the intra-state wars have been incredibly protracted: that between the security forces and armed opposition groups in Colombia has been going on for 38 years and involved mainly civilian deaths. In such cases, do armies confront each other, or is it a matter of guerrilla bands? Is it a civil war between political, religious or ethnic groups, or a liberation movement operating initially from outside the country concerned? Many recent wars have involved attempts to eliminate conventional forces by attrition or conversion: the antagonists have aimed not at the acquisition of territory, but rather to win over the local population to their viewpoint, and to get rid of those who cannot share it. Again, are democratic or totalitarian groups involved, or is it a conflict between groups with differing political ideologies? The transition from totalitarianism or militarism to democracy, or vice versa, can involve a period of instability during which violence may easily break out. Is the violence between organized groups of individuals, or between undifferentiated mobs? What sorts of weapons are involved? How organized are the warring parties? Were those involved mercenaries, conscripts, or loyal idealists? We could say that war is simply the use of violent means to achieve political ends, but that begs many questions, not the least being what counts as a political end. Should the greed or ambition of a military leader be dignified by being called a 'political end'? In this book we have taken a broad perspective and, in seeking to understand the bases of war, we discuss violent conflict within states and terrorism as well as international war.

The diversity of wars implies even greater diversity in their causes. Only two decades ago the major problem seemed to be the threat of war between the superpowers, with the probability of its leading to a nuclear exchange. Many of the other wars then occurring around the world could be seen as proxy wars, instigated or supported by the major powers. But it now seems that the Cold War situation, while encouraging some wars, had a restraining influence on others. Since the Cold War ended wars have broken out within states and between states in many parts of the world. Many of these started because repressive regimes, formerly supported by one of the superpowers, were challenged from within. Lack of democratic governance, economic factors, the greed of leaders (for instance, the acquisition of drugs in Colombia, diamonds and minerals in Africa, timber in Cambodia), and many other factors have fuelled the flames. And, more recently, actions perceived as involving excessive hegemony by the USA were seen by many as partly responsible for the 11 September terrorist attack resulting in thousands of fatalities.

To give some indication of the scale of the problem, it is estimated that, during the twentieth century, over 100 million people died in armed conflict and a further 170 million in political violence. Although the frequency of wars has decreased since the end of the Cold War, there has been an increase in the proportion of civilian deaths – around 90 per cent according to most estimates. And, though we have mentioned it already, it cannot be too strongly emphasized that casualty figures, though horrifying in themselves, represent only a fraction of the suffering caused by war. For every person killed, it is likely that at least one or two are bereaved, and perhaps thereby scarred for life. Many of those disabled become dependent on others for the rest of their lives. Many combatants never fully recover from the psychological horror of war. Refugees and even the migration of whole populations frequently accompany war. Families are torn apart, with children deprived of the care that they need. Not only did at least two million die as a result of the Rwandan conflict, but a UNICEF estimate indicated that it produced 95,000 unattached orphans and other unattached children. A random survey of these found that 91 per cent had lost family members, and 42 per cent both parents; 48 per cent had been threatened with death themselves, 64 per cent had witnessed massacres, 20 per cent had witnessed rapes and 25 per cent had been injured.

In the next three chapters we consider how modern weapons of mass destruction, and even modern so-called 'conventional weapons', have the potential to make future wars even more devastating than those in the past.

CONCLUSION

Wars are diverse, and there can be no generally accepted definition of what constitutes a war. For that reason alone, one cannot expect the causes of wars to be simple. Whatever the cause, wars are resulting in ever more fatalities and in an ever greater proportion of non-combatant casualties.

2   The Nuclear Peril

THE RISK OF A NUCLEAR WAR

The nuclear age began in August 1945, with the detonation of atomic bombs on Hiroshima and Nagasaki. The vast majority (about 85 per cent) of people alive today (2003) were born into the nuclear age. And since no further nuclear weapons have been used in combat, it is easy to understand that most people believe that we have 'learned to live with the bomb', and there is no need to be worried about it. Indeed, this belief turned into a conviction after the end of the Cold War, followed by the collapse of the Soviet Union in 1989, and the virtual end of the ideological struggle between capitalism and communism. This struggle, which had been going on since the October Revolution of 1918, had been the cause of much tension and even of many wars, mostly in former colonial countries (see pp. 62, 98).

> If the radiance of a thousand suns
> were to burst at once into the sky,
> That would be like the splendour of the Mighty One ...
> I am become Death,
> The Shatterer of Worlds.
>
> *The Bhagavad-Gita*

   That most people are not worried about the nuclear peril is evident from the findings of many opinion polls. An example is seen in the graph (Figure 2) representing results of a public opinion poll in the UK, which has been conducted systematically, every month, for the last 20 years. The graph presents the combined response to two questions: (1) What would you say is the most important issue facing Britain today? (2) What do you see as other important issues facing Britain today? At one time, over 40 per cent rated nuclear disarmament and nuclear weapons as among the most important issues, but the percentage of respondents giving such answers decreased rapidly, and ever since the end of the Cold War has remained very low, at about 1 per cent. From various indicators it would appear that the response in the United States and other countries in the West would be similar.

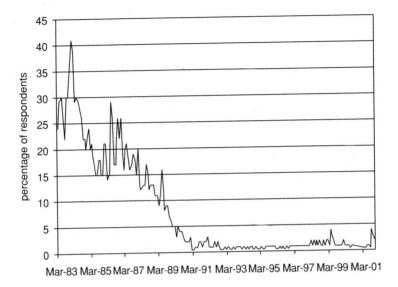

Figure 2   Salience of nuclear weapons issues in UK public opinion

Source: British Public Opinion: A Newsletter Reviewing the Results of Polls conducted by *Market and Opinion Research International* (MORI). Volumes I–XXIV (1983–2001).

The generally held belief that a third world war was prevented by the existence of nuclear warheads, and that their presence in the arsenals is no cause for worry, is an illusion. For one thing, although nuclear weapons were not used in war, many of them were exploded in testing various designs of these weapons (a total of 2,051, see Table 1). In the early years, much of the testing was carried out in the atmosphere, and the radioactive products of these tests, the fall-out, spread all over the globe, exposing people to varying doses of radiation. It has been estimated that the 528 nuclear tests in the atmosphere may cause about 300,000 deaths, mostly from cancer. Not enough is known about human casualties from Soviet tests, but anecdotal evidence indicates that the Soviet authorities were much more lax in protecting the population in the test areas, leading to higher casualty figures.

Table 1   Nuclear tests 1945–98

	Number of Tests		Total Yield (megatons)	
	Atmospheric	Underg'nd	Atmospheric	Underg'nd
USA	215	815	141	38
USSR	219	496	247	38
UK	21	24	8	1
France	50	160	10	4
China	23	22	22	1.5
India	0	4		~0.06
Pakistan	0	2		~0.05
TOTAL	**528**	**1,523**	**428**	**~83**

Source: *The Bulletin of the Atomic Scientists*, November/December 1998.

The main threat, however, arises from the very existence of nuclear weapons. Thousands of these weapons are kept in the arsenals, presumably for deterrence purposes, to prevent a perceived enemy from launching an attack on us, but sooner or later they will be used, deliberately or inadvertently. There is a historical precedent for this: the reason the Allies began developing the atom bomb during the Second World War was specifically to *prevent* its use by Hitler, yet nuclear weapons were used against Japan as soon as they were made. On several occasions we came perilously close to their deliberate use again. Eisenhower considered their use in the Korean War (1952–53), and this was repeated a few years later in the Taiwan crises. China developed its own nuclear weapons in response to what it saw as nuclear blackmail by the USA. Perhaps the best-known event was the Cuban Missile Crisis, in October 1962, when we were a hair's breadth away from a nuclear holocaust. There were also several false alarms: in one case a flock of geese was mistaken for nuclear missiles and triggered an alert, fortunately without serious consequences.

The indefinite combination of nuclear weapons and human fallibility will lead to a nuclear exchange.

Robert S. McNamara (speech at The Royal Society, 1992)

A vivid reminder of the nuclear threat occurred in May 2002, during the India–Pakistan crisis over Kashmir; we were officially warned that a conventional war there might escalate into a nuclear exchange. This crisis has been resolved, but only temporarily; the nuclear danger will remain as long as the conflict over Kashmir continues, or as long as nuclear weapons are held by either side.

Moreover, ever since the events of 11 September we have been told that terrorist groups of the al-Qaeda type may acquire nuclear devices with which to threaten the Western world. This threat too will exist as long as nuclear weapons exist, or as long as materials suitable for nuclear weapons are being stored in many places, not always adequately protected.

Above all, the threat of nuclear weapons being used in combat has increased dramatically following the new doctrines introduced by the G.W. Bush administration. Under these, nuclear weapons have become a standard part of military strategy, to be used in conflict just like any other high explosive; moreover, nuclear weapons may be employed in a pre-emptive attack.

Among most of the people who have studied these problems, there is a general feeling that the avoidance of a nuclear exchange so far has more to do with good luck than with good management. And we cannot rest the security of the world on good luck. The lesson of the past 50 years is that while the probability of a nuclear war occurring at a given moment is very low, the consequences should such a war occur are so grave as to make the risk factor unacceptable. The risk factor is obtained by multiplying the probability of the occurrence of a given event by the magnitude of the harm it would do, should it occur. We, the authors of this book, are convinced that the risk factor, taken over a long period of time, is so high that we must undertake the seemingly unrealistic task of eliminating all nuclear weapons as a first step towards the elimination of war altogether.

In order to persuade the reader of the same, we need to have a look at the consequences of a nuclear war. This was the topic of much discussion in the early years of the Cold War, but it seems to have been forgotten, or pushed into the deep recesses of our consciousness, in later years. It is time for a reminder.

THE DESTRUCTIVE POWER OF NUCLEAR WEAPONS

The blast wave

We must try to convey to you the magnitude of the destructive power of nuclear weapons. The yield of the Hiroshima bomb was about 13 kilotons, which means that the explosive power of the bomb (the blast wave that demolishes buildings and kills or maims people in the vicinity) was the same as would have resulted from the detonation of 13,000 tonnes of ordinary explosives, such as TNT. Our direct experience of bomb explosions is, fortunately, very limited, but we see often enough on television the terrible destruction and carnage produced by suicide bombers or other terrorist groups. The explosive power of these bombs is usually a few kilograms, perhaps a few tens of kilograms, of TNT. We are nauseated by the sight of mutilated bodies caused by bombs with an explosive power *a million times* smaller than that used on Hiroshima.

In war operations, much larger explosives are used. Some of the bombs used during the Second World War had an explosive power of several tonnes of TNT – bombs of that magnitude were also used in more recent wars, over Kosovo, and against the Taliban in Afghanistan. But even in comparison with these, the Hiroshima bomb – a primitive device in terms of modern nuclear warheads – was gigantic, about three orders of magnitude (1,000 times) more powerful than the largest conventional weapons.

It is difficult to imagine what such a quantum leap in destructive power means in terms of human casualties. Above a certain threshold, our senses become numb; a hundred times, a thousand

Figure 3   Hiroshima after atomic bombing

times, a million times, the difference ceases to have any meaning. Stalin is reputed to have said: 'the death of one person is a tragedy; the death of a million people is a matter for statistics'. Perhaps a better grip of the qualitative difference between nuclear and conventional explosions can be obtained by looking at the material damage, the destruction of buildings. The photograph of Hiroshima after the bombing (Figure 3), with the whole city laid waste, gives us a better idea of what nuclear weapons can do.

The enormous destructive power, and the horrendous human casualties, are not by themselves a feature unique to nuclear weapons. The same effects can be obtained with conventional explosives, as for example was the case with the air raid on Tokyo in January 1945. But in the latter case more than a thousand aircraft had to be used, and this makes for a qualitative difference between conventional and nuclear warfare.

Conventional wars are (or used to be) conducted according to certain conventions designed to protect civilian populations. In a conventional air raid, each aircraft has a specific target: a military facility, a communications centre, an industrial object, the destruction of which can perhaps be justified in terms of war strategy. Mistakes occur, of course, and civilians are killed; this is euphemistically referred to as collateral damage. Despite the huge progress in precision bombing since the Second World War, many such mistakes were made in the raids on Belgrade and other Serbian centres during the Kosovo war; but in principle the civilian populations were not meant to be harmed. Unfortunately there have been many departures from this principle. During the Second World War area bombing on primarily civilian targets in Germany and Japan resulted in hundreds of thousands of civilian casualties. This culminated in the use of nuclear weapons on Hiroshima and Nagasaki. A single nuclear weapon produces the same destruction as a thousand bombers, and targets almost inevitably include a large populated area, and enormous civilian casualties are the unavoidable outcome. Nuclear weapons are indiscriminate, and this makes them weapons of mass destruction. The conventions about the conduct of war governing the behaviour of a civilized community include issues such as proportionality in the choice of weapons employed, avoidance of non-military targets, and so on, but these considerations cannot be maintained with nuclear weapons. The use of nuclear weapons is illegal. This was in essence the conclusion of the International Court of Justice when, in its pronouncement on the subject in 1996, it said: ' ... the threat or use of nuclear weapons would generally be contrary to the rules of international law applicable in armed conflict, and in particular the principles and rules of humanitarian law' (see also pp. 141–4, 147–66).

Heat wave

The damage caused by the blast wave is only one of the effects of nuclear weapons. These weapons are also powerful incendiaries; they kill by radiation, and can cause much suffering by the destruction of the environment. All these effects add to the uniqueness of nuclear warfare.

At the instant of the detonation the temperature in the fire ball of the atom bomb rises to tens of millions of degrees (it doesn't make much difference in which scale you measure it) and this gives rise to a wave of heat and light which has been described as 'brighter than a thousand suns'. The thermal radiation causes instantaneous death and starts fires over considerable distances, depending on the explosive yield of the bomb. For bombs of Hiroshima size (or bigger) the area affected by the heat wave is many times larger than the area of lethal damage from the blast effect. The individual fires started by the heat pulse may consolidate into one huge fire covering a large area. Such a firestorm may also coalesce into a single convective column, which blows inwards from an outside perimeter and creates temperatures of over 1,000 degrees Celsius, so that everything combustible within the area is destroyed. Another effect of the firestorm is that it sucks oxygen out of buildings, so that people in deep shelters are suffocated. Overall, in populated areas the heat effect produces many more casualties than the blast wave.

Radiation effects

A third effect of nuclear explosions is exposure to ionizing radiations. This can arise in two main ways: instantaneous and delayed. The first is the emission of gamma-rays and neutrons at the instant of the detonation. People caught in the open at a distance of several kilometres, depending on the yield of the bomb, may receive lethal doses of radiation. Death usually occurs within a few weeks of the exposure. In Hiroshima and Nagasaki, many people who miraculously escaped the heat and blast effects, died from exposure to these radiations.

The second way is from exposure to radiation emitted from the radioactive products of the bomb. The fission process in uranium or plutonium results in the production of vast amounts of radioactive materials (mostly unstable forms of ordinary elements) which decay, giving off beta and gamma rays. The half-lives of these materials cover a vast range: from a fraction of a second to many millions of years. If the detonation occurred at a low enough altitude for the fireball to touch the ground, the soil and other materials are sucked up with the strong after-winds, and get mixed with the radioactive materials. Subsequently, they fall to the ground at distances which depend on the direction and strength of the wind. This deposition of radioactive material constitutes the local fall-out. People in the affected areas may then inhale or ingest the radioactive materials and thus receive internally radiation doses which, although generally not lethal immediately, may result in death from cancer a long time after the event.

For explosions at higher altitudes there is no (or very little) local fall-out. The radioactive products are sucked up to great heights into the troposphere or stratosphere whence they may travel long distances before descending to the ground, where they form the global fall-out. By that time the concentration of the radioactivity is too low to cause acute effects, but the long-term effects, mainly cancers, may affect people for a long time anywhere on the globe.

After a single explosion, the number of victims of global fall-out is likely to be quite small, but if a large number of bombs were detonated – as would have been the case if the warheads in the arsenals accumulated during the Cold War years were used – the cumulative effect of exposure to the fall-out could be very serious; over a long period of time the casualties might be larger than from all the effects described earlier.

Nuclear winter

A fourth effect of nuclear warfare – nuclear winter – arises only when a large number of nuclear weapons are exploded. Huge quantities of dust and soot are thrown up into the atmosphere, at the simultaneous explosions of many high-yield weapons, which could result in the obscuring of much of the sun's rays for a considerable time. The resultant lowering of the temperature could result in an ecological disaster of unprecedented magnitude in the history of civilization. (An event of 65 million years ago, caused by an impact with an asteroid, is presumed to have been responsible for the extinction of the dinosaurs.)

We should point out that in the opinion of many scientists the probability of such an extreme event occurring is very low, but a 'mild' nuclear winter may be more plausible.

Electromagnetic pulse

Among the other effects of nuclear warfare, not directly hazardous to human beings, is the electromagnetic pulse. This is the emission of a short pulse of radiation similar in character to radio waves but millions of times stronger. Despite its short duration it may cause electrical surges and permanent damage to electrical equipment. It does not produce human casualties directly, but the disruption to electric power supplies and telephone and radio communications may add to the chaos after the war; it would certainly affect the chances of survival of injured persons.

THE NUCLEAR ARMS RACE

Having described briefly the effects of nuclear weapons we want now to take up – also briefly – the history of the development of these weapons. In an amazing sequence of events, the initial scientific-technological advances that increased the destructive potential of warfare a thousand-fold (in the fission bomb), subsequently led – driven by mainly political and ideological motivations – to a further thousand-fold increase in the destructive potential of individual weapons (in the hydrogen bomb). Following this, the sheer momentum of the arms race led to the accumulation of tens of thousands of these weapons. Thus, at the height of the Cold War, the arsenals of the two superpowers, the United States and the Soviet Union, contained weapons each with an explosive power *a million times* greater than those available before the nuclear age; and the cumulative explosive power in the arsenals was *four thousand times* greater than all the explosives used in wars throughout the course of history. How has such an unbelievable sequence of events come to pass?

As mentioned earlier, the initial motivation for starting research on the atom bomb (in which one of us, JR, was directly involved) was the fear felt by scientists in the West that Hitler might acquire the bomb and use it to win the war. The intention of these Western scientists was to *prevent* the use of the bomb, by anybody; they never intended that it would be used.

But other groups in the West – statesmen, military leaders, and some other scientists – had different ideas. Thus, General Leslie Groves, the overall head of the Manhattan Project (the name of the US programme for the development of nuclear weapons during the Second World War) saw the atom bomb from the very beginning as a means of suppressing the Soviets. Among the scientists adhering to this view, the leading figure was Edward Teller. His obsessive hatred of communism led him to the belief that scientists have the duty to build up the military strength of the 'free world' in defence against communism.

There was never from about 2 weeks from the time I took charge of this project any illusion on my part but that Russia was our enemy and that the project was conducted on that basis.

General Leslie Groves, *Now It Can Be Told: The Story of the Manhattan Project* (1954)

Such views undoubtedly had an influence on the decision of President Truman to use the bomb against civilian populations, without any warning. The official reason for using the bombs on Japanese cities was to bring the war to a rapid end and thus save many American (and Allied) lives, which would have been lost if Japan were to be conquered by conventional means. But there are plausible views that the war could have been brought to an end without such a military operation. The Japanese were willing to surrender on the same terms (safeguarding the Emperor) that were subsequently accepted in any case. But President Truman ignored these overtures. He was determined to use the bomb as a means of demonstrating to the Soviet Union the newly acquired enormous military superiority of the United States. For this, the bomb had to be used in a way that would maximize its destructive potential.

But this demonstration also had another effect. In people all over the world it invoked a feeling of abhorrence to this new means of indiscriminate mass killing, and a general call for the abolition of nuclear weapons. This call found expression in the very first UN resolution (January 1946), unanimously adopted by the General Assembly, to set up an Atomic Energy Commission entrusted with the task of eliminating from national arsenals nuclear weapons, as well as other weapons of mass destruction.

Foremost among the groups which expressed their opposition to any further use of nuclear weapons were American scientists, including many who had worked on the Manhattan Project. A committee set up by these scientists issued a report which recommended the creation of an International Atomic Development Agency which, *inter alia*, would ensure that the 'Manufacture of atomic bombs shall stop' and 'Existing bombs shall be disposed of ...'

The gist of these proposals was incorporated into the Baruch Plan, the official US policy on this issue, which was presented to the Atomic Energy Commission of the United Nations. The Baruch Plan begins with emotional language stressing the great dangers that have arisen from the development of nuclear weapons and the urgent need to deal with them. However – foreshadowing future US policies on the nuclear issue – the Baruch Plan included certain conditions, which quite clearly would not be acceptable to the Soviet Union. And indeed, the Plan was rejected by the Soviet delegation, and the first international attempt to control nuclear weapons ended in failure.

BARUCH PLAN

We are here to make a choice between the quick and the dead. That is our business.

Behind the black portent of the new atomic age lies a hope which, seized upon with faith, can work our salvation. If we fail, then we have damned every man to be the slave of Fear. Let us not deceive ourselves: We must elect World Peace or World Destruction.

The Soviets were in any case unhappy about having to negotiate from a position of weakness, with the Americans monopolizing the new weapons. They did their utmost to remove the inequality. Through their intelligence agencies, they knew from the very beginning about the work on the atom bomb that was going on in the UK. Already during the war, a few Soviet scientists began research on the atom bomb, and this effort gathered strength very rapidly after the news of the bombs on Hiroshima and Nagasaki. The success of the Soviet Project was greatly facilitated (and hastened by several years) as a result of the spying activities of Klaus Fuchs, who worked on the Manhattan Project in the Los Alamos Laboratory in New Mexico, and regularly reported to the Soviet scientists (through his contacts) about the progress made there. Thus, the Soviets were able to test their first nuclear weapon (an exact replica of the Nagasaki bomb) in August 1949, four years after Hiroshima; much sooner than expected by US politicians and military. The loss of the nuclear monopoly put the United States into a panic, and President Truman – against strong objections, mainly on moral grounds, from senior scientists – decided to go ahead at full speed with the development of the hydrogen bomb.

The hydrogen bomb is based on an entirely different principle from the fission bomb: fusion of light elements. In order to make it work (at least, at the present state of technology), it has to use a fission bomb to ignite it. Actually, work on the hydrogen bomb had begun in Los Alamos by Edward Teller even before the fission bomb was made. With the end of the Second World War, and most scientists having left Los Alamos, work there came to a near standstill; its main task was the preparation of tests of fission bombs. But after Truman's decision, the laboratory came back to life, in large part due to the efforts by Teller, who managed to recruit a new team of scientists.

Unlike the fission bomb, there is no practical limit to the explosive power of the hydrogen bomb. Although the efficiency of the fission bomb was increased by an order of magnitude over that of the primitive Hiroshima bomb (bringing it into the range of hundreds of kilotons), the hydrogen bomb brought the explosive power of nuclear weapons into the megaton range (millions of tons). The first proper hydrogen bomb, successfully tested in March 1954, had a yield of 15 megatons.

This time the Soviets were not behind. The Russian counterpart of Edward Teller (but only in this respect), was Andrei Sakharov who, on his own, solved the problem of making the hydrogen bomb, at about the same time as in the United States. Nikita Khrushchev seems to have been keen on testing ever larger bombs. The Soviet's largest test, in 1961, had an explosive yield of 58 megatons, that is, 4,500 times more powerful than the Hiroshima bomb. (It was actually

---

*Detailed studies have been carried out on the likely effects of the explosion of a single megaton nuclear weapon over Birmingham. The conclusion drawn is that the explosion would lead to the immediate death of about a third of the population, total destruction within a two mile radius of the bomb burst, and barely a house undamaged in the greater Birmingham area ... 'If one could concentrate into one focal moment all the destruction which Britain suffered in the Second World War, the picture would not be as bad as the one that needs to be conjured up when one talks of a single megaton weapon over a city.' In the case of a major attack of two megaton bombs on the UK's ten biggest cities it was speculated that the UK might **never** physically recover from such a blow.*

Solly Zuckerman, *Nuclear Illusion and Reality* (1982)

designed for a 100 megaton yield, but on Sakharov's insistence it was reduced by almost a half, to lessen the dose of radiation from its fall-out; it should be noted that the radioactive fall-out of the H-bomb can also be increased a thousand-fold.)

It did not take long for the Americans and Soviets to realize that there was not much point in having very large H-bombs. Almost any target can be destroyed with a bomb of less than a megaton, so the extra yield of bigger bombs is largely wasted. Although both US and Russian arsenals still contain a few multi-megaton bombs, the bulk of the current arsenals consist of H-bombs with yields of between 100 and 500 kilotons (see Table 2).

Table 2a   US nuclear forces (2002)

Type of Weapon	Range of Yields (kt)	Number of Warheads (active/spares)	Total Yield (Mt)
Strategic ICBM	170–335	1,700 (85)	527
SLBM	100–475	3,120 (172)	479
Bombers	0.3–1,000	1,660 (85)	
Non-Strategic	0.5–170	1,120 (40)	
Stored	0.3–170	2,700	
Strategic reserve		~5,000	
TOTAL		10,682 (+~5,000)	

Table 2b   Russian nuclear forces (2002)

Type of Weapon	Range of Yields (kt)	Number of Warheads (active/spares)	Total Yield (Mt)
Strategic ICBM	550–750	3,011	~2,000
SLBM	100–500	1,072	136
Bombers		868	
Non-Strategic		~ 3,380	
Stored/Reserve		~8,000–10,000	
TOTAL		~8,300 (+~8,000–10,000)	

Source: *Bulletin of the Atomic Scientists*, May/June 2002 (US forces) and July/August 2002 (Russian forces). The US strategic reserve comprises stored plutonium pits and thermonuclear secondaries.

With parity in the destructive capability of the weapons having been achieved by the two superpowers, the main feature of the arms race between them was then the number of warheads each side possessed. Figure 4, which gives the numbers of US and USSR warheads over the course of time, is testimony to the frenzy of the race and to its inherent madness. Within the space of two decades the US arsenal had grown from 3 to 30,000 warheads. Where on the earth could that number of enemy targets be found? At that time many of the weapons were still in the megaton range, so the total yield of the US arsenal amounted to the stupefying figure of 20,000 megatons. Less than one kilogram of TNT is needed to kill a human being; this means that (if evenly distributed) the US arsenals had sufficient power to kill every human being on this planet 5,000 times over!

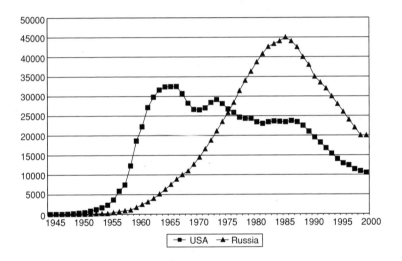

Figure 4   US/Russian nuclear warhead stockpiles, 1945–2000 (numbers of warheads)

Source: *Bulletin of the Atomic Scientists,* March/April 2000.

The main reasons for this ridiculous accumulation were: first, to make sure that enough weapons were left for a retaliatory attack, after a first attack by an enemy; and second, because of the possibility that a large number of one's own weapons would be shot down on their way to attack the enemy. Even so, there is no rational justification for that monstrous accumulation of weapons. In the later stages of the arms race both of these factors had been partly taken care of: one, by ensuring the survival of one's weapons after a first attack, by keeping the warheads in submarines and using mobile launchers, which are much more difficult to locate, and two, by making the failure rate of delivery much smaller, by using ballistic missiles for the attack. This is why after 1965 the number of US warheads began to decrease, while those of the Soviet Union, with their less sophisticated technology, were still increasing until about 1985. But for these very reasons, the decrease in the number of warheads does not mean a reduction of the actual destructive potential.

As mentioned earlier, during the Cold War years there was a general assumption in the West – still widely accepted today – that the possession of nuclear weapons prevented a Soviet military attack. This is one of the deliberately propagated myths of the Cold War. Careful studies by reputable historians from the West have found no evidence for this assertion. The Soviet government would have liked, of course, to see communist regimes all over the world, but they tried to achieve this through propaganda and by supporting subversive groups, mainly in the poor countries.

Table 3   Milestones in the nuclear arms race

Milestone	Year of achievement by	
	USA	*USSR*
Test of atomic (fission) bomb	1945	1949
Deployment of intercontinental bomber	1948	1956
Deployment of jet bomber	1951	1954
Test of practical hydrogen bomb	1954	1955
Deployment of tactical nuclear weapons in Europe	1954	1957
Deployment of nuclear artillery	1954	1980
Strategic reconnaissance for targeting	1955	1962
Test of intercontinental ballistic missile (ICBM)	1958	1957
Deployment of ICBM	1959	1960
Deployment of submarine-launched ballistic missile	1960	1964
Deployment of solid fuel ICBM	1963	1968
Deployment of swing-wing, supersonic bomber	1967	1974
Test of MIRVs	1968	1973
Deployment of MIRVs	1970	1975

All the evidence indicates that the build-up of nuclear armaments by the Soviet government was a response to that by the United States. Almost every step in the nuclear arms race, every technological advance, was initiated by the United States, with the Soviet Union struggling to keep up. As the table of milestones in the nuclear arms race shows (see Table 3), out of 14 key milestones the Soviet Union led the way only in one case. On the average, the Soviets were lagging behind the Americans by six years. But although the USA was usually ahead, it was never satisfied that its offensive weapons would provide full security, and President Ronald Reagan made an attempt to achieve extra security through the Strategic Defense Initiative, otherwise known as Star Wars. (President George W. Bush is now trying to achieve something similar through the Ballistic Missile Defense programme.) A likely response by the Soviet Union to Reagan's plan would have been an increase in its offensive arsenals, to ensure saturation of the defences – a situation that would eventually have led to a catastrophe, were it not for the emergence of a leader with common sense, Mikhail Gorbachev. Listening to the advice of Soviet scientists (among others), he made a rational assessment of the situation, and called a halt to the arms race.

In Chapter 12 we will return to the story of the successes and failures in the arms control negotiations aimed at limiting the nuclear threat, but we hope that the brief review of the nuclear arms race has given you a better understanding of the perilous situation in which human society has found itself. The great advances in science and technology during the last few decades have provided us with the technical means for wholesale suicide. And the absence of cor-responding advances in the social sciences has led to a climate in which such an act can be contemplated seriously.

Surely we must not allow this to happen. As human beings it is our paramount duty to preserve human life and ensure the continuation of the human race.

CONCLUSION

The combination of technological advances and political antagonisms has resulted in the build-up of nuclear arsenals of such unimaginable magnitude that the very existence of the human race might be threatened in a nuclear holocaust. The imminent danger of such a catastrophe has greatly diminished with the end of the Cold War, but nuclear warheads in their thousands remain in the arsenals, and under the policies of the G.W. Bush administration the likelihood of their being used, even in a pre-emptive strike, has greatly increased.

3   Other Weapons of Mass Destruction

Nuclear weapons are part of the category of weapons of mass destruction (WMD) that includes chemical, biological, and radiological weapons. They are distinguished from conventional weapons (mainly high explosives and incendiaries) because of their potential for bringing devastation, death and disease to human societies, on a scale incompatible with survival. Actually, in regard to the scale of devastation, the distinction between conventional weapons and WMDs is somewhat arbitrary. Technological advances are making conventional means of warfare ever more efficient and deadly in terms of the number of human casualties (deaths and injuries) and structural damage, and land mines and cluster bombs can cause injuries and deaths for years after hostilities have officially ended. Perhaps a more important distinction – as the name implies – is that weapons of mass destruction can affect populations over a much wider area, sometimes at large distances from the point of release. There is also a psychological factor: the general abhorrence of poisons and germs and fear of the invisible, such as ionizing radiation. This is probably the reason for the early agreements to ban the use of these weapons, such as the Geneva Protocol of 1925.

We should also note that the phrase 'weapons of mass destruction' is heterogeneous. Nuclear, chemical and biological weapons differ in the extent of the damage that they cause, in their relative impacts on human life and property, in the ease with which they can be manufactured, and in many other ways. At the present state of technology, the destructive potential of nuclear weapons is so great compared with that of chemical and biological ones as to make them unique within the category of WMDs.

CHEMICAL WARFARE

The first practical use of chemical poisons as a tool of warfare occurred early in the First World War. On 22 April 1915, in Ypres, Belgium, the Germans released 180 tonnes of liquid chlorine into the breeze that carried the cloud of asphyxiating vapour towards enemy lines. About 15,000 soldiers became casualties, one-third of these fatal.

When gas masks were used to protect against this kind of attack, other chemical agents, such as mustard gas, which penetrate through the skin, were introduced, calling for other means of protection such as better clothing etc.; the usual sequence of offensive and defensive measures, as in other means of warfare.

Table 4   Types of chemical agents

Lung irritants (choking agents): chlorine, phosgene
Vesicants (skin blistering): mustard gas, lewisite
Nerve gases: sarin, VX, VR
Blood gases: hydrogen cyanide
Sensory irritants: CIV, CS, CR
Psychotropic agents: BZ

Source: Public Health Response to Biological and Chemical Weapons, WHO Guidance (2001).

The chemical compounds for warfare can be classified in various ways. Table 4 contains a list of agents grouped according to the primary organ system that is affected by exposure to them. The principal hazard is respiratory, from the inhalation of vapours or aerosols. They fill the bronchial passages with mucous, causing uncontrollable vomiting, convulsions, paralysis, and respiratory failure. Death results from asphyxia, generally within a few minutes. Nerve agents, such as sarin, penetrate respiratory tissues and are carried through the bloodstream to act on specific target receptors, such as the peripheral or central nervous system. Other agents are able to penetrate the skin and cause systemic effects.

Despite the Geneva Protocol, research proceeded in some countries on new chemical agents and on methods of their delivery. One outcome was the development of binary weapons, in which two relatively non-toxic precursors of chemical agents are held in separate canisters. At the required time, the canisters are broken, for example by using an ordinary explosive, bringing the two chemicals together to form the toxic compound.

During the inter-war period and the Cold War years, huge quantities of various chemical agents, amounting to some 70,000 tonnes (see Table 5) were produced. Their destruction, in accordance with the Chemical Weapons Convention, is posing problems both with regard to costs and environmental pollution.

Table 5   Aggregate quantities of chemical agents declared to the OPCW by member states (31 December 2000)

Chemical Agent	Total Declared (tonnes)
Agent VR	15,558
Agent VX	4,032
Lewisite	6,745
Mustard Gas	13,839
Runcol (HT)	3,536
Sarin (GB)	15,048
Soman (GD)	9,175
Other	1,572

Source: Public Health Response to Biological and Chemical Weapons, WHO Guidance (2001).

Despite the existence of huge arsenals of chemical weapons by some combatants, they were not used in the Second World War, probably because the widespread development of anti-chemical protection reduced their potential effectiveness. Aversion to their deployment, in violation of the 1925 Geneva Protocol, also played a role. However, chemical agents were used in a number of wars, almost entirely in the less industrialized regions of the world, probably because the more sophisticated defence measures were not available. The main incidents in international wars were: Morocco (1923–26); Ethiopia (1935–40); China (1937–45); Yemen (1963–67); Iran–Iraq (1980–88).

THE TOKYO NERVE GAS ATTACK

On the morning of 20 March 1995, ten members of the Aum Shirikyo Cult carried out a hastily prepared attack on commuters on the Tokyo subway system. Eight plastic bags, each containing about half a litre of sarin, were placed on the train floor, and pierced with sharpened umbrella tips. The attackers fled the train at the nearest station. Within 9 minutes the Tokyo Fire Department recorded the first call, and soon the emergency services were inundated with calls for aid from numerous subway stations. Altogether more than 5,000 people sought medical assistance: 12 of the passengers died, and about 500 needed hospital attention.

The last incident was the attack by a terrorist group using the nerve gas sarin on the Tokyo subway system in March 1995.

BIOLOGICAL WARFARE

Biological weapons are microorganisms, such as infectious bacteria, viruses and fungi, intended for use in war because of their pathogenic effects on people, animals or plants. Their chief characteristic, as distinct from chemical weapons, is the ability to multiply in a host over a period of time, thus making it possible for the disease, often lethal, to reach large populations. This makes them potentially very dangerous weapons, in some cases approaching the destructive potential of nuclear weapons.

There are large differences in characteristics of the various microorganisms, for example in virulence (severity of the effect); lethality (the ability to cause death); pathogenicity (ability to cause disease); contagiousness (ability to transmit the disease). Transmission may result from direct contact between an infected and an uninfected person, or can be mediated through contaminated material, such as surgical instruments, or bedding. There may also be airborne transmission, through coughing or sneezing, or via biting insects.

The list of potential biological weapons is very large (the main ones are listed in Table 6) but the important fact is that there has not been any use of them on a significant scale. An alleged use of the yellow fever virus by the Americans in Vietnam turned out to be unsubstantiated.

The biological agent about which there has been human experience is the anthrax bacterium. Its properties make it a germ weapon *par excellence*. It is highly virulent: less than a microgram of it in the body may cause death within a week in 90 per cent of cases; and it is highly stable; its spores can remain virulent in soil, or in storage, for many years, and survive large variations in temperature and humidity. A WHO Report estimates that the release of 50 kilograms of anthrax by an aircraft on a population of half a million would kill 95,000 people and incapacitate 125,000.

Despite the 1972 Convention, which banned biological weapons, research on them – and storage of them – has apparently taken place in several countries. That this was going on in the Soviet Union became known in 1979 when an accident in a laboratory in Sverdlovsk resulted in an outbreak of anthrax; 64 people died in the accident.

A bizarre event occurred in the United States shortly after the 11 September terrorist attacks, but – as it turned out – unrelated to them. A number of people, including prominent politicians, received packages by mail, containing anthrax spores. Twenty-two of the recipients contracted the disease, and four of them died, but the main effect was panic among the public and disruption of postal services which lasted for a considerable time. To this day it is not known who the perpetrator was, but it is suspected that a disgruntled former worker in a US biological laboratory was responsible.

Table 6   Biological Agents

Bacteria	anthrax, trench fever, brucellosis, glanders, melioidosis, tularaemia, typhoid fever, shigellosis, cholera, plague, Q fever, scrub typhus, typhus fever, Rocky Mountain spotted fever, psittacosis
Fungi	coccidioidomycosis, histoplasmosis
Viruses	Hantaan/Korean haemorrhagic fever, Sin nombre, Crimean-Congo haemorrhagic fever, Rift Valley fever, Ebola virus disease, Maburg virus disease, Lymphocytic choriomeningitis, Junin (Argentine haemorrhagic fever), Machupo (Bolivian haemorrhagic fever), Lassa fever, Tick-borne encephalitis/Russian spring–summer encephalitis, Dengue, yellow fever, Omsk haemorrhagic fever, Japanese encephalitis, Western equine encephalomyelitis, Eastern equine encephalomyelitis, Chikungunya, O'nyong-nyong, Venezuelan equine encephalomyelitis, smallpox, Monkey pox, White pox, Influenza
Protozoa	naegleriasis, toxoplasmosis, schistosomiasis

Source: Public Health Response to Biological and Chemical Weapons, WHO Guidance (2001).

> During the century ahead, as our ability to modify fundamental life processes continues its rapid advance, we will be able not only to devise additional ways to destroy life but also become able to manipulate it – including the processes of cognition, development, reproduction and inheritance. A world in which these capabilities are widely employed for hostile purposes, would be a world in which the very nature of conflict had radically changed.
>
> Matthew Meselson, *Averting the Hostile Exploitation of Biotechnology* (2000)

The main concern about germ warfare is that new, much more virulent agents may result from advances in biotechnology, particularly from gene manipulation of known bacteria or viruses. According to one source: 'The outlook for biological weapons is grimly interesting. Weaponeers have only just begun to explore the potential of the biotechnological revolution. It is sobering to realize that far more development lies ahead than behind.' This is particularly worrying in view of the opposition of the United States to a Protocol to the Biological Weapons Convention that would have provided more safeguards to the Convention (see Chapter 12).

RADIOLOGICAL WARFARE (DIRTY BOMBS)

Radiological weapons (other than nuclear bombs) are devices for the dissemination of radioactive materials in order to cause injury or death by exposure to the radiation emitted from these materials. In wartime they could be used either for defensive or offensive purposes. An example of the former would be to make an area inaccessible for enemy troops, inhibit a river crossing, or close a mountain pass.

Offensive uses are more plausible. The objective might be to force the evacuation of populations from cities or other industrial or communication centres, thus playing havoc with the economy and fighting potential of the country attacked. Or it may have a more sinister purpose – to kill a large number of people. These objectives could of course be achieved more effectively with nuclear explosives, but radiological weapons may be preferable if the attacker wanted to avoid the structural damage caused by nuclear bombs.

Radiological warfare has been made feasible by the development of nuclear reactors for the generation of electricity. The fission process which gives rise to the release of energy also results in the production of vast quantities of radioactive materials – the fission products, usually referred to as the nuclear waste – millions of times more than available from the naturally occurring radioactive elements. The plutonium produced in a reactor is of course also a powerful radiological weapon. A third way is to transform normal elements into radioactive species, by placing them in a reactor and subjecting them to bombardment with neutrons.

The use of fission products as a weapon in warfare was contemplated immediately after the first nuclear reactor went critical in Chicago on 2 December 1942. Robert Oppenheimer, the Director of the Los Alamos National Laboratory, requested that the Chicago scientists look into the possibility of producing large quantities of strontium-90 – one of the fission products – and spraying them from aircraft over German soil. He qualified his request with: 'I think we should not attempt a plan unless we can poison food sufficient to kill a half a million men.' Fortunately, this was not then possible, and the project was abandoned for technological reasons, rather than for moral scruples.

No further attempts have been made to use fission products for such purposes, but the employment of radioactivity directly on human beings has become a practical possibility. The growth of the nuclear industry – although much slower than envisaged earlier – has resulted in the construction of some 442 reactors in 31 countries, with a total power capacity of 357 gigawatts net (357 million kilowatts). A typical reactor of 1GW output produces after three years of operation some three tonnes of waste products, most of which is radioactive. It would also produce about 250kg of plutonium per year. At the present time, the total plutonium produced in civilian nuclear reactors amounts to 920 tonnes (in addition to the 270 tonnes of military plutonium). Considering that a lethal dose of radiation could result from the inhalation of 20 milligrams of plutonium, it is apparent that radioactivity is potentially a very potent weapon. This is why a convention to prohibit radiological warfare was proposed by the United States and Soviet Union as far back as 1979, but has not yet come into force.

In practice, however, the use of plutonium to deliver lethal doses of radiation is very limited. For use as a radiological weapon, plutonium would probably be dispersed in the form of an aerosol of finely divided particles. In open areas it would be impossible to maintain the suspension for any length of time. Even a gentle breeze would rapidly disperse it over large areas, making it necessary to use very large quantities of it. For example, to cover a medium-sized town would require about 10 tonnes of plutonium, which rules it out as an acute lethal weapon. However, smaller quantities by a factor of 1,000 (that is, a few kilograms) would be sufficient to require the evacuation of the population and necessitate difficult decontamination measures. This may turn out to be the practical reason for the use of plutonium. Another limiting factor is the long persistence of plutonium (the half-life of its main isotope is 24,100 years). During that time, the aerosol would spread to other parts of the world – including the country that used the weapons – causing long-term effects such as cancer.

The long half-lives of the fission products would also be a limiting factor in the use of these materials. But this objection would not carry weight with terrorists, with their disregard for the sanctity of human life. The use of radiological weapons by terrorists is therefore much more likely, assuming that they can get hold of the materials. Since 11 September, radiological weapons have been colloquially described as 'dirty bombs'. (Note the misleading implication that some other types of nuclear weapon are 'clean', that is to say, produce no radioactive fall-out – this is not the case.) A large quantity of radioactive material is packed into an airplane and detonated, by means of an ordinary explosive, over a city, dispersing the radioactive material and causing many deaths and huge panic. Indeed, panic – arising from the fear of radioactivity among the general public – may be the most effective outcome of the use of radiological weapons. Another way to achieve this objective is to detonate a high explosive bomb over a reactor, or a processing plant, or on the cooling towers holding the spent rods, and disperse their radioactive contents.

INFORMATION TECHNOLOGY WARFARE

Information Technology Weapons, also called cyber weapons, belong to an entirely different category from those discussed so far. They do not directly produce physical damage to people (deaths or injury) but this may arise indirectly, as a result of the collapse of the economic system of a country brought about by the use of cyber weapons. The orderly functioning of modern society is increasingly dependent on the proper performance of a variety of computer systems. The security of a state could be fatally damaged if another state, or a group of terrorists, developed the means to put vital computers out of action.

Information technology warfare is a real possibility: it is defined as an attack, undertaken or sponsored by a national or political entity, on the information technology component underpinning the national infrastructure. The national infrastructure of many utilities, in particular electricity, gas, water, sewage, railways, road transport, air transport, telecommunications, are each dependent on several of the others, and all depend on telecommunication. Banking and financial services are, in effect, further critical national utilities. Local administration and central government, and the health and medical services, are all dependent on the aggregate of these utilities, as is manufacture, commerce and civil life. Even the military services could not survive a breakdown of civil infrastructure for more than a few days.

No system of countermeasures can guarantee complete immunity to an attack by a determined group of terrorists. All that can be achieved is to make an attack significantly harder to undertake and much more difficult to conceal: to limit its initial impact and to speed up recovery to full service.

CONCLUSION

Even at the present state of technology, chemical, biological and radiological weapons can inflict very large numbers of casualties, but the peril may be much greater from future advances, particularly in the biological sciences. Information technology warfare can cause widespread damage that can in turn lead to much hardship.

4 'Conventional' Weapons

In the previous chapters we have called attention to the enormous power of modern weapons of mass destruction. But it is important not to lose sight of the fact that the overwhelming majority of casualities in past wars have been caused by 'conventional' weapons.

On the deck, twitching like freshly caught mackerel, were the bodies of a dozen or more American soldiers. They were covered in the black fuel oil which had suffocated them when they were pitched into the sea.

Morris Brodie ed., *A World Worth Fighting For: Ex-Services Campaign for a Non-Nuclear World* (1990)

The massacre in Rwanda has reminded us that even simple weapons or tools used in day-to-day life can be the instruments of unbelievable horror. The panga or machete alone can be used to cut off ears, limbs, genitals or heads. Terror squads simply armed can produce thousands of casualties. Longbow, crossbow, rifle, howitzer and rocket have made it possible to kill at greater and greater distances. We have seen that four aircraft in the hands of terrorists can kill thousands of civilians. Machine gun and shell can kill many simultaneously. The history of warfare is a history of the use of increasingly deadly weapons – gunpowder, mustard gas, napalm, area bombing, and now nuclear weapons. In the Second World War, a thousand-bomber raid could cause as many deaths as the atomic bomb in Hiroshima. Even the so-called precise bombs, though aimed at military targets, have caused very large numbers of civilian casualties in Iraq.

As pointed out already, the number of casualties is an inadequate measure of the horror of war, but it is as well to recognize the extent to which casualties occur even in wars involving only conventional weapons. Estimates vary widely, but Table 7 shows one estimate of the military deaths resulting from the major wars since 1945. Only one of those wars involved the use of nuclear weapons, and there the deaths that resulted were nearly all civilian. And these do not represent the whole tally – there have been over 100 wars by any

39

Table 7   Wars since 1939 causing 100,000 or more battle deaths

International Wars	Year	Deaths
Second World War	1939–45	16,630,000
Franco-Indochinese War	1945–54	600,000
Korean War	1950–53	910,000
Algerian War	1954–62	100,000
Vietnam War	1965–75	1,020,000
Iran–Iraq War	1980–88	1,250,000
Civil Wars		
Greece	1944–45	160,000 *
China	1946–50	1,000,000 *
Columbia	1949–62	300,000 *
China	1956–59	100,000
Vietnam	1960–65	300,000 *
Zaire	1960–65	100,000 *
Yemen	1962–69	100,000 *
Sudan	1963–72	250,000 *
Guatemala	1966–72	140,000
Nigeria	1967–70	1,000,000
Cambodia	1970–75	190,000
Pakistan	1971	500,000 *
Ethiopia	1974–91	150,000
Lebanon	1975–90	170,000
Angola	1975–91	350,000 *
Afghanistan	1978–92	1,300,000
Cambodia	1978–91	200,000
Mozambique	1979–92	1,200,000
Uganda	1980–88	100,000 *
Sudan	1983–	1,300,000 *
Bosnia	1992–95	250,000 *
Liberia	1992–95	150,000 *
Angola	1992–94	100,000 *
Burundi	1993–	200,000 *
Rwanda	1994	500,000 *

* State battle deaths – total battle deaths (i.e. incorporating fatalities of non-state entities or domestic insurgents in civil wars) unknown. Battle deaths (rounded to nearest 10,000) taken from Correlates of War datasets available at http://cow2.la.psu.edu.

definition in that period, and in some of those the civilian casualties greatly exceeded the military.

And conventional weapons have themselves become more dangerous, especially to civilians. Missiles can be launched from a distance, so that casualties can be inflicted on an enemy with minimal risk to the aggressor. Cluster bombs disperse large numbers

> [After a plane crashed on returning to base after a raid] *In the morning we were organized to comb the fields; if we saw anything which looked human, we pointed it out to the medical staff who picked it up with tongs and put it in a bag. Enough bits were collected to fill two coffins.*
>
> Morris Brodie ed., *A World Worth Fighting For: Ex-Services Campaign for a Non-Nuclear World* (1990)

of bomblets over a considerable area. Quite apart from the immediate damage that they cause, bomblets that fail to explode are a major hazard to civilians. Many died in Afghanistan from unexploded bomblets, and these weapons were used by the USA and the UK in the 2003 Gulf War. Landmines were used extensively in recent wars, and are incredibly difficult to find after the war is over. As a result, they cause large numbers of civilian casualties and farmers are prevented from working their land for many years after the end of hostilities. So-called 'bunker buster' bombs, designed to penetrate many feet of concrete in order to reach enemy shelters, could be equally effective against civilian shelters. And 'Daisy-cutter' bombs, weighing 14,850 pounds (though even larger ones are planned), explode just above the ground and can cause devastation across an area a mile wide. They are indiscriminate in their effects.

Another issue that has arisen in the Israeli/Palestinian conflict, in the terrorist attacks in New York and Washington, and in the 2003 Gulf War, arises from the actions of suicide bombers. Individuals with strong idealistic motivation, confronted with greatly superior force, may give their own lives in order to destroy enemies. Often their sacrifice involves the deaths of civilians. But it can also have insidious consequences, as seen in Iraq. Soldiers who suffer casualties from suicide bombers inevitably become suspicious of all civilians, and trigger-happy. This again leads to the deaths of innocent civilians.

> [The raid on Hamburg by RAF Bomber Command] ... *hundreds, if not thousands, of fires were started ... enormous heat was generated, estimated at between 500 and 1000 degrees centigrade. The tarmac underfoot melted and houses collapsed on every side ... When shelters were eventually dug out of the debris and opened up, almost no bodies were found but just little piles of charred ashes or small pools of glutinous liquid.*
>
> Peter Johnson, *The Withered Garland: Reflections and Doubts of a Bomber* (1995)

In sum, very simple weapons can be and are used to kill large numbers of people. So-called 'conventional' weapons are being constantly improved, and some now have enormous destructive power.

*   *   *   *

CONCLUSION TO SECTION I

In this section we have argued that war, except in very special circumstances, is no longer an acceptable way of solving conflicts of interests. The wars of the twentieth century were destructive enough; future wars could be even more devastating. And, in a number of ways that we shall discuss in later chapters, the world is now a different place. Technological advances in communications and inter-state dependencies mean that wars can no longer be isolated. Most wars occur within states, so that civilians are inevitably affected. Every war produces large numbers of refugees, with all the suffering that that entails. Wars involve an enormous waste of resources that could better be spent on health, education, and other ways that would increase human well-being. And nearly all wars are both immoral *and* illegal.

If war is unacceptable, can it be prevented? War has been present practically continuously throughout human history, and it is easy to be pessimistic. But the difficulty of the task is no excuse for inaction. The apparently impossible has been achieved before. Freedom from colonial rule in India, the outlawing of slavery, the emancipation of blacks in the USA, votes for women in Britain, the ending of Apartheid in South Africa, and the overthrow of communist rule in Soviet satellite states were all achieved through popular action, initiated or guided in each case by only one or a few individuals.

Three means for solving or preventing conflicts can be distinguished: pacifism, conflict resolution, and undermining the factors that cause wars and make war an acceptable way of solving conflicts.

Pacifism, although it can be an important adjunct to other means, is by itself unlikely to be an effective option. Admirable as the pacifist who maintains his stance against popular opinion may be, it is unlikely that the ideology of pacifism could be adequate. But this does not mean that those who are absolutely opposed to the use of force have no role to play. In the negotiations that attempt to bring wars, and especially intra-state wars, to an end, a compromise between the two parties' conflicting aims is unlikely to produce a viable solution: the wisdom of those who have stood outside the conflict can play an important role. These could include pacifists, but it would be essential that they understood the political realities. Those who choose not to become engaged must therefore equip themselves to play a constructively pragmatic role at a later stage.

Attempts to resolve conflicts offer hope of success in individual cases. We shall see later (Chapters 14 and 15) that mediation by a third party can sometimes bring a peaceful solution. However, most wars do not have simple causes, but involve complex networks of causes acting within a state of preparedness for war, together with an acceptance of its inevitability, at least in the long term. Disentangling the entrenched views of the several parties involved, views whose origins may extend back into past centuries, is always likely to be a formidable and lengthy task. But by the time the processes of negotiation intrinsic to conflict resolution can reach a conclusion, it may be too late. And the best solution for all involved may not correspond to the expectations of the parties in conflict. That, of course, does not mean that attempts to resolve conflicts should be abandoned, but rather that they must be undertaken as early as possible if they are to have any hope of success, and that they should not be seen as a universal panacea.

Preferable by far is to find ways to eliminate the causes of war, thereby creating a world where potential differences in interests are resolved without violence by negotiation at an early stage, and wars simply do not happen. In promoting awareness of the causes of war, and in eliminating them, education must play a major part. Education for a culture of violence must give way to education for a culture of peace. But education, though essential, will not be enough. And although politicians or military leaders are usually the prime movers in war, history shows that eliminating war is not a matter that can safely be left solely in their hands. Indeed it cannot be a matter solely for politicians, for wars cannot happen unless individuals are willing to go to war, or allow themselves to be coerced into doing so. Leaders depend on their followers, even in totalitarian regimes. Prevention of war requires action both at the grassroots and at the political level. And it is insufficient merely to wait until war is imminent and then try to resolve the conflict. Given the world as it is, with war an ever-present possibility, means for conflict resolution are essential. But we shall do even better if we are aware of the causes of war and do our best to remove them.

II
What Makes War More Likely?

5 Causes of War and the Role of Weapons

CAUSES OF WAR

What caused the Second World War? Why did the Germans invade Poland? Was it because the Germans needed *Lebensraum?* Was this perceived need really a matter of Hitler's political ambition? And how was it that Hitler thought he could get away with it? Was it because Germany had been allowed to re-arm in spite of the restrictions imposed after the First World War? Or because Britain and France had been too slow to realize the necessity of rearming to face Hitler's Germany? And why did they not trust the Soviet Union as an ally in spite of a 1935 Franco-Soviet agreement to collaborate to contain Nazism? Was that lack of trust related to the outbreak of the Spanish Civil War in 1936? Or to the influence of friends of Germany in positions to bring pressure to bear on their governments? These are but some of the many causal chains that could be explored, and each of them would be found to have many branches. Clearly, understanding the causes of any war is a very difficult task.

Approaches to this problem can be divided into three groups. The first involves looking back over recent decades or centuries to see if there are any circumstances, alone or in combination, that are related to war breaking out with a greater frequency than the average. This approach has limited usefulness in the present context. Factors critical for one outbreak may be irrelevant for another, and most wars depend on a large number of circumstances coming together simultaneously. And because both the nature of wars and political systems have changed so much over the last century, and are changing even more rapidly now, the statistical analysis of the circumstances surrounding past conflicts can have but dubious value for forestalling the future.

A second type of approach involves an historical analysis of particular wars, attempting to tease apart the multiplicity of factors operating in each one. Here the emphasis is not on generalities, but on understanding particular instances. For example, while the historical sequence of events preceding the First World War is well known, it does not adequately explain how a Balkan conflict escalated into a world war. Close historical analysis suggests that, from one point of view, it was a combination of the following: belligerence of the German military, miscalculation by the German politicians, treaty obligations, an imperialist culture, the perceived need to acquire markets, competition between capitalist economies, misperceptions and illusions by political leaders, and the instability of the European political system that had been induced by the growth of German power. Each of these must in turn have had many causes. Such an approach is capable of producing a deep understanding of the many interacting factors operating in the particular case examined, including distinctions between structural factors, predisposing factors, and triggers, though often these merge. But, again, such an approach does not lend itself to generalizations that could be useful in forestalling future wars.

A third approach – and the one adopted here – is to focus on some of the factors believed to be causes of war, and to examine the extent to which they seem to be either necessary or sufficient and, more importantly, how they interact. Thus the following chapters discuss a number of factors often believed to have contributed to the outbreak of wars, assess the evidence, and discuss the relations between them. This approach throws into relief the interdependence of, and mutual interactions between, the factors considered. For instance, we shall see that: state propaganda exploits individual aggressiveness, which contributes to the willingness of individuals to go to war but usually plays but a minor role in battle; that poverty is seldom a primary factor, but again may contribute to the probability that a country or group will go to war; that environmental factors may interact with sovereign prerogatives; and that perception that a rival is achieving weapons superiority can prompt escalation of preparedness or a pre-emptive strike.

But of course no one approach will give all the answers, and this one skirts some problems and raises others. Full understanding of wars requires insight into the many perspectives from which the situation is perceived: leaders, politicians, combatants and non-combatants on both sides, and outsiders will each see and interpret the circumstances in different ways. Furthermore, these perspectives are likely to interact: while most causes of war operate through the perceptions of leaders, leaders are influenced by the social climate in the society, and they both influence and are influenced by the perceptions of the military and of the population at large. These are issues best tackled by the historian dealing with particular wars.

So wars have multiple causes – chains of interacting, mutually supporting causes that can often be traced back, even across generations, into the remote past. Some causes lie in the history of the warring parties, old hatreds and injustices fomented and carried forwards into the current generation. Some lie in present circumstances, such as a persisting shortage of oil, need for room for expansion, a religious revival. And yet other causes can be seen as triggers immediately precipitating the violence – the assassination of an archduke is said to have triggered the First World War. Some causes are social or political, others individual, like the ambitions of a leader. And often causes are to be found that lie between those two – such as the interaction between rival political groups. Just because of this complexity, actions of many kinds and at many levels are needed if wars are to be eliminated. We discuss these in Section III.

Although it is fruitless to search for *the cause* of any particular war some factors often seem to be paramount. In this and the next five chapters we examine some of these. We shall find that some are not so important as they might seem, and that most of those we consider are insufficient to cause war on their own.

Here we are concerned with how the possession of weapons is not only necessary for war, but can be conducive to war.

THE ROLE OF WEAPONS

The only conditions absolutely necessary for the occurrence of war are the availability of weapons and individuals willing to use them. Not only are weapons necessary, but their possession may lead to wars that would not otherwise occur. If one state attempts to procure a new or enhanced military capability, this could be seen by other states as a threat, and provoke a pre-emptive strike. Or, to cite a danger predicted in the Cold War era and which now looms again, the development by one country of a means to intercept hostile missiles may lead a rival to increase the number of missiles that it possesses beyond those with which the defensive system could cope. In addition, with trigger-ready modern long-range weapons there is always the possibility that one will be launched accidentally, or by a deranged local commander: the perception of an incoming missile by the other side might provoke retaliation and lead to full-scale war.

These dangers have become particularly acute with the development of modern weapons with their enormous destructive potential, as described in the previous three chapters. The military applications of the advances in science and technology have created a dangerous situation, conducive to preventive wars. In a world in which military power is a determining factor in national security, any attempt by one state to procure a new military capability may be seen by other states as a potential menace, and this might lead to a preventive war. We have witnessed this in the recent crisis over Iraq. Past attempts by Saddam Hussein to acquire nuclear weapons and his use of chemical weapons against his own people were reasons for the determination by the US government to bring down the regime in Iraq by military means. In current US nuclear doctrine nuclear weapons could be treated like any other high explosives to be used to stop an aggressor, or even pre-emptively, if there is a suspicion that a state with an undesirable regime wants to acquire weapons of mass destruction.

Of course quite simple weapons may be sufficient to cause very large numbers of casualties. But weapons of some sort are essential, and wars create a demand for weapons. Few countries manufacture weapons themselves, so most wars are fought with weapons imported, legally or illegally, from elsewhere.

So far as arms-manufacturing states are concerned, the acquisition of armaments is normally a political decision, but in democratic countries governments may be under considerable pressure from several sources. Not surprisingly, the military leaders endeavour to ensure that they have the best equipment available. This is likely to require government investment in research, as well as in the actual purchase of weapons. Second, governments must be seen by the electorate or population to be safeguarding the security of the country and maintaining its prestige, and this may be interpreted in terms of having well-armed forces. Third, the arms manufacturers, acting in their own interests, lobby both their own and other governments to maintain or increase the strength of their armed forces. In addition, the arms manufacturers may be supported by sections of the electorate who are connected directly or indirectly with the armament industries and who see any decrease in arms production as threatening their employment or other interests. As a result of these pressures, some countries tend to be much more heavily armed than would be necessary to preserve an adequate defensive capability. As an obvious example, during the Cold War both superpowers built up enormous arsenals of nuclear weapons, far in excess of what could be seen as necessary for defensive purposes. At present the USA, Saudi Arabia and some East Asian states are known to spend vast amounts on arms. In North Korea and in the former Yugoslavia (Serbia and Montenegro) over 20 per cent of the gross domestic product is spent on arms.

States that do not manufacture the weapons that they need must purchase them abroad. Here pressure may come from the arms-manufacturing countries. Since the development and production of modern weapons is a very expensive business, governments of countries that manufacture them attempt to defray the development costs, and thus the cost of the weapons they buy, by encouraging arms firms to sell their products abroad. To this end they arrange 'arms fairs' where weapons are displayed. In addition, to encourage foreign governments to purchase weapons from them they may offer incentives – perhaps aid or investment in development projects. Sometimes a country's arms dealers export to both sides of an ongoing conflict. Over 50 suppliers were involved in the Iran/Iraq war, at least 20 of them sending arms to both sides.

Finally, parties to civil wars, freedom fighters, and such like, purchase their arms through arms dealers. This often involves clandestine negotiations and the despatch of the weapons from the manufacturing country through indirect routes to avoid restrictions placed on arms exports. In the resulting web of intrigue the operators try to maximize their own profits, persuading their customers to buy the arms they have for sale as superior to those of the other side. The dealers thus escalate the scale of violence (see Chapter 12).

CONCLUSION

Every war depends on multiple interacting causes, but one factor is essential – the availability of weapons. While very crude weapons may suffice for the massacre of largely defensive civilians, as in Rwanda, modern wars increasingly demand more sophisticated weaponry. But the size of a country's stockpiles is not always governed by apparent necessity. Whether we are considering states that manufacture weapons, or those that do not, or groups within states, there may be pressures for a state to possess more weapons than are needed. And weapons, once possessed, have a way of being used.

6   The Political System and its Leaders

In a sense, nearly all wars are politically caused, but this generalization can be interpreted in more than one way – in terms of the world's political system, or in terms of the actions and personalities of leaders.

THE INSTITUTION OF NATION-STATES

So far as the world's political system goes, it has been argued that conflict, often leading to war, is intrinsic to a world composed of sovereign states. The number of recognized states is now 192, and the count is rising. National self-determination is now recognized as a 'right' by the United Nations. Many past wars have been connected with national (or nation-state) identity: many recent wars have been concerned with secession from a nation-state because of perceived sub-group identity. The nation-state, as it has evolved during the last few centuries, is bound by definition to preserve its identity: it has to stress its separateness from other nation-states. Sovereignty is the foundation of its existence. So one of its main functions is to ensure the security of its existence against threats from other states. That means that the nation-state must retain the means with which to wage war, and a military establishment is almost universally held to be an indispensable institution – Iceland and Costa Rica being honourable exceptions to this.

To the historian of past centuries this generalization, that the existence of nation-states is highly likely to lead to war, would seem valid. However, there are several reasons why it should not be taken as a guide for the future. First, within Europe, the principal cradle of inter-state wars in the past, war between states now seems inconceivable. The close ties between members of the European Union, the common currency shared by many European countries, and their economic interdependence, make the use of violent means to settle conflicts of interest improbable. The tragic lessons of the two world wars in the twentieth century have undoubtedly augmented the determination by European states not to use military means to resolve conflicts of interest. And within the rest of the world, very few inter-state boundaries are now in dispute and, with a few exceptions (see below), attempts by one state to annex additional territory in the Third World are improbable. States may still covet the resources of other states, but the probability of resort to violence in an attempt to acquire them is much less than it used to be (Chapter 8).

A second reason why the history of inter-state rivalries may be a poor guide, and why inter-state wars are likely to be relatively less frequent in the future, lies in the processes of globalization. As we shall see (Chapters 9 and 11), the greatly increased facilities for communication arising from the rapid progress in information technology, and the growth of multi-national corporations, are among the factors increasing economic, political and cultural links between states. However, in Chapter 9 we shall point out that the effects of globalization are not wholly benign.

Third, arising from their increasing interdependence, the power of nation-states to do whatever they like within their own borders has decreased in many parts of the world, and especially within the European Union. This diminishes their ability to raise funds to support armies. A decrease in the sovereignty of states, in so far as it could make them more susceptible to control by supra-national bodies, seems to be an inevitable consequence of changes in the world's political system – and one not to be discouraged (see also pp. 63–4, 89–90, 135–6).

Of course, none of this should blind one to the continuing possibility of wars between states. Although they failed, the attempts by Iraq to invade Kuwait, and the Soviet Union to invade Afghanistan, and the rumbling conflict between India and Pakistan, not to mention the situation in the Middle East and the invasion of Iraq by the USA and UK, are sufficient evidence against such a view. The increase in the number of small weak states by partition or secession may also be a cause of instability. And the rise of international terrorism has provided another plausible cause for war between states, though it is to be hoped that the incursions into Afghanistan and Iraq by the USA and its allies will not form a precedent. Clearly, there must be no complacency: the point being made is that the lessons of history are becoming less reliable indicators of the future as wars within states become relatively more frequent.

As previously described, in recent years the majority of wars have been internal to states. Of the violent conflicts occurring in different parts of the world since the end of the Cold War, the vast majority have been so-called 'civil wars' – though, as we shall see, there may also have been outside influences at work. Such wars within states often appear to be due in part to political failure – to the inability of the current government to satisfy the needs or political aspirations of groups within the state. A survey of recent violent conflicts within states suggests a number of conditions that may be conducive to intra-state war in particular cases. These include a political, economic or ideological system that discriminates, or is seen to discriminate, against religious or ethnic groups within the state, and impending economic failure increasing competition between individuals and groups. Warlords, intent on personal gain, may exploit such conditions. Conflict may also be triggered by the collapse of an autocratic regime, weak government, and corruption within the government or the bureaucracy. Such problems are especially likely to arise in autocratic states and in states undergoing the transition to democracy.

Most states are based on a capitalist economic system, and two very different arguments have been advanced in favour of the view that capitalism needs warfare. A few words about these points of view are necessary, though neither bears close examination.

First, in the past a functioning international economy has made it necessary for a powerful state to guarantee free markets and to enforce international rules within which international economic activity could be conducted. Since the fifteenth century this role has been occupied by European powers: Portugal, Spain, Holland, France and Britain, sometimes more or less without dispute but more usually with two in contention. Now it is the USA that is in command. On this view it has been argued that the role of the dollar as the key currency within the international trading system, and continued access to oil and other essential supplies, are now safeguarded by the military power of the USA. But, even if this were true, there are good reasons why it should not be taken for granted that the role of the USA as an international policeman is to be encouraged. It would clearly be better if that power lay with the United Nations and, in any case, globalization (see pp. 89–94, 135–6) is likely to lead the world away from the domination of any one country. In the near future the global economy is likely to be dominated by competition between the USA, the European Union, and Japan, and perhaps later by China and India. Beyond that is anyone's guess.

A second type of support for the view that capitalism needs warfare lies in the suggestion that capitalism, in attempting to match supply and demand, generates excess industrial capacity and thus unemployment. To ameliorate this, and to prevent popular dissatisfaction, states increase spending. Military spending is particularly suitable for this purpose because it can increase demand without increasing the supply of either capital or consumer goods – in fact, just because it is wasteful. However, military spending is not the only possibility. In Germany and Japan, probably as a consequence of their defeat in the Second World War, state expenditure accounts for over 60 per cent of the national expenditure, but the money is spent on education, welfare and infrastructure rather than predominantly on weapons. Hope for the future must lie in the elimination of weapons of mass destruction, on international control over conventional arms, and on the development of new forms of economic cooperation that take into account the needs of the Third World.

Thus, the view that capitalism needs war should not be taken too seriously. However, we shall see later (pp. 93–4) that, according to some economists, capitalism can lead to an increase in poverty, to a larger gap between rich and poor, and to disruption of the world system, with a consequent increase in the incidence of wars.

TOTALITARIANISM VERSUS DEMOCRACY

The history of the twentieth century suggests that some types of political organization are associated with a greater involvement in war than others. Thus both the Italian invasion of Abyssinia (now Ethiopia) and the German invasion of Poland were initiated by dictators. Perhaps the personal ambitions and autocratic natures of the leaders of totalitarian regimes are responsible for their disregard for the lives of their own citizens and their expansionist policies. Hitler, Stalin and Mao are obvious examples. Certainly, during the Cold War era the totalitarian nature of the communist regimes lent support to the view in the USA that the Soviet Union was bent on expansion, and communism was regarded by many as a threat to democracy. This not only led to the injustices of McCarthyism in the USA, when the slightest hint of communist sympathies could lead to indictment, but was also used by the 'hawks' in the USA to justify a continuing build-up of nuclear weapons.

By contrast, the data suggest that, for many centuries, democratic countries have been unlikely to go to war with each other, conflicts being more often initiated by autocratic rulers or dictators. Democracies recognize the common values that they share, and aspire to ensure basic rights for their citizens, making it less likely that the people would be willing to go to war. That it is relatively unusual for democracies to go to war against each other does not necessarily mean that democracy itself prevents war: other explanations for peaceful co-existence between democracies are possible. It could be that peace makes democracy possible, or that those who create and support democratic regimes are also less willing to be recruited. Nevertheless, collective decisions taken by elected representatives reduce the possibility of ambitious or headstrong leaders leading their country into war.

Furthermore, democracies are likely to be especially effective in preventing wars. They are likely to possess practices of tolerance and conflict resolution for dealing with their own problems, and these can be applied to the situations of states in conflict. And in recent decades, their shared values have enabled democracies to form alliances and agreements that enable them to intervene (given UN approval) when conflicts threaten elsewhere. We shall return to this issue in later chapters.

There is, however, an important exception to the generalization that democracies are conducive to peace. If any state, including a democratic state, seeks to dominate, militarily, economically, ideologically or culturally, other states, there is likely to be trouble. The position is especially dangerous if the state in question believes, or rationalizes its ambition in the belief, that its particular style of governance is superior to any other, and should be imposed on all others. Britain took this role in the nineteenth century, Nazi Germany and the Soviet Union tried to in the twentieth, and it is happening with the USA at the present time. Under the George W. Bush administration the USA believes that its own particular brand of democracy – involving cut-throat capitalistic competition on a principle of the devil take the hindmost, and enormous differences between rich and poor – is superior to every other culture. It seems impossible for the present US leaders to believe that its own brand of morality, involving a primary emphasis on individual freedom and unfettered competition, is not what everyone desires. Or are these beliefs merely a whitewash for a desire for American aggrandisement? We shall return to this issue repeatedly in the following pages.

THE ROLE OF POLITICAL LEADERS

Quite apart from the structure of the world's political system, there is another reason why wars are to be seen as politically caused, namely that virtually all violent conflicts stem from the actions of leaders. Wars do not happen unless the leaders of one or both sides perceive that they have the strength and resources to resolve a conflict of interests violently and thereby to gain more than is achievable through negotiation. Hitler, building on foundations laid over the preceding decade, perceived or invented a need for more German *Lebensraum* and more German influence and, building on racial prejudices, initiated actions leading to the war in 1939. His views were supported by powerful sources in several democratic countries that saw Hitler as leading the war against communism. Neville Chamberlain, UK Prime Minister, supported by some cabinet colleagues, felt that peace, coupled with Britain's military weakness, justified appeasement of German ambitions and so kept the country out of war at the time of the Munich agreement, but later reluctantly took it into war in 1939.

Similarly, wars within states are usually initiated by leaders or by charismatic figures who embody the desires (or manipulate the desires) of part of the population. Thus almost invariably it is a decision by political or military leaders, the government that they represent or the party they lead, that precipitates a state of war, though the hands of the leaders are often forced by their constituency or followers. Since the trials of the Nazi leaders at Nuremberg after the end of the Second World War, the responsibility of leaders for the initiation and conduct of war has been recognized in international law.

The decision to go to war depends on how the leaders, individually or as a group, interpret the situation, and this will be influenced in turn by the culture and historical context in which they are living. A minor incident, viewed in the context of past persecution or perceived political injustice, may be seen as symbolic and as justifying or even requiring a violent response. In the same way as, at the individual level, blasphemy is seen as punishable by death in some cultures but not in others, so a border infringement, or the threat of a reduction in oil supplies, will be seen as justifying military action by some but not by others.

The complexity of the situation in which leaders or governments find themselves when war is impending requires emphasis. In the case of international war, leaders may have to weigh up international prestige, the probability of success, possible national gain, internal domestic issues, their own careers and many other imponderable factors acting against one another. They may feel a need to defend their country's existence, or that its power is threatened, or that its honour is at stake. They may have to consider the possible responses of hitherto unallied nations, and of politically divergent groups within their own country. Often their decisions are based on data that are incomplete and ambiguous, and they lack, almost inevitably, much of the information needed. Their interpretation of the situation may be influenced by their own personalities and ambitions and also by wishful thinking, facilitated by each side trying to conceal its true strength and intentions, with the frequent result that each underestimates its opponent. They may be affected by misperceptions or wishful thinking about the probable actions of the potential enemy and by irrational assessments of the probable outcome. They may be angry, or afraid. They are often very tired. For a variety of such reasons, the decisions of leaders may be very different from those of an objective outside observer. Hitler's continued striving for victory after defeat at Stalingrad was neither wise nor rational.

Political leaders or governments are usually guided by a group of advisers. And their advice may not be good advice. For example, we are fortunate that Winston Churchill turned down the advice of Lord Halifax and his colleagues to surrender after the fall of France in 1940. Whilst one might expect that measured discussion between the members of a group would improve the wisdom of any decisions taken, that is by no means always the case. The group's deliberations may be affected by stress induced by the importance of the issues, the ambiguity of the information available, and the personal biases of the members. Normally unaggressive individuals may choose aggressive means to solve a situation when the volume of information and the complexity of the situation seem to make rational deliberation impossible. There is experimental evidence that members of small groups, in coming to agreement, tend to reach decisions that are not only more uniform, but also more extreme, than those that would have been expected from the initial views of the group members. It has been convincingly argued that some political fiascos, such as President Kennedy's invasion of Cuba at the Bay of Pigs, and Chamberlain's policy of appeasing Hitler, were due to such group effects in decision-making. Clearly, such difficulties in making decisions may have an important influence on the incidence of wars.

There can be no better example than the manner in which the USA, the Soviet Union and Cuba came within a hair's breadth of nuclear disaster in 1962. The Soviets had secretly deployed nuclear missiles and bombers in Cuba. Their presence was discovered by aerial surveillance, and the Americans prepared to launch an attack. Just in time, as the decision to attack was to be taken, Khrushchev announced that he was removing the missiles. Years later, a series of meetings between high-ranking participants from all three countries showed that the decisions had been distorted by misinformation, miscalculation, and misjudgement. For instance, the Soviet Union believed falsely that the USA intended to invade Cuba; the CIA had reported no tactical nuclear warheads on the island, when there were in fact 162, and most of these had just been moved from their storage sites to positions close to their delivery vehicles; the USA had believed that the Soviet Union would never move missiles outside its borders; the Soviets believed that they could move the weapons without detection; and Kennedy's advisers, in urging an air and amphibious attack, did not believe that this would have elicited a military response from forces in Cuba and probably elsewhere in the world. Uncontrollable escalation might have been almost inevitable.

That raises the question of the extent to which governmental decisions depend on the unanimity of support that they expect from the population. In most cases going to war requires a united country, or a united group within a nation-state, on whose support the leaders feel that they can rely, though Tony Blair took the UK into the 2003 Gulf War in spite of considerable opposition in the country. Sometimes, however, it seems that lack of support for the leaders can help to precipitate a state of war. There are few causes of group solidarity more effective than the perception of an outside threat, and leaders have been known to exploit this in order to consolidate their own positions. Commentators have argued that public dissatisfaction with the policies of the Junta was on the point of erupting into organized revolution when Argentina invaded the Falklands: public anger was then redirected towards the British. In a similar vein, when Richard Nixon was under pressure because of his controversial role in the Watergate scandal, he alerted his troops ostensibly on account of the Yom Kippur War between Israel and Egypt, and public attention was thereby directed outwards. It has also been suggested that the new leaders of the republics emerging from Yugoslavia needed war to maintain power over their own populations. Of course, in such cases the evidence is circumstantial, and it is unlikely ever to be possible to establish with certainty that the action of the leaders was intentionally directed towards safeguarding their own positions.

In the modern world, in which many industrial and commercial organizations see themselves as international, or even state-independent, additional problems arise. The organizations' interests may conflict with governmental interests: industrial efficiency and competitive edge may be pitted against the public good, and it has even been suggested that their influence over the government may be greater than the government's influence over them.

Another problem that complicates matters for decision-makers concerns the role of outsiders. While it is easy to think of war as involving two opposing sides, it is seldom that simple. Outsiders often play a significant role. The two superpowers played an important role in the wars in Africa and South America during the Cold War era. The Irish government has influenced events in Northern Ireland, as did also the UK government, though the latter was hardly an outsider; the UK, Greece and Turkey have all influenced the conflict in Cyprus; and the European community influenced the course of the wars in the former Yugoslavia. In such cases, the third parties often have their own axes to grind. Furthermore, wars take place in a world with many influential international agencies and organizations, such as NATO, and under the spotlight of the international media. And of course, many wars would have been very different without the availability of arms from abroad – the Israeli–Palestinian conflict being an obvious example.

Political leaders and their colleagues may profit financially from war, though recently this has been a factor in the maintenance of a state of war rather than its initial cause. Angola and Liberia are examples. In Angola the war was originally ideologically motivated and both sides had superpower support. However, the leaders of both sides stood to make rich pickings from diamonds, oil, or other resources and, as superpower support dropped away, the situation became self-perpetuating. The financial resources obtained provided both the incentive to prolong the war and the means to do so.

Quite apart from their role in decision-making, leaders may also be symbols, both for their own group and for the opposing one. The importance of charismatic leaders was never more clearly demonstrated than by Hitler, who led Germany inexorably towards war through the 1930s; or by Winston Churchill, when he became Prime Minister of Great Britain at a moment when the USA was hanging back and the British Commonwealth was without allies and facing defeat. (Interestingly, Churchill was rejected by the popular vote as soon as the war was over.)

There is, of course, another side to the coin. Just as personally ambitious and misguided leaders can lead to conflict and violence, so it is wise leadership that recognizes the just claims, necessary for peace, of all parties involved. This is especially the case in the transition from authoritarian rule to democracy.

There could be no clearer example of this than in the Republic of South Africa's transition from Apartheid to democracy. Many had predicted that bloodshed was inevitable when the non-white majority gained the representation and control it had been denied for so long. Nelson Mandela's courage and statesmanship enabled him to guide the country towards a solution that did the maximum justice to the demands of all parties. And he achieved this without giving expression to the rancour he himself must have felt over the humiliation and injustice that he had suffered during his imprisonment.

CLANDESTINE POLITICAL ACTION

It sometimes happens that one state wishes to bend another to its will, but does not wish to be seen taking overt military action, even though political pressure and other means may have failed. In such a case it may use clandestine action. Throughout the colonial period, European powers tried to persuade local leaders to take their side: such activities were particularly salient in Africa, and in the attempts by Russia to gain access to the Indian Ocean and by Britain to prevent it. During the Cold War period both of the superpowers strove to extend their influence in other countries, usually by combating or promoting communism. They operated behind the scenes to foster and influence wars between and within states. Such operations included financial and technical assistance, the supply of arms, assassination of influential political figures and the training of combatants. For instance, the United States, sometimes aided by Britain, covertly opposed the Soviet Union's invasion of Afghanistan by providing arms to the Taliban and thereby assuring their victory – a move that they subsequently came to regret.

AUTONOMY OF GROUPS WITHIN STATES

So far we have been concerned primarily with conflicts between states, but we saw in Chapter 1 that most cases of armed conflict now occur within states. Any collection of people that sees itself as an entity is likely to want to control its own destiny. Groups within a state may see themselves as distinct entities by virtue of a history, culture, religion, ethnicity or language that differs from the rest of the population. Discontent over lack of security, prosperity or involvement in political decision-making may fuel a desire for independence or greater autonomy. When a state contains a sizeable religious or ethnic minority, and especially when a state fails adequately to satisfy the needs or aspirations of all its peoples, a minority may feel that it could do better on its own, and seek to secede, or at least to obtain a degree of independence. Tensions then arise in the clash between the desire of such a minority group to determine its own destiny and to pursue its own way of life, and the desire of the central state authority for continuing control. Often the minority group desires to secede.

Since 1945, many countries have achieved independence from their former colonial masters. In the post-Cold War era, tensions within states have been frequent, and in many cases have led to violence and even protracted war. Where one of the major powers had supported a repressive regime from behind the scenes, the minority was better able to try to assert its demands when that support was withdrawn. The nationalist movements within the former Soviet Union, and the break-up of the former Yugoslavia, are clear examples.

A somewhat different sort of situation resulted from the demise of the Soviet Union in the Baltic countries. Many Russians had moved into Latvia, Lithuania and Estonia during the occupation – both in the occupying forces and as civilian residents. When independence came in 1991, problems arose. Each of these Baltic states threatened to impose restrictions on its Russian residents, and tensions ran high. It was only preventive diplomacy co-ordinated from a number of independent sources, together with generous financial aid from the USA to help in the repatriation of the Russians, that led to a solution. The case of Chechnya, however, is very different. Its strategic importance, and the probability that secession would lead to a domino effect amongst neighbouring regions, has led the Russian government to refuse its desire to secede: the result has been a long and bloody war. This has included terrorist attacks in Russia itself, like the taking hostage of a theatre audience in Moscow – an action that was brutally suppressed with a considerable number of casualties.

A state government is inevitably unwilling to lose control of a section of its population or part of its territory. The granting of autonomy would infringe the state's integrity and diminish its own strength and sphere of influence. And at the moment, quite apart from such self-interest, state authorities can claim legitimacy in resisting demands for independence from minority groups. By definition, every state has been seen to have the right to control affairs within its own borders. That is the basis of the concept of sovereignty, enshrined in the Charter of the United Nations. State sovereignty and the self-determination of a constituent group are incompatible, for sovereignty and self-determination of a group within it are contradictory principles in international law. International law, based on the concept of sovereign states, cannot recognize an unqualified right to secede because to do so would undermine the legitimacy of the states themselves.

As a consequence, the United Nations is virtually prohibited by its Charter from interfering in the internal affairs of sovereign states (UN Charter, Chapter 1 Article 2:7). We say virtually, because there is some ambiguity: it has responsibility 'to determine the existence of any threat to the peace', and 'to maintain or restore international peace and security' (Chapter VII, Articles 39–42). But the fact that the Charter is based on the concept of sovereign states means, for instance, that the Kurds, who live in four different countries, have no existence so far as the UN is concerned.

CHARTER OF THE UNITED NATIONS

Chapter 1: Purposes and Principles
2.1 The Organization is based on the principle of the sovereign equality of all its Members ...
2.7 Nothing contained in the present Charter shall authorize the United Nations to intervene in matters which are essentially within the domestic jurisdiction of any state ...

Many now question the emphasis on sovereignty in the United Nations Charter. In the modern world, a disturbance of the status quo within any one state may have widespread repercussions. Even a change in its government may affect other states, and civil war is likely to have serious effects in other countries. International forces influence the prosperity of every state. So whether they wish it or not, nation-states are losing aspects of their sovereignty as the inter-relations between nations become more important. Globalization (see pp. 89–94, 135–6) promotes international links, and tends to diminish the internal power of individual governments.

The rights of any one state must therefore be tailored to those of others, so that the concept of the nation-state is becoming gradually less applicable in the modern world. Boutros Boutros-Ghali, in drawing up 'An Agenda for Peace', when Secretary-General of the UN, argued: 'The time of absolute and exclusive sovereignty has passed.' Instead he emphasized that leaders of states should find a balance between the needs for good internal governance and the requirements of an ever more interdependent world. The (unsuccessful) UN intervention in Somalia was seen as justified by the internal chaos in the country.

Nevertheless, states are prone to resist secession. Repression, or lack of responsiveness to the demands of the minority group, is likely to make the situation worse. If the feelings of the minority group run high, the resulting tension all too often leads to violence that may be severe and protracted. This may take the form of sporadic attacks on conspicuous or symbolic targets, in which case the combatants are seen by the minority group as 'freedom fighters', but are labelled as 'terrorists' by the majority. The IRA in Northern Ireland has been a clear recent example, though some degree of regional autonomy for the Province may now be achieved. The Basques in Spain have had a degree of autonomy, but not enough to satisfy the extremists, who employ 'terrorist' tactics. Such violence may escalate into all-out war. This happened in the case of the Tamils in Sri Lanka, though resolution seems to have been achieved. Escalation is especially likely if the minority group has support from the outside, as happened in a number of countries during the Cold War (see p. 85).

Without outside support, the minority group is unlikely to be strong enough to achieve complete independence, though it may achieve a degree of autonomy. Out of 30 attempts by ethno-nationalists to achieve independence or unification with ethnic kin between the end of the Second World War and 1990, only 14 achieved regional autonomy, and the conflicts lasted on average 14 years. Only in a few cases has the minority group acquired peacefully a considerable degree of autonomy from the rest of the country.

In any case, secession can prove to be an unsatisfactory solution unless the seceding group is homogeneous and contains no sub-groups, which are likely to claim self-determination in their turn. If it is heterogeneous, secession can spawn a sequence of problems. There may be difficulty in defining the limits of the population that wishes to break away, and the limits of the territory that they should occupy. What division is both fair and viable? What are the precise conditions in which a group should be allowed to break away? Could it form an enduring unit? And would there be groups within the seceding unit that would in turn demand their own autonomy? If the group is characterized by some criterion of culture, religion, or ethnicity, will there be minorities left on either side of the new border? Will it involve the movement of population, with all the suffering that that can cause? For such reasons, attempts to secede by force are rarely seen as justified by the state.

In some cases, war has been avoided by a degree of devolution. The granting of autonomy may then be a partial matter. It may involve the use of a different official language, the practice of a different religion, a different form of education, control of its own resources, its own system for the administration of justice, and so on. In such cases the minority group can acquire peacefully a considerable degree of autonomy from the rest of the country. At the same time, a close relation between the parent country and the newly recognized group can be maintained. This may take a number of forms. The central body may retain the power to limit or withdraw the autonomy if it sees fit to do so, though this can lead to continuing tension. Or the arrangement may be a federal one, with the division of power written into the constitution, as in Quebec within Canada and the Sikh in the Punjab, but in most cases tensions persist. But there have been successful exceptions. Switzerland, which adopted a federal constitution in 1848, is an obvious case. Bavaria and Saxony have retained many of their cultural traditions and a good deal of constitutional power.

When a reasonably amicable agreement can be reached, all is well. The division of Czechoslovakia seems to be a case in point. But, from the number of cases where it has not been possible, it is clear that full recognition and acceptance of the powers of the UN to arbitrate, or if necessary intervene, in disputes within states is highly desirable.

TERRORISM

We shall not attempt to define terrorism, because the use of this label depends on one's political perspective. As has often been said, one man's terrorists are another man's freedom fighters. Perhaps terrorism can best be specified by its aim – to injure or kill a few in order to frighten many others. By this criterion the IRA and the Irish National Liberation Army on one side, and the Ulster Volunteer Force and Ulster Freedom Fighters on the other, are all freedom fighters, although fighting against each other. So are the Palestinian suicide bombers, and so also are the Israeli tank crews that terrorize Palestinian villages, and indeed any troops who set out to teach a lesson to those who disagree with the regime.

Terrorism is both immoral and illegal, and can only be understood as the result of unbearable perceived injustice, and as involving actions by individuals or groups who lack the resources for conventional military action. Religion or ethnicity often serve as an excuse, but poverty, suppression of freedom or powerlessness are usually the root causes. It is usually a way of waging war against a superior power, and can be seen as a reaction against the political system or its leaders. And this carries the further danger that the superior power will use its strength as an excuse for aggression against states which are said to hold terrorists, as has recently happened in Iraq.

Terrorists must be condemned because they kill innocent civilians, and do so often without warning. But one can perhaps ask whether terrorist activities are more reprehensible than the indiscriminate use of tanks and bulldozers to destroy them, or the state terrorism used in the strategic bombing of cities in the Second World War. Violence too easily breeds violence, and the long-term prevention of terrorism must involve the removal of the causes for discontent.

We shall have occasion to refer to terrorism in a number of contexts later in this book.

CONCLUSION

Given the system of nation-states, each looking after its own interests, conflicts of interest between them are always possible, and may escalate into violence. However, the interdependence of states in the modern world is making this increasingly unlikely. Furthermore, it seems that democratic states are less likely to go to war with each other than are totalitarian ones, and the number of democratic states has been increasing. Danger spots remain, however.

The role of leaders in initiating war is, of course, crucial. But it must be remembered that leaders are fallible. When war impends they are subject to many conflicting demands, and must make decisions with inadequate information. Leaders may initiate clandestine political action to avoid overt war.

Given that each state is responsible for maintaining its own integrity, groups that feel themselves to be underprivileged may resent the state's authority and resort to violent means to gain what they perceive to be their rights. States have been seen as having sole authority for exerting control over affairs within their own borders, and intervention by the United Nations or other outside body has been seen as permissible only if international peace or security is threatened. However, under Chapter VII of its charter the UN has authority to intervene if there is a threat to, or breach of, the peace. At the present time the concept of national sovereignty is being increasingly questioned and thus the appropriateness of intervention on humanitarian grounds accepted.

Groups which lack resources and see themselves to be improperly deprived or underprivileged, may resort to terrorism. While it is necessary to punish the offenders, it must be remembered that violence breeds violence. In the longer term it is essential to identify the motivation of the terrorists' activities, and to rectify the perceived injustices from which they feel themselves to be suffering.

7   Culture and Tradition

A country's political system and its leaders are not the only factors related to the probability that it will be involved in violent conflict. Aspects of its culture, and cultural differences between societies, are also important.

CULTURAL FACTORS RELATED TO VIOLENCE

Is military prowess valued in the society, or is violence denigrated? The cultural climate not only reflects the country's past history but also influences the probability of the country becoming involved in war.

There are very few countries in which war seems never to occur: this is a controversial issue, but it is claimed that the Inuit of the Canadian Arctic, and a few hunter-gatherer societies living in tropical or sub-tropical regions elsewhere, never engage in inter-group violence. The Inuit appear to have a variety of cultural devices that contribute to this condition. These rare pre-industrial societies that shun war have probably become peaceful either because of their relative isolation, or because their circumstances have been such that the probable gains from war were perceived to be less than the costs. However, the absence, or relative absence, of war does not necessarily mean that human potentials are different in these societies. Rather cultural mechanisms have developed such that individuals are less prone to display violence, and the societal structure is less conducive to it. For instance, these societies tend to be egalitarian and to have an anti-violence value system. This means, for example, that combative sports are rare or non-existent; the norms governing day-to-day behaviour are such that quarrelling, boasting, stinginess, anger and violence are stigmatized, while generosity and gentleness are encouraged. These norms involve an accepted contrast between the peaceful members of the society and the violent outsiders, who are portrayed as evil and dangerous. Outsiders who attempt to interfere are resisted, but such societies appear not to initiate violence.

By contrast, in classical antiquity war was part of normal life in the Greek and Roman eras. For two or more centuries war was a structural element in the organization of the Roman empire, and the state was almost continuously at war. Religion and cultural and moral values were suffused with a warlike ethos. Of the adult citizens 10 to 15 per cent were continuously committed to active military service. Political decisions rested with citizens with sufficient wealth to equip themselves for war. Many of the wars were primarily expansionist, and were often a consequence of the personal ambitions of commanders, willingly supported by their armies. Such wars brought enormous wealth not only to individuals but also to the state, and became a fundamental factor in its economic organization.

It has often been suggested that a settled way of life, together with the need to protect grazing land or stores of grain, made wars between groups more frequent, but, even if true, that cannot be the whole story. Archaeological evidence from pre-agricultural societies certainly indicates that war was not unknown. And in the modern world states have differed markedly in the frequency with which they have engaged in war. No doubt this is related to the nature of the political system that they have, but there is also a relation to the cultural climate within the state. In the Western world a few countries, like Switzerland, are prepared for war but have a long history of neutrality. Sweden, formerly militaristic, became committed to neutrality by a deliberate political decision, while at the same time retaining a significant military capability. However, the desires of both Sweden and Switzerland for neutrality did not prevent their becoming involved economically, politically, and in intelligence operations in the Second World War.

At the other extreme, some countries have, or have had, a long tradition of militarism. Nietzsche saw the warrior as epitomizing human life at its best. And at the beginning of the twentieth century Social Darwinists, naively applying the theory of animal evolution by natural selection to the international arena, regarded war as a route to progress, armed struggle providing the test of which nation deserved international supremacy.

Cultural attitude as used here is, of course, a nation-wide concept, and must not be taken to imply that all individuals have common attitudes. Even in the most aggressive cultures, and when their country has been actively engaged in conflict, there have been some with the moral strength to hold out against violence which they considered immoral or unjustifiable.

In addition to cultural attitudes towards violence, the structure of societies is related to the incidence of violence within them. More violent societies tend to be those that do not have generally accepted systems for controlling their internal affairs and the behaviour of their citizens. They tend to lack relations between individuals and successive layers of government, and the institutions that might provide such relations. They are without well-established social groups, like churches, trades unions or social clubs, whose members have respectful relationships with each other, seeing themselves as in some degree dependent on each other and with a communal obligation to each other. Such societies could also be described as lacking in 'social capital', and are less likely to have democratic governments.

In general, militarism towards outsiders seems to be related to attitudes towards violence within the society, and to the extent to which violence is legitimized. For example, some states practise capital punishment, and others do not: in some of those that do, executions are made into a public spectacle. In Europe, the centuries-long decline in violence has been related to, among other things, a decreasing tendency for states to use violence in punishing criminals. In a later section we shall see that legitimized violence within the society does indeed tend to go with militarism and involvement in war, though the connection is not a direct one (p. 96–8).

ETHNICITY

Current events in African countries, and especially the Republics of South Africa and Zimbabwe, have brought home to Europeans how powerful the forces of ethnic prejudice can be, and how hard it is to eliminate them. That ethnic prejudice can still also contribute to war in Europe was amply demonstrated in the disintegration of Yugoslavia (see below). A recent study has shown that countries exhibiting 'ethnic dominance', where one ethnic group makes up the majority of the population, are at risk of civil war. Anti-Semitism has been around for at least 2,000 years, and today racial violence persists in most European cities. What is the basis of this antipathy to outsiders?

The way individuals see themselves is related to how they see the group to which they belong. Even apparently trivial issues may affect this relationship: football fans walk taller if their team wins, but feel themselves to be diminished if it loses. Their self-esteem is not only influenced by their evaluation of their group, but also affects it: if they feel proud of themselves, they feel proud of their group.

Conflict and war necessarily involve distinctions between 'Our group' and 'The other lot'; between the in-group and the out-group. Individuals identify with the group to which they belong, and therefore see a threat to the group to which they belong as a threat to themselves (and in some cases a threat to the self may be seen as a threat to the group to which one belongs).

Group loyalty of this sort arises even when the two groups are picked at random, as when individuals are assigned at random to different football teams. But often, indeed usually, the differences between in-group and out-group are made concrete in terms of differences in language, politics, colour, culture and/or religion. In Northern Ireland the labels used are 'Protestant' and 'Catholic', in Apartheid South Africa they were 'Black', 'Coloured' and 'White'. Such differences serve as badges by which the two groups differentiate themselves as discrete social categories. They stand for what the conflict or war is 'about'. Although the differences may in fact have many sources – history, ancestry, class, customs, economic status and interests, for example – they are often referred to as 'ethnic' differences. Thus, although 'ethnic' was originally used to contrast a nation from outsiders, it has come to have a more general usage, and does not necessarily imply a racial or any other immutable difference.

Ethnic differences within a group can lead to two forms of discrimination, 'direct' and 'indirect'. 'Direct discrimination' involves simply dislike or hatred of the other group, which often stems from feelings of past or present injustice, or from a threat seen to be posed by the other group. 'Indirect discrimination' results rather from the structure of society, and is not necessarily based on ill-will. For instance, in a multi-ethnic community an all-white business that recruits by word of mouth is likely to recruit whites, with the result that non-whites feel that they are discriminated against. Indirect discrimination, therefore, may be a powerful source of ill-will even when it is not caused by ill-will. The situation may be made worse if the members of one group feel themselves to be deprived in comparison with the other. This can lead to fear, anger and aggression, which may be turned against the other group, superimposed on the basic feelings of difference between 'Them' and 'Us'. It is not possible to do justice to the full complexity of the factors leading to ethnic prejudice here, but it will be apparent that they are far from simple.

During the colonial era in some parts of the world, the seeds of inter-group conflict were sown by the drawing of international frontiers without regard to tribal and cultural links or differences. In Africa international boundaries were established with virtually no regard for pre-existing tribal distinctions, and in some cases inter-group rivalry was encouraged on the divide-and-rule principle. A similar situation occurred in both Western and Eastern Europe after the two world wars: an arbitrary boundary was drawn across Germany, and groups that saw themselves as culturally distinct were united in Yugoslavia.

When members of different cultural groups find themselves in the same administrative area, difficulties are likely to arise. Peoples with quite different cultures, or with a long history of rivalry and conflict, do not take readily to being forced to live on close terms with each other, or to supporting a government concerned with the general good. Although the Organization of African States (now the African Union) has supported the international boundaries imposed during the colonial era, such boundaries are likely to be of far less significance to the individuals concerned than those based on religious or ethnic differences, making the establishment of a new national identity an almost hopeless task, and providing a basis for long-term intra-state group rivalries. The boundaries between the cultural groups are maintained psychologically, and in many cases – especially if one group sees the other as having more power – strife ensues. The horrors in Rwanda and Yugoslavia, and the long-drawn-out conflict between Tamils and Sinhalese in Sri Lanka, provide recent and tragic examples. The Hutu/Tutsi distinction in Rwanda was formalized and exacerbated by the introduction of identity cards by the Belgian colonial administration. At the time of writing, the creation of a unitary government that crosses rival tribal units in Afghanistan is fraught with difficulties. Solutions to such problems have not been easy to find: it has been claimed that, if national boundaries were to be defined by ethnic identities, the Balkans alone could produce over 100 new states.

Conversely, a political boundary may separate individuals who see themselves as members of the same group, and in the course of time prove to be insufficient to eliminate a desire for unification – as in Korea and Vietnam. The Kurdish people have become divided between four nation-states, and thus find themselves not only unable to join together as a Kurdish nation, but also unrecognized by the United Nations. The break-up of the Soviet Union made possible a renewal of historic ties between groups within the Soviet Union and peoples in bordering states. In such cases, if conflict does break out, the situation may be exacerbated by differences in ethnic or religious allegiances between the majorities on either side: this has happened in Kashmir, where the concept of a Kashmiri identity seems to be vanishing because of the Hindu/Muslim divide. Conflicts of the type discussed here are often associated with a demand for self-determination.

Although in such cases the ethnic characteristics are seen as part of the essential natures of the two sides, permanent and unchangeable, they are likely to involve a mixture of objective characteristics, such as race, language and religion, with subjective ones constructed, in some cases deliberately, to foster differentiation between the two groups. The fluid nature of group markers is well illustrated by the case of anti-Semitism, for – at different times – the Jews have been described as a religious group, a race, and an ethnic category and as members of the State of Israel, even if only ideologically. Inter-group differences that seem fundamental to the group members may seem trivial to outsiders: nowadays the issues that divided Protestant from Catholic in past centuries hardly seem to merit bloodshed.

The disintegration of Yugoslavia was a gradual process, and turned people who had been good neighbours for decades into deadly enemies. It started with economic crises: unemployment was high, standards of living had fallen dramatically, and the situation could be exploited by ambitious leaders. This led to competition between the republics, and this in turn to independent control of television and radio by the republics, challenges to federal authority, and the establishment of militarized 'territorial defence units' in the republics. All this was accompanied by increasingly vehement ethnic propaganda. For example, Svetlana Slapsak, a Serb, argued in the *International Herald Tribune* (27 May 1993) that the bestialities of war in what used to be Yugoslavia were triggered by words – clichés put forward by intellectuals and taken over by politicians. 'To nationalist Serbian writers Albanians were "bestial," Croats "genocidal," Slovenes "slavish," Slovenians and Croats in return called Serbs "barbaric," "Balkan" and "Byzantine." These phrases were soon recycled by journalists, and young conscripted soldiers were sent off to war with such slogans ringing in their ears.' Hugh Beach (personal communication) comments: 'Note that Serbs, Croats and Bosnians are all southern Slavs, speaking the same language, genetically indistinguishable, separated only by the area in which they live, their religion (Catholic, Orthodox, Muslim), and a bloodstained history.' In the former Yugoslavia this conflict provided a frightening demonstration of the way in which communities that had been intermingled and friendly could be transformed into warring factions, with propaganda enhancing so-called ethnic differences between them. In due course, this led to genocide or 'ethnic cleansing', and attempts to eliminate or remove the opposing group became an overt war aim.

Even earlier, Turkey's expulsion of Greeks and Armenians could be described in the same terms. In Rwanda, the early victims seem to have been Hutu opponents of the government, but hostility between the Hutus and the Tutsis was fanned by unscrupulous politicians: up to a million people, mostly Tutsis, were massacred. Some forms of ethnic cleansing have had a long history, for invasion often involved the elimination of the existing population, and the establishment of most modern states has a record of ethnic conflict somewhere in its history. British history is one of successive invasions, many of which were accompanied by attempts to exterminate or exclude the previous inhabitants.

In this way ethnic (or religious, see below) differences are used to justify or exacerbate tensions whose roots lie in the more immediate issues of poverty and unemployment. They provide a convenient way of finding a scapegoat for current ills. In the past, the Jews have been used as scapegoats in the West. In recent centuries the imperial powers (mainly Britain) have been blamed, with more justification, for past and current problems in countries in Africa and the Far East.

On a small scale, this transference of blame can occur 'by mistake': an attack on an individual for some other reason may be ascribed by the victim or the victim's friends to ethnicity, and lead to reprisals against those of the same ethnicity as the attacker. More often, ethnicity or religion is used by those with influence to foment inter-group hatred, as noted above. The safest route to the prevention of ethnic tension involves the creation of a workable distribution of economic opportunity and political power between the groups in conflict (see Chapters 6 and 15).

Ethnicity, then, is a label used to characterize the differences between two groups in conflict, differences that are seen by those involved, and presented to outsiders, as natural, timeless, and immutable. So immutable, in fact, that new information is twisted to accord with stereotyped preconceptions. Usually, however, the conflict has little to do with the characteristics that seem to differentiate the groups, but is based on quite different, often economic, causes. Ethnicity is then merely used as a basis for political mobilization or social stratification. Its importance is reconstructed and exaggerated for political purposes. Many of the characteristics on which the differentiation depends, if not fabricated, are given enhanced significance in the cultural traditions and in the propaganda used to foment the struggle.

The problems are particularly severe when two groups, which see themselves both as nations and as ethnic groups, come into conflict over territory, self-determination, or culture. This has been and is the case with the Palestinians and the Israelis. The Jews, who have come to Palestine from many parts of the world, see themselves as a nation for historic, religious and ethnic reasons. A Palestinian national identity has been created, largely as a consequence of the conflict, during the last 50 years. Many on both sides assume that the two sides have contradictory collective memories and goals. The core of the present situation is that the Jews have fulfilled their goal of establishing a state of Israel, while the Palestinians are living in a state of Israeli occupation or control. It is difficult to see how this can be resolved unless the Israelis relinquish the territories conquered and illegally occupied in 1967 and allow the formation of a Palestinian state. Many individuals see this to be in the mutual interests of both sides and as the only way forward: as so often happens, the way is blocked by extremists on both sides.

RELIGION

Religious differences are often seen as an aspect of ethnicity, but not infrequently act independently as a fuel to sustain the institution of war. Cromwell's New Model Army was inspired largely by religious fervour. Some religions have advocated war against outsiders. Thus, before Muhammad was powerful he advocated tolerance, and the Quran cites him as saying 'To you be your religion, and to me my religion' (109:6 Yusufalis translation). But later the message he gave was quite different: one should 'kill the disbelievers wherever we find them' (2: 191), and 'fight the unbelievers until no other religion except Islam is left' (2:193). Such precepts were, of course, associated with attempts to spread Islam by conquest. Fortunately, only a small proportion of the most fundamentalist Muslims attempt to follow these precepts literally, and many now see the *jihad* as a war against evil rather than human opponents. However, so long as some still subscribe to them, they remain a threat to the rest of the world, and one must hope that the metaphorical interpretation will prevail.

It is perhaps salutary to remember that the Judaeo-Christian Bible carries similar passages. The divine instructions in Deuteronomy (20, 10–18) required the Israelites to subjugate or kill all males in the cities that they encountered, and the destruction of hundreds of cities and the slaughter of thousands of men and women is recorded with approbation. The Old Testament is full of accounts of bloody battles, and the imagery of the book of Revelation refers continually to war and death. Although the Crusades acquired imperialist and economic aspects, they were primarily religious wars in which Christian countries attempted to gain control of their 'holy places'. Many of those who participated had a motivation not so different from that of the modern suicide bomber, so that a late thirteenth-century Dominican preacher commented that 'by this kind of death, people make their way to heaven who perhaps would never reach it by another road'. The Crusades continued in one form or another for over 300 years and caused enormous suffering. The record of Christian persecution of the Jews, and of the internal strife exemplified by the Spanish Inquisition, provide a similar picture. All this in spite of the fact that the early Christians had accepted a form of pacifism – possibly the best policy in a period of persecution – until the conversion of Constantine allowed Christians to accommodate to militarism. In Christendom, St Augustine's need to justify participation in war led to the concept of the 'Just War', namely one necessary to avenge injury or to maintain earthly justice. Even today Christians still use militaristic metaphors – the Christian is often depicted as a soldier 'fighting the good fight'. Though such phrases would perhaps be better dispensed with, we have no difficulty in seeing them as metaphors. Hopefully, this will soon become true for all advocates of all religions.

Often secular ideals of patriotism and territorial rights are closely interwoven with religious ideals, so that support for the 'Just War' is derived from a mixture of the sacred and the secular. This is seen in a most extreme form in the belief of some right-wing Israelis that certain territories belong to the Jewish people by divine right. Such religious prejudices are firmly embedded in cultural traditions. Amongst Christians, anti-Semitism finds its roots in St John's Gospel, and was exacerbated by Luther, while Pope Innocent III equated Muhammad with the apocalyptic Beast of Revelations. Secular propaganda has parasitized these prejudices for political ends. But even within Christianity seemingly minor points of doctrine have been seen as adequate justification for persecution and even war. The conflict in Northern Ireland, although depending basically on differences in political, economic and cultural aspirations, is represented as, and has become, a conflict between Protestants and

Catholics. Religion has become the basic feature of identity, religious symbols being used in the rhetoric of 'otherness', so that there is a close affinity between religious and political loyalty. During the recent period of intermittent violence, Catholicism was seen as the enemy of the Protestant community, and any Catholic became a legitimate target – and vice versa.

Religious labels are especially dangerous in that they both legitimize war and portray it as a sacred endeavour. Religious belief can motivate and sustain violence, even in situations of great personal danger. Combatants can draw on religious images and symbols to explain their actions – images that justify their own actions and demonize the enemy. A basic problem for leaders in wartime is to convince their followers that they should risk their lives in battle: religion can present reward in an after-life as an incentive for sacrifice. Hence the dedication, almost incomprehensible to an outsider, of the suicide bomber.

Christianity is used in a similar way by equating death in war with Christ's sacrifice on the Cross. One of the more popular pictures in Britain in the First World War portrayed a dead soldier, lying at the foot of the Cross, with a small and nicely sanitized bullet hole in his head. Beneath were the words 'Greater love hath no man than this.' Even Hitler's ideology used the religious vocabulary of sacrifice in appeals to the German people to tolerate losses for the sake of the German *Volk*. The propaganda used by both sides in the world wars often carried the assumption 'God is on our side.' And religion has played a major role in the commemoration of those who died in war. War memorials, which nearly always have religious associations, not only help survivors to make their peace with the dead and comfort next of kin, but also add to the determination of the combatants: since the Greeks it has been recognized that men may be more willing to confront danger if they know that their sacrifice will be recorded. The role of religion in supporting wars is the less surprising when one remembers that separation of church and state is a relatively modern development. In most societies the religious system and the social system have been indivisible.

Religious images do not act alone. Religion is often conflated with ethnicity, and with politics and economics, for the issues underlying conflict are seldom simple, and religion can act as a powerful unifying label. The warlike potential of fundamentalist conceptions of religion often depends on a confusion between religion and politics. The politicized use of religion as a legitimizing ideology can mask underlying social reality and provide a cover for pre-existing patterns of inequality. As mentioned previously, this is clearly demonstrated by the Israeli/Palestinian conflict, in which religious, social, economic and territorial issues are inextricably interwoven. Similarly, the terrorist activities of the al-Qaeda, though carried out by a fundamentalist religious group, stem from basically political and economic motivations.

The tragic attacks on the World Trade Center and the Pentagon show how religious and secular issues become entwined. As noted earlier, the motivation for the attacks seems to have been primarily political – anger at the presence of Western troops in Saudi Arabia and unilateral support by the USA for Israel. According to some estimates, 200,000 Iraqis died during or immediately after the 1991 Gulf War, and it is alleged, although unsubstantiated, that a million civilians have since died as a result of the sanctions imposed by the victorious powers, and numerous further deaths have occurred during and after the 2003 Gulf War. These estimates may be far from accurate, but they are embedded in the consciousness of many in the Islamic world.

Religious factors have played an important part in uniting bin Laden's followers. Here an historical perspective is helpful. In the nineteenth century national leaders, who were not fundamentalists, arose in the Islamic world. In the twentieth century, conflict with Western beliefs surfaced. Standard Oil was nationalized in Iran, and the CIA attempted to intervene. This exacerbated anti-Western feeling. There followed the attempted Anglo-French invasion of Suez. Such incidents provoked uprisings leading to the end of non-fundamentalist leadership in many Islamic countries, and the power of the Mullahs increased. Further interference by the CIA in Afghanistan helped to provoke an international *jihad*, assisted by Pakistan. Islamic warriors were recruited from all over the world, motivated by their common Islamic inheritance. (Although Islam has its sectarian divisions, Muslims see great commonalities among themselves in a way that Christians do not, and injustices in some part of the Islamic world can be felt throughout the whole. Thus many, though certainly not the majority of Muslims, were pleased when the news of the 11 September attack came through.) For many of these warriors the political motives were forgotten, but the Western materialism and way of life provoked religious anger and jealousy (see also pp. 81–2, 166–8).

Thus, the causes of the terrorist attacks on New York and Washington can be traced back through history. The common religious basis provided a powerful unifying factor, and gave the movement much of its strength.

OTHER IDEOLOGICAL ISSUES

It goes without saying that a decision to go to war will depend on the perceived importance of the goals. If they include resources, much will depend on their scarcity, and the availability of alternative supplies. The conflict is likely to be more intense if the resource in question is shared by the parties concerned – for instance, if the problem concerns water supplies and both depend on the same river system. But, as we have seen, such tangible goals are often coupled with ideological ones that help to rally the population, and sometimes the ideological ones seem to be primary. Indeed, religious, ethnic, nationalistic and other ideological goals can be extraordinarily powerful, and it may be hard to deflect the parties in conflict from pursuing them. Although entangled with more secular issues, they may come to be seen as primary, and they can also be used to justify torture, rape and genocide.

The ideological issues involved in conflicts within states are diverse. One, as we have seen, is the desire for independence. Although the Basque country is often seen to be a violent part of the world, the actual levels of non-political interpersonal violence are similar to or lower than those in Spain and France. It is political violence, fuelled by the desire for independence, that is conspicuously higher there than elsewhere. The same could be said of the conflict in Northern Ireland, where political issues are closely interwoven with religious and economic ones. In Cambodia, insistence that the population should embrace an extreme form of Marxism led to the slaughter of millions who did not accept this. Internationally, the Cold War can be seen as concerned primarily with political ideology, though again other issues were also involved. And antipathy to communism in the USA had dreadful repercussions on freedom of opinion within its own borders, as well as on the internal affairs of other countries, such as Chile. This antipathy is still instrumental in maintaining tension in relations with Cuba through the imposition of sanctions, which continue in spite of Cuba's record in social services, and in spite of its improving relations with other Caribbean countries.

A related question is that of national pride. All nations, and indeed groups within nations, take pride in their achievements and in those of their citizens or members, and it would be a sad world if that were not the case. The claim that the human need for political/national superiority is a major cause of war is certainly an overstatement, but national pride can affect the incidence of war. The escalation in the stockpiles of nuclear weapons far beyond military requirements during the Cold War era can be seen as due in part to the national pride of the leaders of the two superpowers. Patriotism is seen as a desirable and praiseworthy emotion. Unfortunately, as we shall see later, it is often coupled with nationalism, in the sense of the tendency to denigrate others. Though the two are separable, in the sense that an individual can be high on one but not the other, they do tend to go together. Love for the culture and traditions in which an individual has grown up may fuel hatred for a country that threatens them, at the same time that nationalism, belittling the other party, increases confidence that victory is assured. In many cases, of course, such issues are closely interwoven with the religious, ethnic, and other ideological ones.

As always, one must be aware that causal relations may operate in both directions. War, or the threat of war, may enhance national pride, and that in turn increases the belligerence of those affected. In Britain, and at first also in Germany, the bombing of civilians during the Second World War resulted in an increase in their national pride and in their resolve – the 'We can take it' effect. Amongst the initial reactions to the appalling attack on the World Trade Center in New York was a feeling that national pride had been infringed, and there was an unprecedented demand for national flags as well as for immediate retribution. This certainly contributed to the feeling that 'war' was inevitable.

RETRIBUTION

'Getting one's own back', or the propensity to take revenge for injuries received, is a very basic aspect of human behaviour. In many pre-industrial societies lacking a functional legal system, the threat of revenge has been the best form of defence, and has been essential in maintaining personal relationships within the group. Indeed, threat of revenge for anti-social action was probably the principal means by which social cohesion was maintained in early human groups. In general, individuals feel morally obliged to take revenge on others who have harmed them or their kin – and not only their kin in the current generation but also their ancestors in preceding generations. This has been called the 'diachronic transference of pain', because people act as if they could feel the pain inflicted on previous generations. Often it is more than an individual matter, and involves families or larger groups.

The propensity is still with us; in parts of Europe the blood-feud is still part of the culture. Not surprisingly, therefore, revenge has provided a common motive for violence and war, dating from early hunter-gatherer groups to the present day. It can operate at every level from the family or kin-group to the state. For instance, revenge for past injustices still plays a major role in Northern Ireland, and memories of past conflict between the two groups are kept alive by annual marches and demonstrations. The same is true in the Balkans. In such cases, the versions of history espoused by outsiders, non-combatants and distant observers, may be quite different from the historical understanding held by those involved. Differences involving narratives of supposed injustices that have their origins in the distant past are used to characterize the groups in conflict. As another example, the divisions between Greeks and Turks in Cyprus are epitomized by the two Museums of National Struggle on either side of the divided capital of Nicosia. The museums present contrasting views of history, each integrating the history of Cyprus with their respective motherlands, each presenting the past as a narrative of national struggle, each with its own national heroes. The school text-books describe history in culturally biased terms, encouraging respect for and identification with the respective national heroes, and hatred for the other group. The present generations on each side have felt that the injustices they perceive to have been inflicted on preceding generations are still current and affect them. As a result, individual acts of violence have been responded to in a highly emotional way, and intercommunal violence has been seen as requiring direct retaliation in kind which has both immediate and symbolic significance. We shall mention again later how biased education, especially the teaching of history, can lead to chauvinism and xenophobia.

As discussed above, perceived injustices must be included as contributing to the recent attacks on New York. Unforgivable as the horrendous attacks on the World Trade Center and the Pentagon on 11 September 2001 were, revenge for perceived injustices perpetrated by the West certainly played a part (and revenge, perhaps stemming from injured pride, was seen by many Americans as justifying subsequent US actions). It is also now widely known that the USA, largely through the agency of the CIA, has sought to manipulate the governments of a number of other countries. And the British record is far from clean, even though the colonial era is long past. It includes repression in Malaya, the forcible removal of the population from Diego Garcia to make room for US air bases, and the supply of arms to repressive regimes in Indonesia and elsewhere. None of these facts excuses in any way the horror of 11 September, but they do indicate the need for the powerful nations to adopt a new attitude to those weaker than themselves.

CONCLUSION

Some countries are more prone to violent conflict than are others, though traditions of belligerence are by no means immutable. Cultural differences, both between and within countries, can also provide bases for disagreement. Differences in perceived respect for human rights have recently hindered political negotiations between the USA and China, but such cultural values may be products of a long historical development and slow to change. Agreement about human rights is more likely to come after political agreement than before, and its absence should not be allowed to delay the latter. Disputes are often associated with differences in ethnicity and/or religion, though these are often used as convenient labels for differences in circumstances, such as financial well-being or perceived privilege. Individuals identify with such labels, and feel themselves to be harmed by perceived injustices towards previous generations: revenge can then become a powerful motive for engaging in conflict.

8 Resources: Territory and the Environment

In the past, the pursuit of natural resources was a major goal of imperialism. Wars were engendered in connection with the command of the spice trade, the pursuit of gold in Central and South America, or the transport of slaves across the Atlantic. Sometimes these resulted from the initiatives of individual adventurers, but more often from national aggrandisement. Competition between the European nations for spheres of influence overseas sometimes involved land battles in Europe or sea warfare, with the loser ceding colonies to the victor. Even in the twentieth century some wars have concerned territory or resources. Germany and Italy sought to expand the territories that they controlled to gain *Lebensraum;* the need for oil and other natural resources was a potent factor in Japanese expansionism before and during the Second World War; and oil fields were central in the Iraqi invasion of Kuwait, and probably in the response to that invasion.

Mineral and oil resources are still potential causes of conflict. Cobalt and uranium in southern Africa, and phosphate in the north, have played a role in recent conflicts. Oil is an even more serious issue, and is likely to remain so until renewable sources of energy can be more fully exploited. It is estimated that the USA will soon have to increase its imports of oil by 60 per cent, and most oil is in regions that are unsympathetic to the USA, and, in some cases, politically unstable. The efforts of the USA to increase its military power in such regions may be a not unrelated phenomenon.

But although competition over resources other than oil is now less likely to lead to violent confrontation between the industrialized nations than was the case in the past, that does not necessarily imply that this will always be the case. Human pressures on natural resources and on the environment are increasing with the growth of the world's population. The human population increased nearly four-fold during the twentieth century and energy consumption increased twenty-fold.

Nowadays, competition usually seems to be a matter of political manoeuvring rather than violent confrontation. This, however, may be misleading in the longer term. About two-thirds of the world's oil resources, and most of the easily obtainable ones, are in the region of the Gulf: Western support for the élite and undemocratic government in Saudi Arabia, stemming largely from the West's need for oil, has been a major source of resentment for the al-Qaeda terrorists. And the resolve of the Bush administration to invade Iraq was at least in part due to a desire to influence the control of oil.

But although the competition for 'empire' persisted until 1945, since the mid-nineteenth century the causes of imperialist wars have usually been more diffuse, the acquisition of resources being still sometimes present but often secondary to the more general aims of extending influence, opening up overseas markets for manufactured items, and providing opportunities for emigration. Often the aim was to obtain resources and primary products in exchange for manufactured goods. At the present time real or feared territorial claims still cause tensions in a few parts of the world. The long-standing semi-war between India and Pakistan concerns their borders in Kashmir; Greece and Turkey have found it difficult to reconcile their claims on Cyprus and the Aegean; North and South Korea, artificially created and supported by powers with different political ideologies, have so far been unable to reconcile their differences; and China's invasion of Tibet has led to continuing tension, and its relations with minority populations both inside and outside its borders are far from equable.

Territorial acquisition has been important in another way in some recent intra-state wars – namely as a means of political control. Revolutionary groups may try to gain control of areas not initially by conquest but by political indoctrination or conversion. One method, conspicuous in intra-state wars in Central and South America, has been to attempt to provide improved conditions, thereby inclining the population to accept the group's ideals and to distance itself from the central government. Sometimes those who do not cooperate may be killed, as in the former Yugoslavia. In some cases, such as the civil war in Mozambique, other forms of population control may be used as well – terror, or expulsion of dissenting populations by force or by destruction of the environment.

More direct economic motives, as well as ideological ones, have been important in the conflicts between the USA and some South and Central American countries, which were seen to have expropriated US firms that had been exploiting the country's natural resources. In these cases the more powerful nation avoided the appearance of being at war by using less conspicuous means to gain its ends. These included on the one hand bribery, military and civilian advisers, and economic and military aid, and on the other covert operations and the promotion of civil war in order to displace regimes seen as threatening US interests or differing from US ideology. To this end the CIA was maintained as an aggressive, covert and ruthless organization. It contributed to the overthrow of the President in Iran (1953), and a coup in Guatemala (1954). It intervened in the elections in the Philippines (1953) and temporarily destroyed democracy in Ecuador (1961), the Dominican Republic (1963), Brazil (1964), Indonesia (1965) and Chile (1973). And, as mentioned earlier, it was active during the Russian invasion of Afghanistan. These operations probably had mixed motives, including hostility against regimes with ideologies different from those of the USA, and fear that the USSR might establish bases in the country in question, as well as economic interests in natural resources and opportunities for development. Before the end of the Cold War the Soviet Union used similar methods, though perhaps less effectively.

In the Third World, politico-economic (in a broad sense) causes for conflict are still potentially important, and war has been made more probable by the availability of arms in the aftermath of the Cold War, the Iraqi invasion of Kuwait being a case in point. In the wars that have caused so much suffering in Africa in recent decades, the acquisition of resources – diamonds, oil, gold, or other minerals – has been of central importance, not so much in the initiation of conflict as in its continuation. While, during the Cold War, many intra-state wars were supported by the two superpowers, this support was withdrawn when it came to an end. As a result, the government and the economy tended to collapse, if it had not done so already. However the rival leaders were able to continue the war from local resources, either directly or by extortion. Thus the civil war in Angola, originally ideologically motivated and supported by the superpowers, was kept going by the warlords of both sides who, by perpetuating the conflict, were able to obtain the necessary financial support and to amass personal fortunes from the country's wealth in oil and diamonds. International companies may also have profited from the situation. Other examples involved diamonds in Sierra Leone, cocaine in central South America, and lapis lazuli and opium in

Afghanistan. In addition, violence was also often used directly to acquire funds – by robbery, kidnapping, looting and such like.

In some cases, financial resources for continuing a conflict have been obtained from outside. This may have come from relatives or nationals living abroad. In other cases it may come from those who see themselves as having ties with one of the factions: for instance, the activities of the IRA have largely been made possible by contributions from Irish Americans. Finally, humanitarian aid donated by outside powers may be appropriated or 'taxed': the Bosnian Croats are said to have required 27 per cent from aid passing through their territory.

ENVIRONMENTAL RESOURCES

In recent decades the depletion and degradation of agricultural land, over-fishing, wasteful use of mineral resources, the depletion of fresh water, and pollution of the environment have been important causes of unrest and potential conflict. Environmental deterioration tends to widen the gap between rich and poor within states, and between rich and poor states. Poor states are particularly vulnerable because their populations contain a high percentage of children, and they lack the resources to provide temporary alleviation for crop failure. The consequences of crop failure may have spreading repercussions. For instance, poor crops may lead farmers to attempt to clear more land in less productive neighbourhoods. This may involve moving up slopes, leading to accelerating deterioration in the environment. Resource scarcity may lead to armed clashes, which may in turn be destructive of fragile ecosystems, and lead to the destruction of water systems and rainforest – as seen recently in southern Mexico. These problems are likely to be exacerbated in the future by the effects of global climate change, though these cannot yet be established with precision.

Environmental degradation has led to conflict in the past, and could do so again. It has even led to the collapse of civilizations, as with some ancient Mesopotamian civilizations, and in more recent centuries the Anasazi in the southwest of the present USA. The natural riches of Easter Island allowed the early Polynesian settlers to establish a flourishing civilization. But since then the island has been completely deforested and its resources degraded. Because of the island's isolated position war was not on the cards, but the result was a decrease in the population from about 20,000 to 2,000 by the time the first European settlers arrived. It is not beyond the bounds of possibility that a similar crisis could arise in the future on a global level.

The dangers may be particularly acute where natural resources are shared by two or more nations. Disputes over water have provided many examples. More than a billion people in many areas of the globe have no access to fresh water, and many more lack adequate sanitation. Over 260 river basins are shared between nations, and the sharing of water resources has been one of the factors in wars in the Middle East. The use of water from a river which crosses the international boundary has been a cause of friction between Spain and Portugal; Turkey and Syria have been in dispute over the waters of the Euphrates; Ethiopia and Sudan have been uneasy about Egyptian claims to a larger share of the Nile waters; and water resources have been an issue in relations between the USA and Mexico.

In southern Africa the growing population of South Africa, and its demand for a higher living standard, has necessitated major water conservation measures and water transport from beyond the national boundaries. The Kunene River, shared by Namibia and Angola, could give rise to problems. Complex systems of pipelines for transferring water between river basins have been proposed, some of the proposed pipelines crossing international borders in a part of Africa that, at the moment at least, is inherently unstable. For instance, plans to link the Congo River across Angola to Namibia with a pipeline would involve three countries. Disputes in these parts of southern Africa have been going on for a considerable time. As examples, the Okavango River forms part of the boundary between Namibia and Angola: a proposal for a pipe to extract water to relieve water shortages in Namibia is opposed by Angola, and also by Botswana which lies downstream of the proposed pipeline. A dispute between Namibia and Botswana over the Sedudu/Kasikili Island in the Chobe River involved military confrontation and had to be taken to the International Court of Justice; and Namibia and South Africa have disputed territorial and other water-related rights along the Orange River. The last two cases are complicated by natural changes in river courses and by mineral deposits in the present and past river beds.

Such examples show that water is a potential source of conflict but, in actual fact, so far wars over water have been virtually non-existent. Although water resources have been a frequent cause of dissent, in recent times they have led to violence in only a few cases: when Syria tried to divert the headwaters of the Jordan away from

Israel in the 1960s, and in a dispute over the Cauvery River in Sri Lanka. However, while it may be that at present water scarcity is unlikely to be a sufficient cause of war, the shortages are likely to become more acute. In many places the aquifers are being depleted, and the consequences of global warming are unpredictable. In any case, inequities in access to water can lead to poverty, shortened lifespans, and misery. In general, resource inequities can increase local or international disputes, create refugees who attempt to cross borders, and render a nation more vulnerable to economic or military aggression. Environmental scarcity may augment the differences between rich and poor, and lead to mass migration, which may in turn be part of a causal network leading to war.

Another cause of conflict lies in the pollution of one country by the industrial activities of another. There have been disagreements between the USA and Canada, and between the USA and Mexico, arising from the acid rain produced by industrial production in one country falling on the other. Similar problems are likely to arise between China and both Koreas, and could arise between the UK and Scandinavian countries. Pollution of the seas through the release of nuclear wastes is another source of friction between the UK and its neighbours. Although such issues have not so far led to violent conflict, the spreading effects of environmental pollution and deterioration make it a real possibility for the future. In addition, global pollution, leading to climate change, rising sea levels, drought in areas that are at present fertile and floods in others, is an increasing threat. This will affect the poor more acutely than the rich, and may well lead to insurgency against the latter and their international supporters.

CONCLUSION

Competition between states over territory is less likely to lead to war than was formerly the case, but politico-economic causes of conflict are still important, especially in the Third World.

Over-use of resources and environmental degradation is also likely to be a contributory cause of conflict, especially when it involves disputes over water resources.

9 Economic Factors: Globalization and Poverty

GLOBALIZATION

We suggested earlier that, in a changing world, it is dangerous to use the past to predict the future. The acquired independence of the former colonies, together with their increasing access to modern weapons and the likely response of the community of nations, have made it highly improbable that the industrialized countries will try to use force to obtain resources in Africa or South America or to acquire new markets for their products. This, of course, is not stopping them using political or economic means to achieve their aims.

However, the world is changing with great rapidity in yet other ways that could breed conflict. 'Globalization' refers to the ways in which happenings in different parts of the world are becoming progressively more interconnected. The increasing efficiency of communications means that information can now be transmitted to distant parts of the world at almost no cost. This has had an enormous impact on the commercial and industrial worlds, for commercial organizations can now establish branches, and operate more readily, in markets in distant countries. Modern information technology has made it much easier to transfer money across the world, so that stock and money markets in different countries are closely linked. As a consequence, in the second half of the twentieth century multinational companies have grown and multiplied, and capital markets have become increasingly internationalized. These changes, together with liaison between the military forces of different countries and the development of communications, have led to a network of common and reciprocal interests that makes war amongst the developed nations seem much less likely. Within Europe, especially, the degree of economic unification makes violent conflict between states improbable. However, it must also be noted that, as companies become more powerful, their influence over government increases: they can use their wealth to influence political elections and political decisions, and they can encourage both arms manufacture and interference in other countries that is unwelcome to its inhabitants. Corporate influences tend to dominate the well-being of the people as a whole. This has surely been the case with the USA.

In the second half of the last century many economists welcomed globalization, taking the view that policy-makers should aim above all for growth: inequalities might get worse as a result, but that would stimulate competition and might be a necessary sacrifice in the interests of longer-term average prosperity. In their view, the benefits would be best achieved by allowing global trade and investment to expand, and by encouraging free movement of trade and capital. By referring to gross global changes, some economists argue that the expected benefits have been realized. The average individual now lives longer, is better educated, and is better off financially than was the case a few decades ago. However, such improvements, though correlated with globalization, probably depended much more on other factors, such as the advances in medical science, and in some places on the so-called 'green revolution' and other practices in agricultural science. Increased educational opportunities for some are, in part, a positive consequence of globalization and the use of information technology. The advances in communication intrinsic to globalization can acquaint members of different cultures with each other's way of life, and thereby enhance cross-cultural understanding. Globalization could be associated with a recognition of the common humanity of all peoples, and thereby diminish conflict between groups.

We shall return to some positive effects of globalization in Chapter 11. However, as mentioned above, in practice it has proved to be a two-edged sword. Moreover, the very rapid rate of progress in information technology may contain a threat to global security. As with all new technologies, it is initially very expensive and thus accessible in the beginning only to those who can afford to pay. About 90 per cent of all computers are at present in the industrialized world, mainly in the United States. The language of the Internet is predominantly English, although this language is spoken only by 10 per cent of the world's population. The benefits of information technology are therefore available, almost exclusively, to the English-speaking nations, resulting in the less developed countries falling back very rapidly in technological attainment.

In the area of information technology – with the many benefits that accrue from it – there is thus a widening gap between the rich and the poor countries, and some analysts see this as a portent of a catastrophe for civilization. A widening gap between nations is a source of aggravation in international relations, a likely cause of strife, tension and even war. Hence, it is alleged that the rapid growth of the Internet might itself become a cause of war, a war that has been described as between 'the West and the Rest'.

We do not subscribe to this pessimistic conclusion. While not denying that the wide gap resulting from the uneven access to information technology is potentially dangerous to world security, we see this as a temporary drawback, a transitional obstacle. In addition, this drawback is more than offset by a potential benefit – information technology is leading to progress in education at all levels (though this has been lamentably slow at tertiary levels, Figure 5) and better education is essential if we are to build a better world (see Chapter 13).

In a number of other ways, globalization has exacerbated factors that are conducive to war. It has resulted in an integration of the world economy such that some commercial firms are not subject to democratic control in any one country, and the role of the state is compromised. Many of the larger transnational corporations are now more powerful than some of the nation-states within which they operate, and have an undue influence on the policies of the latter. Of the largest economies in the world 51 per cent are transnational corporations, and only 49 per cent nation-states. The power of the multinationals in the USA influences political decisions and indirectly enables that country to go its own way, with little regard for the rest of the world. The diminished power of states can involve a diminished ability to control the use of force. Multinational conglomerates are interested in profits, and this often takes priority over the welfare of the inhabitants of the countries where they operate. Of course, it is the poor who suffer most.

The close linking of financial markets has meant that an upheaval in one region can throw vast regions of the world into chaos. This did in fact happen when the East Asian economies crashed in 1998: the immediate effect was that the demand of these countries for raw materials dropped, and this affected the economies of other countries. The more recent collapse of the oil giant Enron in the USA, and accounting irregularities in other major businesses, have had repercussions around the world.

Furthermore, globalization can lead to potentially dangerous forms of competition, especially competition in technology, that carry a great deal of human misery in their train. For example, the multinationals may be in competition with, and more powerful than, local

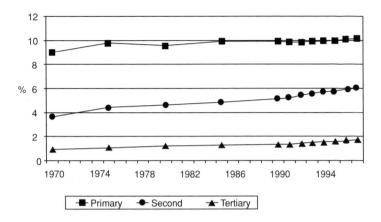

Figure 5 Enrolment ratios by level of education

Source: UNESCO Statistical Yearbook 1999. UNESCO uses 'gross' enrolment ratios (the ratio of students enrolled in a given level of education regardless of age, to the population of the age-group officially corresponding to that level of education) as a general indicator of the level of participation in education.

industries. This may cause unemployment in the countries to which they export their products. The industrially advanced nations are better able to pioneer technological advances than those less technologically sophisticated, and the latter may find themselves in a position of dependency. The ability of large companies to produce foods and other products more cheaply than traditional local enterprises may also be detrimental to the countries where they market their goods by increasing unemployment among those who cannot acquire more modern skills in the latter. The drive of large companies to market their own products may even undermine the health of populations in the Third World: encouraging mothers not to breast-feed their children by export of breast milk substitutes has had a detrimental effect in the Third World because the substitute lacks the health-giving properties of mother's milk. In general, the World Trade Organization has attempted to establish fair trade, but some of the richer countries have imposed their own restrictions to favour their own interests. The result has been that high tariffs on imports to the Western world prevent poorer nations from profiting from their traditional industries. The tariffs imposed by France and the USA, particularly those on the food products and textiles produced by smaller or poorer countries, have had a thoroughly detrimental effect on the latter.

While large companies may transfer some of their operations to less well-developed countries because labour is cheaper there, and thereby alleviate unemployment in the latter, countries which are not chosen to participate in this way, like those of sub-Saharan Africa, tend to fall even further behind. Thus globalization tends to increase the disparities between those who profit from it and those whose worlds are still tied to localities. While some countries have expanding economies, for many others the economy is contracting.

After the end of the Second World War the newly acquired independence of former colonies gave great hope to the Third World. However, a number of factors, including the greater technical expertise of the former colonial powers and the desire of Third World countries for technical equipment, including arms, gave the already industrialized countries further advantage, and – as mentioned earlier – in many cases the gap between the rich and some of the poorer nations increased. Globalization has failed to result in equality of opportunity between the developed and the developing nations.

Not only has globalization been accompanied by little if any diminution and often by increases in the differences in wealth between rich and poor countries, during the last two decades of the twentieth century it has been accompanied by an increase in the gap between rich and poor people within countries. This has been the case even in the USA, where nearly 40 per cent of the nation's wealth is now owned by 1 per cent of the households. This is partly due to the fact that the movement of unskilled jobs to countries where workers demand lower wages has resulted in fewer unskilled jobs in the USA and other industrialized nations. As would be expected (pp. 96–8), in a number of countries the expanding gap between rich and poor has been accompanied by an increase in individual violence and growth in the prison population. Social safety nets have become less effective. These trends appear to have been related to policies advocating the unrestrained magic of the market place, resulting in the increased wealth of the rich countries, and especially their richer members, at the expense of the poor.

In addition, since technological expertise lies primarily in the West, globalization involves the spread of Western values and ideas. This has resulted in resistance to Western influences in parts of the world where the cultures and traditions are very different from those in the West. Globalization and the increased efficiency of communication have highlighted the differences in standards of living, making more apparent to many living in less developed parts of the world the depth of their poverty and lack of political freedom in comparison with the West. Globalization is often seen as an aspect of Western imperialism, bringing resentment at the intrusion of alien practices, augmenting demand for the preservation of local cultures and religions, and thus producing a tendency for groups to mobilize round religious, ethnic or racial identities. As we shall see, this may lead to a resurgence of fundamentalism, which may be exploited by political leaders.

In summary, while globalization is unlikely to be a direct cause of war, the changes it involves exacerbate many of the factors that make violent conflict within or between states more likely. While it is unlikely to go away, efforts to ameliorate its deleterious effects are essential.

POVERTY

Differences in wealth, both between countries and between individuals within countries, are enormous. Contrasting the fifth of the world's population that live in rich industrialized countries with the fifth that live in the poorest, the per capita income differs in a ratio of the order of 100:1. Worse still, the gap is getting larger, as is evident from the graph in Figure 6, which shows the variation of the ratio of per capita income between the richest and poorest countries over the past 30 years. According to a recent estimate, nearly one-fifth of the world's population has to live on less than two US dollars a day. Nearly 2.4 billion people lack basic sanitation, and one billion lack adequate water resources.

Vast differences in wealth are also to be found within countries. One way to show this is to rank the households within a country from the richest to the poorest, and then to compare the income of the household at the bottom of the top 10 per cent of the population with that of the household at the top of the bottom 10 per cent. During the 1990s in the UK the bottom household in the top 10 per cent was 4.6 times better off than that at the top of the bottom 10 per cent; in the USA the figure was 5.6, and in Mexico 11.6. Though reliable data are not available, the difference between the household at the very top and that at the very bottom must have been even more dramatic. Such differences within a country mean not only that the rich are vastly better off than the poor, but also that the

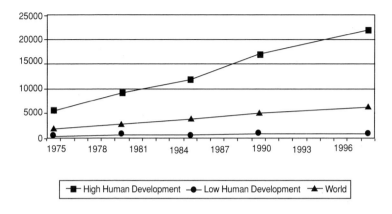

Figure 6   GDP per capita (US$ 1995)

Source: Based on data taken from *Human Development Report 2000* (New York: Oxford University Press, 2000). The data is derived from GDP and population data collected for the World Bank and published in its *World Development Indicators 2000*. 'Human development' refers to the 'Human Development Index', a composite index developed by the UNDP based on longevity, educational attainment, and per capita GDP.

poor are constantly confronted with the contrast. The patterns of world trade, mass production technologies in the industrial nations, patent laws, and many other factors are tending to increase the gap between rich and poor.

It is difficult for people living in affluence to imagine the lives of the very poor. The latter may live in constant fear of starvation and at the same time display extraordinary fearlessness in protecting their needs or those of their children. They may be faced with decisions as to who in their family shall live and who shall die. Infanticide may become an acceptable course of action. If conditions become clearly hopeless, they may become passive, accepting their fate. Alternatively, they may become fiercely competitive, and train their children to become similarly competitive. This competitiveness may be accentuated if the poor live side by side with the affluent, or have access to television, so that their noses are rubbed in the differences in their circumstances. (Of course, intense competitiveness is also found amongst the affluent members of a society, especially those who have recently acquired their wealth; it is indeed the driving force of capitalism.)

Is poverty, or wealth differentials, conducive to war? Some wars have been between countries, or between groups within countries, in which average incomes of one side were very low and income differences between groups high. A positive correlation between poverty and war has therefore often been suggested, but the evidence is equivocal and the arguments go both ways. On the one hand, it is argued that people become fiercely competitive when resources are scarce. The frustrations consequent upon poverty, especially acute when comparisons are made with others more fortunate, can stimulate aggressiveness, and make it easier for leaders to incite their followers: the poor may feel that they have nothing to lose in going to war. The poor's ignorance of worldly affairs may make it easier for leaders to persuade them that war will be in their best interests. But an alternative view is also possible. Others have pointed to evidence that, as noted above, with increasing poverty and deprivation, and especially if deprivation is extreme, people become passive, seeing their fate as inevitable and beyond their control. If poverty enhances the sense of powerlessness and vulnerability, it is unlikely that a population which already feels that life is difficult would welcome war.

Discussions at the socio-economic level have been similarly equivocal. Since wars are expensive, some argue that national poverty must render international war less likely. Indeed, financial resources with which to make or purchase military hardware are essential in most cases, so the country or group must have the necessary resources before it chooses the way of war. The First World War was made possible by a period of great economic progress in Europe. (Civil wars may provide exceptions to the generalization that war needs a large financial backing.) On the other hand, a country or group with inadequate resources or markets may see war as the only solution to its difficulties, as with the Japanese invasion of Manchuria in the 1930s and its entry into the Second World War. A country would be especially prone to take the path of war if it saw its rivals as militarily weaker than itself. (Of course, in the twentieth century it became only too apparent that causation could operate in the other direction. War is both expensive and destructive, and can lead to the impoverishment not only of the vanquished but also of the victor.)

Thus, mere argument at both the individual and socio-economic levels is indecisive. And in fact, the historical record provides no hard evidence to show that poverty, or that a difference in wealth within a society, is *directly* related to the probability that that country will be involved in war. While some developing countries with exceptionally high disparities in income have suffered disastrous civil wars, there are many others with a similar disparity that have not. But is it possible that the question we are asking is too simplistic? We have stressed repeatedly that the causes of war are seldom unitary, and that war results from complex networks of interacting factors. It may be argued that most major internal violent conflicts are immediately caused by bad leaders, though social conditions are also important in making conflict possible: poverty, or marked discrepancies in wealth within the population, can be a powerful element in those social conditions. As argued in the next paragraph, there are in fact strong indications that a marked difference between rich and poor is part of a network of inter-related factors that link the conditions within a society to militarism.

In the first place, non-industrial societies that are often at war, unlike the peaceful societies mentioned in Chapter 7, seem consistently to have high rates of inter-personal, within-group violence. Such societies tend to engage in violent sports, have corporal and capital punishment, and male children are typically socialized for aggression. In industrialized societies, cross-cultural studies, using the homicide rate as the index of violence within the society, show a relation between homicide and inequalities in income. (By contrast, there is no consistent evidence that homicide rates vary in relation to industrialization, urbanization, unemployment, population density or cultural heterogeneity.) In turn, in both agricultural and industrial societies high rates of homicide are related to frequent involvement in wars. In other words, there seem to be links between wealth differentials (at least in industrialized countries), interpersonal acts of violence within the society, and legitimized acts of violence by the society as a whole, such as capital punishment and militarism. The links between these probably concern the manner in which children are brought up. Impoverished parents are unable to give children the sensitive care that is conducive to a prosocial, cooperative temperament, and moreover such parents may encourage selfish assertiveness as a way to get on in a hard world (see pp. 102–3).

Thus, there appear to be linkages between the incidence of homicide within a society, various characteristics of the society including especially the wealth differential, and involvement in war, either civil or inter-state. Of course, the fact that wealth differentials, homicide and war are often linked still does not necessarily imply a direct causal relation between them, nor does it indicate the direction of any causal influences that may be present. But the relations between these factors are striking. We have already seen that there is a link between attitudes towards violence within a society and militarism, and it is at least plausible that inequalities and an atmosphere of violence within the society make war more likely. That homicide rates tend to increase in both winners and losers after a war suggests that there may also be some influence in the other direction, the actual waging of war focussing people's attention on the enemy and increasing loyalty to the in-group, resulting in a temporary decrease of violence within the society.

So far as intra-state wars are concerned, wealth differentials between different sections of a community may be a basic factor in internal conflicts even when the conflict is popularly characterized in other ways – for instance in terms of race, language or religion. This seems to have been so in the complex case of Northern Ireland. There, the two sides do indeed have different religions and often incompatible political and cultural aspirations but, underneath that, many members of the Catholic community have seen themselves as underprivileged in housing and employment, and the grudges of earlier generations are seen as current. Currently, there are signs that some Protestants are dismayed by the prospect of the Catholics increasing in population and resources.

Inequitable distribution of land has often led to conflict – as in Chiapas (Mexico), where impoverished groups rebelled against the government, and in Zimbabwe, where the wealth of white farmers contrasted with the poverty of the Mashona and Ndbele, whose discontent was exploited by the Mugabe government. Poverty also has the potential to act in another way. Together with increases in population, it may cause people to live in marginal environments where they are susceptible to natural hazards – for instance on flood plains (Bangladesh) or areas that are susceptible to earthquakes or volcanic eruption. This increases the demand for more favourable sites, and hence can lead to conflict.

While wealth differentials within societies have played an important though often indirect role in wars within states, their importance in wars between states has so far been much less clear. However, the attack on the Twin Towers and the Pentagon on 11 September 2001 has sounded a warning for the future. Though political issues were said to be primary and religious differences were also involved, and though those directly involved were mostly of middle-class origin, the wealth differentials between the industrial-ized West and some Eastern countries was certainly also a factor. Given modern communications, people in one part of the world can readily compare their situation with that of those in another. But wealth differentials are closely related to power differentials, and the consequences of the hegemony of the USA and other Western countries were undoubtedly also basic. This was indicated by the symbolic combination of the al-Qaeda attacks on financial and military centres, with a third but unsuccessful strike probably aimed at the centre of government.

We have seen that poverty, or wealth differentials, contribute to the causal factors leading to war. Factors that exacerbate the difference between rich and poor must therefore also be seen as (indirect) causes of war. We have already noted that the use of information technology is tending to increase inequalities between the rich and the poor.

Economic decline can also make violence more likely. As resources become scarcer within a society, competition for them increases, and the gap between the powerful and those less powerful increases. This may lead to violence and to deterioration in the state's power to govern. Indeed, the incidence of political violence in poor countries is due as much to poor governance, and absence of the necessary legal institutions and established practices to which the West is accustomed, as to poverty itself. Attempts to help countries at risk of economic decline must, therefore, be made with caution: policies intended to enhance growth can increase competition and augment inequality within the country, and thus increase instability within the society and make violence more probable.

The long-term future may be bleak. Some economists argue that the world's economic system is becoming increasingly dysfunctional. Financial crises have totally (though temporarily) disrupted the financial systems in a number of countries – Mexico, Indonesia, Argentina and Japan. Such catastrophes in one country have worldwide repercussions. A central factor seems to be that production outstrips demand, so that countries compete for markets. This leads both to marked instabilities in the financial system, and to marked economic and social inequalities, and this is not corrected by the poorly structured financial institutions and/or inadequate monetary and fiscal policies. Attempts to increase consumption exacerbate the environmental degradation caused by increasing population pressure and industrialization. And the competitive spiral leads to a need for increasingly complex skills. Those able to deploy such skills profit, but not everybody can, and many must accept lower paid jobs or unemployment. The discrepancy between rich and poor increases. More efficient and more complex institutions are required to manage the spiral of growth, and from time to time these inevitably fail.

CONCLUSION

Territory and resource competition, formerly major causes of war between industrialized nations, have become less so, but their place has largely been taken by political and economic competition for influence and markets. But needs for resources can be powerful sources of discontent, leading to conflict and perhaps to violence. Such needs are being exacerbated by environmental degradation, water shortage being an important example. Globalization, while having some positive consequences, is increasing the gap between rich and poor, and wealth differentials are related to discontent and conflict.

Looking back over the four preceding chapters, it will be apparent that none of the factors considered is *the* cause of any war, and no war has a single cause. Rather wars break out because a multiplicity of factors come together – competition over power; disputes over borders; ethnic, religious, or other cultural tensions; revenge; wealth differentials and other economic issues; environmental competition and degradation; weak governance; a perceived power differential between the opposing parties coupled with the failure of negotiations and many other issues. Often one of these is seen to be central, or is used by leaders to bolster support from the population, but would not be sufficient if the threshold for war had not been lowered by the presence of some of the others. Furthermore, the chain of events may be long, indirect and tortuous: for instance the 'transference of pain' may cross many generations; and resource shortages may lead to poverty, poverty to migration, and migration to violence.

The causes of war are thus not to be found at any one of the traditional levels of explanation – individuals, states or the international system. Rather it is necessary to analyse the relations between these levels, exploring the manner in which war is related through cultural and group processes, through relationships between individuals, to the basic propensities of individuals.

10   War and Human Nature

AGGRESSION AND AGGRESSIVENESS

Whatever the ostensible reason or reasons for which a group goes to war, a war cannot be fought unless there are people willing to fight it. Because war requires soldiers to kill enemy soldiers, it has been supposed that it is human aggressiveness that causes wars. In this chapter, we shall argue that, at least in the case of major international wars, that is not the case, and that the human propensity for aggression is not directly responsible even for the behaviour of combatants.

During the Cold War, which stemmed ultimately from ideological differences, politicians, trying to justify increasing their stocks of nuclear weapons, claimed not only that it was necessary to keep up with the other side, but also that human aggressiveness makes wars inevitable. This is an extension of the long-held view that the inherent aggressiveness of individuals is held in check only with difficulty, and is liable to burst forth from time to time in organized war. Therefore, a nation must arm itself to meet any emergency, but this justification for war, for that is what it amounts to, is simply wrong for several reasons.

To begin with, it involves a semantic error. We refer to an individual who intentionally harms others as 'aggressive', and may ascribe his behaviour to 'aggressiveness'. We also refer to a nation that attacks another as 'aggressive', and may refer to the aggressiveness of that nation. But 'aggressiveness' means something very different in these two situations. They have little in common other than that harm is caused. The causes operating when Bill strikes Bob are very different from those operating when an army marches across a national boundary. The physiological and psychological mechanisms causing Bill's behaviour have nothing in common with the chains of command in the invading army. We use the same term because both cases have in common similar (presumed) intents and likely consequences, but the two instances have nothing else causally in common.

Another reason why it is erroneous to argue that human aggressiveness requires us to depend on armaments for our safety is that it implies a false view of human nature. We all have the capacity to behave aggressively. That people do sometimes harm others is made only too clear to us by the daily newspaper and television reports of violence, murders, rapes and muggings. But these are newsworthy only because they are unusual. If burglaries or muggings were common, if they happened on every street every day, they would cease to be of interest. Things we take for granted do not get into the newspapers. For most of the time, most people are kind, sensitive, cooperative, caring, helpful. The newspapers give us a view of those other people out there, those strangers we usually do not know, who do evil things, when for the great majority of the time our everyday experience tells us that the whole world is not like that. The truth is that we all have the potential to show consideration and kindness to others, to behave 'prosocially' as well as to be selfishly assertive and aggressive. The important question, therefore, is what makes the balance swing one way or the other, towards prosociality or towards the selfish assertiveness that can lead to aggression.

That is a big question, and could take us very far afield. It is sufficient for the present context to indicate that the balance between prosociality and selfish assertiveness is affected by three groups of factors that mutually interact with each other. First, individuals tend to be more prosocial if they have been brought up by one or more caregivers (usually the mother and father) who are sensitively responsive to their needs and exercise firm but reasoned control. Conversely, people brought up in a harsh, insensitive and rigid atmosphere, or by parents who exercise too little control, often tend to be selfishly assertive and aggressive.

Second, the balance is affected by current circumstances. If life is difficult, if the necessities of life are really hard to come by, selfish assertiveness is likely to become more prominent. Not surprisingly, these two factors are linked, because parents living under harsh conditions find it difficult to be sensitive caregivers to their children and may encourage their children to be self-seeking. The children are then likely to grow up to be selfishly assertive like their parents.

Third, how individuals behave is influenced by the culture in which they are living: for instance, in a challenging environment, like that experienced by those who pushed out into the American West in the nineteenth century, assertiveness and independence were seen as virtues. One can suppose that people behaved assertively in part because they had been brought up in a manner conducive to such behaviour, partly because circumstances forced it on them, and partly because such behaviour was esteemed in the culture. And it works both ways, because the cultural climate not only affects the behaviour of individuals, but is itself affected by how people behave: aggressive behaviour can create a hostile social atmosphere and a value placed on selfish assertiveness, while when people behave kindly and cooperatively the atmosphere tends to become easier and more prosocial. Earlier in human history, when social conditions were more consistent and homogeneous than they are now, this would have been a system that worked well. Children would grow up to be relatively more assertive and aggressive if conditions were such that assertiveness would serve them well, and relatively more cooperative if that was likely to be a good strategy. Unfortunately, the current atmosphere of competitive capitalism in the West pushes the balance towards selfish assertiveness.

Of course, these are crude generalizations, and the interacting factors are more diverse and more complex than described here. But the point being made is important: in so far as the aggressiveness of individuals is important, either in supporting war or in actual combat, its salience amongst individuals is affected by the social environment.

To come to yet another reason why it is erroneous to ascribe war to individual aggressiveness, we must ask just how important individual aggressiveness is either as a cause of war or in the behaviour of combatants. It is important here to distinguish between 'aggressiveness', on the one hand, and 'aggression' or 'aggressive behaviour', on the other. 'Aggression' and 'aggressive behaviour' are descriptive terms referring to actions intended to harm others, directly or indirectly. If Bill hits Jack intentionally, that is an example of aggression. Often the term 'aggression' is extended to include verbal abuse. 'Aggressiveness' refers to the capacity or motivation to harm others. We have seen that humans have the potential to be kind and considerate, and also the potential to be selfishly assertive. Selfish assertiveness in the form of fear, greed, envy and so on, may arouse aggressiveness, the motivation to harm others. Only rarely does aggressiveness lead to aggressive acts independently of any other incentive. While war inevitably involves aggressive behaviour, the important question is how that behaviour is motivated. The answer depends very much on the sort of war being considered. In Chapter 1 we emphasized that wars differ along many dimensions, but for present purposes we may consider a spectrum from tribal raids, through loosely organized (but immensely destructive) wars like the outbreak in the former Yugoslavia or the genocide in Rwanda, to the two world wars.

In the tribal case, the combatants may be inspired to violence by hope of capturing women or cattle or by desire for revenge. In some cases a firm resolve to secure the reward, or to enhance their status amongst their peers, may fuel their aggressiveness, in others they may work themselves up with dancing, ritual, or drugs into a state where they are motivated to behave aggressively. Duty or loyalty towards the group plays at most a minor part in motivating their aggressive behaviour, which is primarily a tool to obtain their objective. Aggressiveness is not the basic cause of the slaughter, but when sufficiently aroused aggressiveness may take over, and individuals kill for the sake of killing. And violence feeds on violence: as we have seen, revenge is a powerful instigator of aggressive behaviour, and its effects are by no means limited to tribal societies.

In this context, the wars in Yugoslavia and Rwanda were intermediate between the conventionalized picture of tribal war given above and the world wars. They involved cultural groups that had previously lived apparently amicably together. The cultural differences, highlighted by political propaganda, provided the combatants of each group with an incentive and even a duty to attack the other. The war in Bosnia-Herzegovina was at one point a matter of territorial conquest, with a degree of central control, but escalated to extreme levels of brutality, often seemingly inflicted at the whims of local perpetrators – though they later tended to claim that the violence was forced on them by circumstances or by their superiors. The brutality was aimed at humiliating, terrorizing and killing the enemy population in order to remove it from the territory. It was rationalized by the views that 'they would do it to us if they could' and that the contested land 'is ours, really'. In both the former Yugoslavia and also in Rwanda, organized war in which the combatants saw the conflict in cultural, political or idealistic terms, and perhaps fought as a matter of duty, thus led to the arousal of individual aggressiveness. Often individuals who had previously been neighbours or friends were subjected to indescribable brutality, showing that the aggressive violence was a consequence of the dispute, not a cause. The genocide in Rwanda seems to have been planned at a high level by an élite who, to maintain their own power, induced hatred and fear amongst people who had previously lived together happily. The genocide was implemented by semi-autonomous local military and paramilitary groups. *But it was war that caused the aggression, not aggressiveness that caused war.* Thus, in the context of war, individuals who under other circumstances might behave with compassion can show callous violence. It is a sad aspect of human nature that, given the aura of war, the perpetrators of violence can view their acts in a positive light.

At the other extreme, in the two world wars individual aggressiveness between the combatants played at most a rather minor role. With some exceptions, the primary motivation of the combatants was not to kill the enemy but to do their duty. The tank or bomber crew setting off on a mission was not inspired by a desire to kill, but rather to do what they had been told to do. The infantryman moved forwards because it was his duty to do so, and he could perform his duty more adequately if he killed the soldiers who were trying to stop him.

Of course, there were times when it was necessary to kill in self-defence – when it was necessary to kill or be killed. And, more rarely, there were times when, often inspired by fear or by desire for revenge, naked aggression became primary. In such cases, the alienation from civilian life that is often inherent in military training may have permitted the combatants to disregard values that would previously have been central to them. But in the vast majority of cases the combatants did what they had to do: they fought because it was their duty to fight. And whether or not individual aggressiveness was solely responsible for the aggressive behaviour, *it was the state of war that caused the aggression, not aggressiveness that caused the war.* In any case, those who actually did the fighting whether on the ground, at sea, or in the air, constituted only a small proportion of those involved in the two world wars. The munition, transport and other workers, equally important to the prosecution of the war, also had duties, but duties that did not require them to behave aggressively.

To summarize the preceding paragraphs, the aggressiveness of individuals is not to be confused with the aggressiveness of nations. Aggressive acts play a part in all wars, but individual aggressiveness, while perhaps important in causing tribal wars, and induced in the Yugoslavia/Rwanda wars, plays virtually no role in fully organized warfare.

Studies carried out in the USA in the Cold War period of the 1980s showed that there was very little relation between the aggressive behaviour of individuals and their attitude towards militarism. But the training given to members of the armed forces, at any rate up to the time of the Second World War, was often such as to augment their aggressiveness. Alienation from ordinary life encouraged the abandonment of old values and the acquisition of a new ideology: peer pressure and discipline paved the way for killing. Beyond that, training for hand-to-hand combat involved rushing at a hanging bag of straw and sticking a bayonet into it. When under training, soldiers were instructed to imagine that the sack was an enemy soldier whom they both feared and hated: thereby their aggressiveness was aroused. Training for hand-to-hand combat thus involved learning to manipulate one's own motivation to harm others.

But hand-to-hand combat is rare in modern war, and no such emotional involvement is called for in using a rifle: indeed arousal might be counter-productive, handicapping decision-making and rendering less efficient the use of the weapon. In using the distance weapons that predominate in modem warfare the combatant pulls the trigger or presses the bomb release because it is his duty to do so, given the role he occupies in the institution of war. Military discipline, together with loyalty to buddies, leaders, unit, country and cause, together with pride and fear of punishment, combine to ensure that combatants do their duty – and overcome fear for their own lives. Some studies show that the fear of killing may be more important than the fear of being killed, and after battle soldiers may perceive their own actions as involving a dirty but necessary job.

A case of special interest concerns the kamikaze pilots who deliberately crashed into American ships, thereby sacrificing their lives. While the popular image has been of ultra-nationalistic young men eager to die for their emperor, a detailed study of some of their diaries shows that to be far from the truth. Many, perhaps most, dreaded dying, but saw themselves as caught up in the forces of history. Their patriotism was buttressed by pride in their masculinity, accumulating peer pressure that prevented them from backing out, and the honour bestowed upon them as members of an élite. Propaganda employed a traditional symbol causing them to picture themselves as falling cherry blossoms.

What, it may be asked, about the Holocaust? There is no simple explanation for the behaviour of those involved. There seems little doubt that many of the guards involved were sadistic and enjoyed inflicting pain and killing. But careful study has shown that a number of other issues were involved. The guards were encouraged to see themselves as members of an élite, so that cruelty to Jews or gypsies, whom they saw as inferior beings or non-persons, became part of their code of values and helped to confirm their social identity. There was a chain of command, with the threat of punishment for non-compliance hanging over them. And the duties of those involved were carefully subdivided, so that most individuals were responsible for only a small section of the chain of events, leading from the manufacture of the chemical, through the transport of the victims on the trains, to the shutting of the doors of the gas chambers. Apparently this reduced the feelings of responsibility of those involved. Finally, the concentration camp guards excused their actions to themselves, and subsequently to their interrogators, by believing that they were doing their duty for the Reich. Even Eichmann saw his role in the extermination of European Jews as justifiable. But while psychological explanations may help to make the guards' behaviour understandable, there is absolutely no implication that it makes it excusable.

The imposition of a duty to kill enemies is not the only way in which war stimulates aggressive behaviour. It also legitimizes killing. That this also spills over into peacetime is shown by the fact that murders tend to increase after a war is over. The most probable explanation for the increase is the legitimization of violence by the institution of war. A very few unfortunate combatants, traumatized by their experiences, remain predisposed to violence after the war is over.

In summary, then, we have argued that human aggressiveness is not an important cause of wars, though aggressive behaviour may be instigated by the war situation. In the next section we argue that this occurs largely because war as an 'institution' imposes on the incumbents of some of its roles the duty to do violence to others, though the importance of 'duty' varies with the type of war, and is most marked in major international wars.

WAR AS AN INSTITUTION

We have argued that, in this spectrum from tribal conflict to international war, duty plays an increasingly important part in the motivation of the combatants. This can most easily be understood if we see war as an institution with a number of constituent roles. That requires a brief digression.

Every institution involves a number of roles, with the incumbents of each role having recognized rights and duties. In our society, marriage is an institution with constituent roles of husband and wife, each role having recognized rights and duties. There are some things that each partner is expected to do, and others that he or she has a duty to do, and each has a right to expect the other to perform the duties appropriate to the role he or she occupies.

As another example, Parliament is an institution, with constituent roles of Prime Minister, Cabinet Ministers, Members of Parliament, the voting public, and so on, the incumbents of each role having particular rights and duties. One duty of the Prime Minister is to chair Cabinet meetings; one of his rights is to receive loyalty and a degree of respect from his colleagues. It is both a right and a duty of each member of the voting public to cast a vote on election day.

In the same way, major wars can be seen as institutions, with many constituent roles, the incumbents of each role having their own jobs to do. The politicians, generals, munition workers, transport workers, signals personnel, scientists, technicians, doctors and nurses are an integral part of the total effort, with their own roles in the institution of war. They do what they do because it is their duty to do so. But while it is the duty of the munition workers to make weapons and ammunition, and of the transport workers to convey them to the front, it is the duty of the combatants to use the weapons to kill. In wars like the Second World War and the Korean War, aggressiveness may be a quality to be encouraged; it may play some part in short-term interactions; and it may be induced by fear or revenge, but at most it is a very secondary issue. When aggressiveness does come to the fore, perhaps induced by fear but sanctioned by those in command on the spot, it is not condoned by the authorities or by the public – as with the massacre of Vietnamese villagers at My Lai.

Institutions do not simply exist. They must be continuously maintained and supported, though the forces that do so may be either intrinsic to their structure or external to them. The institution of marriage is maintained internally by the behaviour of married persons and externally by legal, moral and religious conventions and rules that may be enforced. The institution of Parliament not only depends continuously on the actions of the incumbents in its several roles, but also is embedded in the (unwritten) Constitution of the country. What maintains war as an institution capable of motivating individuals to see it as their duty to risk their lives in combat, and to overcome their moral scruples against killing? Not surprisingly, the factors are numerous, and we may consider them in several categories.

Individual everyday factors

Too often war is trivialized by kitsch, and this has the effect of making it seem ordinary and acceptable: shell cases are used as umbrella stands, torches or cigarette lighters are disguised as hand-guns.

Many of the expressions used in everyday life have military origins and associations. We use expressions like 'digging in', 'outflanking a rival', 'keeping your head down', and so on. And in wartime the horrors are muted by euphemisms: bombing attacks are described as 'surgical strikes', 'killing' is described as 'taking out the enemy', and civilian casualties of bombing or shell fire are referred to as 'collateral damage'. We even talk of the 'war on want' and 'fighting for peace', thereby giving respectability to the military metaphor. A trivial issue, perhaps, but the way in which we think is shaped by the language that we use, and the use of such metaphors contributes in a small way to maintaining the institution of war as a respectable, or at least acceptable, possibility. Just as the removal of sexisms has contributed in a small way to greater equality between the sexes, so may the rejection of 'warisms' help to minimize the power of the institution of war. Indeed, it is more than a matter of making war seem ordinary, for warisms in everyday speech contribute to a picture of the world as a place of competing groups, using violent means to compete for power and resources – a picture that can create its own reality.

Many, but not all, films and books about war give it a positive image. They nearly always focus on the victors, while the defeated are merely cardboard figures. War is depicted as the scene for the manly virtues – courage, fortitude, stoicism. Many films convey a mythology of glory, excitement, and new surroundings, which may act as a lure for new recruits. Death is portrayed, but seldom the disintegrating terror that may precede it. Using 'high diction' the 'dead' become the 'fallen', 'soldiers' become 'comrades'. Of course some books and films, of which *All Quiet on the Western Front* is the classic example, attempt to portray the full horror of war. A number of films about the Vietnam War follow in the same tradition, but these are exceptions. In any case, it is difficult for the filmmaker to get it just right: the effects of portraying war are difficult to predict. For while vivid realism may encourage violence, too little sanitizes war, and too much numbs the senses. And no film or book can capture the intensity of combat when lives are at stake. The photographs taken by war correspondents that show its true horrors are mostly kept from the public.

War toys capitalise on the fascination of mechanical devices for boys, as well as on the macho image of the brave soldier. War is made to seem like a harmless game, and as a normal part of life for grown-ups. Board games are often based on militaristic themes, battles re-enacted with toy soldiers. Computer games, often involving extreme, though admittedly make-believe, violence in virtual reality present an increasing problem.

Psychological mechanisms protect many veterans, when reflecting on the past, from the full horrors of their experiences. They are able to construct narratives that minimize the suffering they have experienced and emphasize the comradeship, justifying and glorifying their participation. Many soldiers see war as an essentially masculine business; and in some cultures fighting has come to define manhood. A Marine Colonel, speaking against the recruiting of women in the USA, has been reported as saying: 'When you get right down to it, you have to protect the manliness of war.' But for some veterans the reality remains central, too awful to be spoken about.

In the past, history has often been taught largely as a history of wars and battles, and espoused military values. It reinforced the myth of the warrior hero. Links between religion and militarism were often assumed. History supported the picture of the world as composed of conflicting groups. In the West, perhaps even more important than what is taught has been what was not taught. The achievements and conquests of past civilizations and empires were emphasized, but not the slaves and serfs on which they were built. Educational programmes seldom taught the poor of the world about roads to economic justice that do not involve violence. They taught about cultural differences, which may lead to cross-cultural understanding, but did so without emphasizing the common ground of humanity on which those differences rest. Most importantly, in discussing war, they too often took the view of generals and politicians, not that of the combatants who suffered its agonies.

Such issues, each perhaps trivial on its own, contribute to the cheerful acceptance of war by so many recruits who are subsequently disillusioned by its reality.

Pervasive cultural factors

Closely related to these individual everyday factors are cultural or societal characteristics that affect the attitudes of individuals to war. Perhaps the most all-pervading are national characteristics, as mentioned already in Chapter 7. Citizens of different countries characterize differently their countries' attitudes to war. In some, military might is applauded, in others the pervading climate is one that values peace. Change in the cultural climate can occur, and may be associated with an increase in militarism. For example, Japan had a long period of peace lasting from 1600 to 1853 CE. The ruling samurai had explicitly rejected the adoption of Western guns, and the rest of the population was debarred from the use or possession of arms. In the late nineteenth century these restraints were dropped and the government indoctrinated the peasantry with an 'emperor ideology', and a military élite developed. This transition from an agricultural to an industrial society may have involved an emphasis on militarism to support a threatened social order. More importantly, the businessmen, facing an impoverished domestic market, sought markets abroad. This ran into the problem of Chinese nationalism, and the markets could be secured only by military means. However, after the Second World War Japan amended its constitutional outlook and again became peaceful.

In other cases, there has been an enduring change to a more peaceful position. Sweden, for instance, though retaining conscription, has changed over the centuries from militarism to being one of the most peace-loving of Western nations. This is said to have been due to a deliberate act by members of the nobility who, tired of the belligerence of the king, arranged for the succession to go to a Frenchman who could be counted on not to go to war with Napoleon. These public attitudes are important because militarism in the society, and the very existence of armed forces and the status given to them, can be taken as legitimizing war as a means of solving conflicts. In the case of Sweden this tendency is countered by the well-established policy of neutrality, but elsewhere can augment the possibility of war: Iraq is an example. Militaristic traditions not only tend to be perpetuated and influence decisions, but they are also incorporated into the self-concepts of individuals, who see themselves as having in some degree the characteristics of their country.

It is probable that most people, for most of the time, have believed that war may sometimes be necessary to preserve national integrity or the international order. In time of war or impending war, governments use a variety of types of propaganda to enhance this belief, and to persuade their citizens that the war is just. Colonial wars were often justified by presenting an image of the local population as intrinsically barbarous and violent, while the conquerors, who had of course been the original invaders and had the more destructive weapons, were presented as intrinsically peaceful. In some cases, particularly that of the Spanish invaders of Central and South America, they have presented themselves also as righteous missionaries, converting the heathen. Reciprocally, anti-colonialists have used reverse images to justify bloody rebellion. Comparable myths have been used in virtually every war, including the two world wars and recent intra-state conflicts. Often, war is justified by ethnic or religious hatreds passed down through the generations, and served up again in an accentuated form for the current cause. Such propaganda techniques make the war seem just, and it then seems to follow both that it is the citizens' duty to fight or to contribute to the war effort, and that victory will be achieved.

The effectiveness of such myths depends on channelling national pride and traditions, religious beliefs and the demands of the situation to serve the national cause. They succeed because they use images and concepts with a universal appeal – images that exploit psychological characteristics common to all people. Some of these are concerned with attitudes to one's own and to other groups.

It is helpful here to distinguish 'patriotism' involving love of one's own country, from 'nationalism', a term used to imply a feeling of superiority and need for power over other national groups. Carefully designed questionnaire techniques used in the USA during the Cold War period showed that patriotism and nationalism, though correlated, could be distinguished. Individuals scoring high on patriotism would endorse such items as 'I love my country' and 'I feel great pride in that land that is our America'; while those scoring high on nationalism endorsed items like 'The important thing for the US foreign aid program is to see that the USA gains a political advantage.' At that time (the late 1980s), individuals high on nationalism were more willing to use nuclear weapons against the enemies of the USA, but less willing to risk their lives for their country, than those high on patriotism. High scores on patriotism but not nationalism were associated with a strong attachment to their fathers in both men and women. Nationalism is associated with higher values placed on military power, dominance, and economic opportunity, and lower values on political democracy, than patriotism. Nationalism involves thinking not so much 'My country is wonderful', as in 'My country is the best and others are inferior' terms. It implies international competition, without concern for those who fail in the competition.

Regrettably, much less common was a third attitude, internationalism. This was indicated by the occasional endorsement of such items as 'If necessary, we ought to be willing to lower our standard of living to cooperate with other countries in getting an equal standard for every person in the world.'

Nationalism can be a powerful force. It can be strengthened if education is controlled by the state, and if it is associated with a commonly held set of cultural attitudes. For such reasons it has become a potent force in some developing countries or groups within states. When different cultural groups are artificially grouped together within a state, they may feel that their cultural heritage is being suppressed or submerged in that of the larger entity, and 'patriotism' enhances 'nationalism' as they seek to express their identity as a group.

Nationalism tends to be self-perpetuating in that the more power a nation has, the more its members see it as special, the more they tend to protect their own interests, and the less they care about the welfare of others. It may thus be augmented by the competitiveness of capitalism. Nationalism legitimizes interference in the affairs of other countries when it is to the advantage of one's own. It provides the bases for espionage and undermines mutual trust between nations. Organizations like the CIA are justified by 'national interest'.

Although stemming from basic social aspects of human nature, both nationalism and patriotism are stimulated by propaganda. This is especially the case in times of war or impending war. Customs such as saluting the flag and playing the national anthem, parades and ceremonies, enhance love of one's own country, but may also invite comparison with, and thus denigration of, others. In the UK during the Second World War the national anthems of all the allies were played frequently, presumably with the aim of fostering the sense of collective endeavour. Parades and ceremonies arranged for the purpose of augmenting patriotism are often associated with pleasant experiences in the presence of others, often family or close friends. Identification with the group thus engendered facilitates incorporation of the values of the group, and in due course these may demand sacrifices from individuals for the sake of the general good.

Members of the same group are often referred to in kinship terms, as in the phrase 'Brothers-in-arms', and patriotism is augmented by the perception of the country as the 'mother-country' or the 'fatherland', and by the unconscious perception of fellow-countrymen as kin. It can thus be seen as a facet of the tendency, common to virtually all humans (and most animals), to give preferential treatment to blood relatives. Nationalism is augmented by categorization of the enemy as such, and by propaganda portraying them as evil, dangerous, and even as sub-human: such images depend for their effectiveness on the group processes discussed, and on natural propensities to fear strangers and defend oneself. Portrayal of the enemy as sub-human, evil, and lacking in individuality helps to justify aggression against them, while at the same time fostering increased self-esteem among the in-group and perception of themselves as righteous. The Japanese, in the decades leading to the Second World War, were educated to believe that foreigners were evil. After Pearl Harbour the country was flooded with propaganda portraying citizens of the USA and the British Commonwealth as immoral weaklings, thereby encouraging all aspects of the war effort and enhancing the aggressiveness of the military.

Propaganda actively encouraging aggression is less common, but is sometimes used – for instance, a US First World War recruiting poster showed a gorilla-like creature carrying off a woman with the words 'Destroy this mad brute, Enlist.' The enemy is often personified, and in some cases the leader or other prominent figure is demonized. In the First World War the Kaiser, in the Second Hitler and his lieutenants, and in the Gulf Wars Saddam Hussein, were demonized and their soldiers seen as sharing their guilt. Nationalism is fostered also by propaganda emphasizing the physical and cultural superiority of the nation to which the recipients belong: this both implies the inferiority of the enemy, giving soldiers additional courage, and can be used to justify or conceal atrocities committed on the enemy.

More rarely, propaganda is used to ameliorate the perceived horrors of war. During the First World War a form of poster art that served to create a myth of war enthusiasm circulated in France. It provided a form of patriotic art, for use on birthdays and other occasions, representing the French soldier as part of a gallant historical tradition, sanitizing war, emphasizing the joys of military leave, and portraying national unity.

Other issues, such as ethnicity and national religions, used in propaganda to support the institution of war, were discussed earlier. In general, it must be remembered that perceived reality is constantly being re-created, and propaganda plays a large part in this. Values may be constructed *post hoc*: they may be manipulated by leaders to augment motivation or constructed by individuals to justify their actions.

The military–industrial–scientific complex

Dwight Eisenhower, former President of the USA, pointed out that the complex of the military, with the industry that supported the military, had a pernicious economic, political and spiritual influence, was self-propagating, and could have an unwarranted impact. He referred to the 'military–industrial complex', but in practice, scientists and engineers play an essential role in the arms industry. Indeed, it can be argued that scientists, in improving old weapons and inventing new ones, drive competition in military hardware between rival states (discussed in more detail below). It is, therefore, more appropriate to refer to the military–industrial–scientific complex. This complex of organizations is perhaps the most potent force supporting the institution of war, and can itself be seen as an institution, consisting of a number of nested sub-institutions, each with its constituent roles. The nature of the military–industrial–scientific complex differs greatly between countries, but has great stability, which only powerful forces external to the complex can disturb. For example NATO, originally conceived as an alliance to counter aggression from the Soviet Union, responded to the end of the Cold War not by seeing its task as done and disbanding, as was the case with the Warsaw Pact Organization, but by extending its perceived sphere of responsibilities.

One factor in the maintenance of this stability is the career ambitions of those involved. The incumbents of each role in each sub-institution act as they do in order to achieve the life-goals to which they aspire. This is most obviously true in industry, where many individuals are motivated primarily, though not necessarily solely, by the desire to forward their careers. But one must not underestimate the importance of career ambitions also for scientists, who seek recognition, or for the military, where individuals seek promotion by advancing or supporting the goals of the organization to which they belong.

In addition to career ambitions, within each institution the behaviour of individuals is controlled by regulative processes intrinsic to the institution itself. These are of several types. In industrial institutions they may involve individual goals associated with the roles individuals occupy in the organization, and are often supported by rewards for performance. In the military more coercive rules are also conspicuous, failure to conform leading to retarded promotion or disgrace. And in science the prestige from colleagues acquired as the result of successful research provides an incentive. In each case, norms and values, accepted by the individuals involved, shape the meanings given to events and actions.

These regulative processes are such as to give the institution legitimacy. The military operates within a series of accepted rules, empowered by the use of symbols that authenticate their very existence. Military procedures are such as to legitimize the institution itself, and the hierarchical nature of every army ensures that, at every level, it is in the interests of leaders to maintain the system. Loyalty and patriotism are inculcated by tradition and patriotic propaganda, and play an important role. Scientists are guided (or should be guided) by universally accepted and largely internalized standards of scientific integrity as well as extrinsic rewards, while industrialists adopt a frame of reference that legitimizes their activities: in both, adherence to the rules, mandatory or generally accepted, is a necessary prerequisite for individual success.

Of special interest are the psychological processes by which the incumbents of roles in the military–industrial–scientific complex disengage themselves from the moral implications of their actions. In many countries, the military can now legitimately claim a primarily defensive or peacekeeping role though, as we have already seen, euphemisms are often used to conceal the consequences of their actions. In some instances military industrialists and scientists can also claim to be working in the cause of peace, though such an excuse covers only part of their activities. But the arms dealers can have no such justification for their actions. The armament industry involves not only a network of roles involved in the manufacture, storage, and sale of arms, but also procurers of legitimization for the export of arms and of spurious end-user certificates. A description of one dealer, who supplied despots with weapons, assassination equipment and terrorist technology, was revealing. His activities were masked under the euphemism of supplying 'consumer needs' in a business with the sanitized name of 'Intercontinental Technology'. He admitted that he deliberately avoided thinking about the human consequences of his trade, tried to justify it by comparing it favourably with the selling of napalm, and claimed that he was basically neutral and commercial so far as the uses of his weapons went. One should add that this sort of moral disengagement is not peculiar to the arms trade, but is found equally in many other branches of industry, such as tobacco manufacture.

As discussed earlier, arms research and arms production are expensive enterprises, and the governments of arms-producing nations encourage their firms to sell abroad in order to reduce their own procurement costs. The resulting arms trade certainly facilitates war, the availability of weapons increasing the probability of violence at the societal as well as at the individual level, but the reverse effect also operates, war facilitating the arms trade. And in many arms manufacturing countries defence interests become important in the economy, the industries providing jobs as well as weapons. The manufacture and sale of arms is supported by advertising campaigns, some of which have gone so far as to claim that sophisticated weaponry saves lives – though this must surely apply to those that use them, not to those whom they are used against.

Military, industrial and scientific organizations are interwoven in many and often subtle ways, so that the three components of the military–industrial–scientific complex reinforce each other. This is ensured by the time necessary for the development of new weapons. Each of the industrial nations seeks to deploy weapons superior to those of its adversaries, real or potential. Scientists are employed to devise them. Because development is a long, costly, and risky business, governments find it necessary to grant special terms to the arms firms, who compete with each other. The military request new weapons, and later must approve and accept the products. Democratic control is eroded because secrecy is involved at each stage, and the accountability of governments thereby diminished. This is especially the case with weapons of mass destruction.

Important, also, are the three-way relations between the military–industrial–scientific complex within each country, public opinion, and the political system within that country, and its relations with other countries in other parts of the world. The assumption by the defence community that war is an ineradicable characteristic of human societies in itself helps to perpetuate the institution of war, and the strength of that institution augments the probability of war. Even in time of peace economic arguments are often used: war industries are seen as providing a major impetus to the economy. Communities become dependent on arms industries, and protest vigorously when military bases are closed. Trade unions become caught up in this, and challenges to military production are seen as imperilling jobs. Within both democratic and non-democratic states the defence interests have a powerful influence on politicians. The probability of war influences the relations of society with the military, and thus also with the defence industries and their scientific support.

During the Cold War era the escalating stockpiles of the two superpowers provided each other with an incentive for yet further escalation. When it ended there was hope for widespread reductions in armed services but, while some occurred, nuclear disarmament proceeded only slowly. The efforts of non-governmental organizations (NGOs) seeking to dismantle the military–industrial–scientific complex were disregarded by politicians. When the threat of war receded, the uncontrolled disposal of many excess weapons by the members of the former Soviet Union provided material for war in other parts of the world.

THE ROLE OF SCIENTISTS

In Chapters 2 and 3 we have shown the terrible threats to human security arising from the military applications of science. But the scientific community was very slow in acknowledging its responsibility for these applications. Up to the end of the eighteenth century science was largely the pursuit of gentlemen of leisure, who communicated their observations to other gentlemen with similar hobbies. The purpose for these pursuits was sheer curiosity – the same that drives scientists today – but with no proclaimed practical aims.

The detachment of scientists from general human affairs led them to build an ivory tower, in which they sheltered, pretending that their work had nothing to do with human welfare. The aim of scientific research, they asserted, was to understand the laws of nature; since these are immutable and unaffected by human reactions and emotions, these reactions and emotions had no place in the study of nature.

The ivory tower mentality was perhaps tenable in the past, when a scientific finding and its practical application were well separated in time – the time interval between an academic discovery and its technical application could be of the order of decades – and implemented by different groups of scientists and engineers. Pure research was carried out in academic institutions, mainly in universities, and the scientists employed there usually had tenure; they were not expected to be concerned about making money from their work. Taking out of patents occurred very seldom and was generally frowned upon. This enabled academic scientists to absolve themselves from responsibility for the effects their findings might have on other groups in society.

For a different reason, the scientists and technicians who worked on the applications of science were mainly employed by industrial companies whose chief interest was financial profit. The employers seldom raised ethical questions about the consequences of the applied research, and the employees were discouraged from concerning themselves with these issues.

All this has changed. The tremendous advances in pure science, particularly in physics, during the first part of the twentieth century, and in biology, during the second half, have completely changed the relation between science and society. Science has become a dominant element in our lives. It has brought great improvements in the quality of life, but also grave perils: pollution of the environment, squandering of vital resources, increase in transmittable diseases, and above all, a threat to the very existence of the human species on this planet through the development of weapons of mass destruction.

The hugely increased role of science in the life of the community, brought about by the great discoveries in science, has in turn resulted in an immense increase in the magnitude of the scientific endeavour; a process of positive feedback, in which success breeds further success. Thus we have seen an exponential growth in the number of scientists and technicians; in the number of publications; in the number and size of scientific meetings. In parallel with this there has been a radical change in the methodology of scientific research, its scope, its tools, its very nature. We can truly speak about a scientific revolution.

Governments, always on the lookout for ways to reduce spending, were only too eager to unload on industry some of the burden of scientific research. Gradually this resulted in a definite shift in the way scientific research was supported. Universities were told that they had to seek financial support from industry; indeed, that their research must be such as to be financially self-supporting. In some disciplines, such as molecular biology and genetic engineering, much of the research is now being funded by industry, largely the pharmaceutical industry, and the main purpose is to secure patents from the discoveries. Financial profit, rather than intellectual advancement, has become a major motivation for research.

An important outcome of the change of emphasis in scientific research is the narrowing of the gap between pure and applied science. In many areas this distinction has become very difficult to discern. What is pure research today may find an application tomorrow and become incorporated into the daily life of the citizen next week (or even earlier if it has military value). Scientists can no longer claim that their work has nothing to do with the welfare of the individual or with state politics.

Scientists should not make such claims, but many of them do. Amazingly, many scientists still cling to the ivory tower mentality, they still advocate a *laissez faire* policy for science. Their logic rests mainly on the distinction between pure and applied science. It is the application of science that can be harmful, they claim. As far as pure science is concerned, the only obligation on the scientist is to make the results of research known to the public. What the public does with them is its business, not that of the scientist.

PRECEPTS OF *LAISSEZ FAIRE* SCIENCE

Science for its own sake
Scientific inquiry can know no limits
Science is rational and objective
Science is neutral
Science has nothing to do with politics
Scientists are just technical workers
Science cannot be blamed for its misapplication

John Ziman, *Scientists, the Arms Race and Disarmament* (J. Rotblat ed., 1982)

As already shown, the distinction between pure and applied science is largely non-existent. And the amoral attitude adopted by those scientists is unacceptable. It is, in our opinion, an immoral attitude, because it eschews personal responsibility for the likely consequences of one's actions.

We live in a world community with ever greater interdependence; an interdependence due largely to technical advancement arising from scientific research. An interdependent community offers great benefits to its members, but by the same token it imposes responsibility on them. Every citizen has to be accountable for his or her deeds; we all have a responsibility to society.

This responsibility weighs particularly heavily on scientists for the very reason that science plays such a dominant role in modern society. Michael Atiyah, former President of the Royal Society, has further developed the rationale for the special responsibility of scientists. In his 1997 Schrödinger Lecture, he said: 'Scientists will understand the technical problems better than the average politician or citizen, and knowledge brings responsibility.'

Both in that lecture and in a Presidential Address to the Royal Society, Atiyah also stressed the need for scientists to take responsibility for their work for yet another reason: the consequences to science of having a bad public image. The public holds scientists responsible for the dangers arising from scientific advance: nuclear weapons are a menace and the public rightly blames the scientists; human cloning is distasteful and viewed by the public as immoral, and science is castigated for the few scientists that want to pursue it.

The general public, through elected governments, have the means to control science, either by withholding the purse, or by imposing restrictive regulations harmful to science. Clearly, it is far better that any control should be exercised by the scientists themselves.

It is most important that science improves its public image, that it regains the respect of the community for its integrity and re-establishes trust in its pronouncements. Scientists must show by their conduct that it is possible to combine creativeness with compassion; letting the imagination roam with caring for fellow creatures; venturing into the unknown yet being fully accountable for one's actions.

CONCLUSION

Wars are not caused by human aggressiveness, though wars are a cause of aggressive behaviour. People are willing to go to war in part because they see it as their duty to do so because of the role that they occupy in the institution of war. Although wars differ in many ways, one can trace a continuum from wars between pre-agricultural societies, through the terrible recent conflicts in Rwanda and Yugoslavia to the two world wars, with duty becoming progressively more important along it. The institution of war is supported by aspects of everyday behaviour, by pervasive cultural factors, and by the military–industrial–scientific complex.

Although aggressiveness does not generally contribute to the incidence of war, it has an indirect influence in several ways: the enemy is personified by propaganda, so that individuals perceive the enemy as though the enemy were a hostile individual; and aggressiveness contributes to the effectiveness of propaganda used to elicit public support for war.

At a time when scientific advances could result in the development of weapons of unprecedented destructive power, it is incumbent on scientists to be conscious of their social responsibility and not knowingly to carry out research that might cause harm to society.

III
What Should Be Done
to Eliminate War?

11 What Stops Countries from Going to War?

In Section II we discussed some major issues that are often seen as causes of war. Many of these are present for a great deal of the time. Why, then, do wars not erupt more often? If that were all there were to it, one might expect an almost continuous state of war. One issue here, already emphasized in previous chapters, is that a conflict between two groups does not usually lead to actual hostilities unless several of these factors are present together. Most wars are caused by a complex network of interacting events and circumstances. But, in addition, there are other counteracting factors that make, or are believed by some to make, violence less likely: these are the subjects of this chapter. We shall argue that in some cases belief in their effectiveness in preventing violence is valid only in some circumstances, or that it is based on wishful thinking.

DEMOCRACY

Chief among the elements alleviating the risk of war is a democratic state. Democracy is desirable not only because it brings greater freedom and good governance to its citizens but also because, as we saw earlier, conflicts of interest between democratic states are less likely to lead to violence than conflicts involving non-democratic ones. There are a number of possible reasons for this. An obvious one is that democratic states tend to share certain values of a type that make them less ready to go to war with each other.

Another characteristic of a democratic state is its ability to put a brake on tendencies to resort to violence. Democracy emphasizes peaceful norms of behaviour, with the people's will usually expressed by the balance between different views rather than by violent demonstration. Democratic governance necessarily requires mechanisms to solve internal problems by negotiation – negotiation that may take place at many levels, from the inter-individual to the governmental one. These norms and skills, honed within the society, can be carried over to international situations, and can give a priority to solving conflicts with other groups or states by negotiation, without recourse to violence.

In a democracy the people choose their government, and (in theory at least) they can replace it if they so will. In addition, in a smoothly running democracy all the major groups in the society participate in the major institutions, and this in itself reduces the likelihood of internal disagreement, or of the imposition of a minority view. It is, therefore, not so easy for democratic leaders to start a war if the majority of the people are not behind them, though this probably happened in the UK in the 2003 Gulf War.

Democracy has the potential, too seldom realized, to ensure that the benefits of prosperity are distributed equitably in the population. This does not necessarily mean equally – some individuals have different needs from others – but in a way that is seen to be fair. Though democracy often fails in this respect, at least it has more potential than totalitarian governments.

Democracy in poor countries is usually, but not invariably, coupled with political and civil liberties, and it has been shown that these are usually related to increased life expectancy at birth, enhanced infant survival, reduced birth rate, and greater income per head – in fact with better overall welfare. Liberties are thus related to lower levels of factors related indirectly to unrest and interpersonal violence, and thus to war (see pp. 96–8).

In true democracies, and most countries that call themselves democratic fall short in some respects, the military are under civilian control. In addition, true democracy is accompanied by a legal system, which is perceived as just and is administered by a judiciary, which is not (or should not be) appointed by the political leaders. The judiciary, therefore, has the potential for limiting the activities of the political leaders as well as those of the general population. In a totalitarian state, by contrast, order is maintained by force, and the use of violence by the police may be legitimized, or at least may not be prevented, by the state. As we have seen (Chapter 9), violence within a group is often associated with violence between groups.

Thus, democracies should be able to set an example and to promote norms over such issues as development, human rights, and especially weapons proliferation. In recent years, alliances of democracies, notably the European Union, have acted with a mandate from the United Nations to prevent war in or between other countries.

However, democratic procedures are not infallible. Too often democracies have refrained from, or delayed, active intervention, seeing their own interests not to justify the costs involved. And democracies have played a major role in the arms trade. In addition, those democracies with a colonial past inevitably face special problems when they offer help to countries in difficulty: their intervention may be viewed with suspicion because of their exploitative past and their perceived self-interest. And every intervention, whether by a democratic state or any other, that lacks the authority of the UN is undermining the proper status of that body.

Democracy is in fact a matter of degree. That voting procedures can be perverted by the current government or its adherents has recently been demonstrated in the quasi-democratic state of Zimbabwe. Belarus, Cameroon, Togo, Uzbekistan and several other one-party states have allowed elections, but permitted only limited opening for political competition. The CIA, often acting without US Congressional knowledge or approval, has aimed to interfere in the electoral processes of foreign governments. Although the USA is often seen as a paradigm of democracy, appointment to the Supreme Court is a political matter. The President of the USA is often able to act without involving parliamentary politics or public debate: Reagan's actions in Central America are examples. Similarly, some decisions taken by the UK government, such as many of those concerned with arms procurement, have been taken, and are being taken, by *ad hoc* committees whose proceedings are secret even from the rest of the Cabinet. Such procedures are said to be necessary in the interests of 'national security'. That may or may not be valid, but it is clear that democracy, with all its virtues, is a delicate flower, and must be tended with care.

The number of fully democratic countries increased dramatically in the last century (Figure 7). In 1900 no state had universal suffrage for competitive multiparty elections. Some countries had potentially democratic systems, but with restricted voting rights. For instance, the UK denied votes to women, and the USA to black Americans. In total 25 states had restricted democratic practices, accounting for only just over 10 per cent of the world's population. Most countries were monarchies, colonies or protectorates. At the present time 120 out of the 192 countries in the world have electoral democracies, and contain over 60 per cent of the world's population.

Other forms of governance can be classified as follows: restricted democratic, monarchies, authoritarian regimes, totalitarian regimes, colonial and imperial dependencies, protectorates. Figure 8 shows the percentage of the countries under the different regimes (a) in

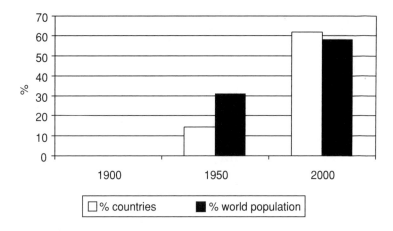

Figure 7   Proportion of democratic governments elected by universal suffrage

Source: *Democracy's Century: A Survey of Global Political Change in the 20th Century*, Freedom House (2000).

1900 (when the total number of countries was 130); (b) in 1950 (154 countries); and (c) in 2000 (192 countries).

As the other side of the picture, totalitarian and other non-democratic regimes have certain characteristics that may make them more prone to war. Assertive individuals who acquire power and become totalitarian rulers are in a position to use their power to further their own interests or satisfy their own vanity. It must require ambition to become a totalitarian ruler, and a totalitarian ruler's ambition cannot be checked by the will of the people. If the people are unwilling to go to war, there are many means that he can use to persuade them.

The promotion of democracy must, therefore, be an important aim for the international community. We shall see later that this is likely to be problematic in states that have only recently achieved independence. The conditions of transition may involve many difficulties including a considerable chance of internal dissension. The lack of an appropriate infrastructure may make it easy for an ambitious individual to seize power and involve the country in internal or external disputes. And we shall argue below that the promotion of democracy does not mean the self-serving imposition by powerful states of apparently democratic regimes in Third World countries.

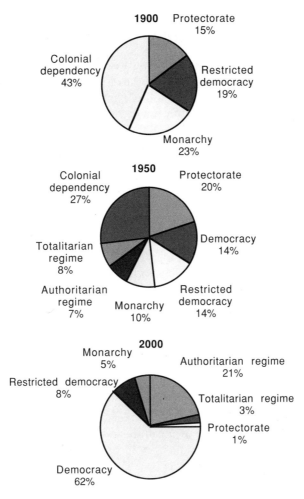

Figure 8 Changing forms of political system in the twentieth century

Source: *Democracy's Century: A Survey of Global Political Change in the 20th Century,*
Freedom House (2000).

OVERCOMING CULTURAL DIFFERENCES

Groups or states that share a common culture or religion have common values and should be able to understand each other. It is often assumed that countries that share a common culture or religion will be unlikely to go to war with each other. Unfortunately, this is by no means always the case and, as we have seen, religious or ethnic *differences* have too often been a cause of, or excuse for, war (Chapter 7).

Wars between countries sharing Christian beliefs have been common enough, and although at the moment there seems to be a feeling of brotherhood amongst the Islamic nations, wars between Islamic countries have certainly not been unknown in the past. Wars between the Ottomans and the Arabs extended over many decades, and recently the devastating war between Iran and Iraq involved two Islamic countries, though with different Islamic sects predominating in each. More recently, though it hardly qualified as a war, the Hazawaras, a Shi'ite group in Afghanistan, were persecuted by the Taliban government before the latter's defeat.

Although conflicts between states are seldom if ever caused solely by cultural differences, such differences are often there as predisposing factors, or are used by leaders to facilitate their purposes. And cultural differences in attitudes to human rights have proved an obstacle to agreement between major powers. For instance, easy relations between the USA and China have been hindered by the apparent disregard of Western values in China (see also pp. 75–9). And most Westerners found abhorrent the values and practices of the Taliban. What are the consequences of this for relations between states, and what should be done?

Should we try to eliminate cultural differences? That would mean destroying local cultures, and the loss of much that is valuable. Is it then possible to reconcile all people to recognize and accept differences between their own culture and those of others? In this section we suggest that, though an apparently desirable goal, that will not be one easy to achieve.

In some parts of the world the contrast between their traditional cultural values and Western capitalism and materialism has resulted in a new sense of dignity and identity, which has promoted antipathy to the West. To many in East Asian societies Western values have come to be epitomized by fizzy drinks and fatty foods, by selfish individualism, imperialism, and the hegemony of the USA. So far as some sections of the Islamic world are concerned, the materialism, individualism and apparent lack of spiritual values in the West are utterly distasteful. This has facilitated the growth of religious fundamentalism. The spread of Western attitudes has enhanced the appeal of Islam's basic values, codes of behaviour and doctrine. Thus globalization, far from producing global uniformity, has increased the feeling of solidarity amongst members of many non-Western religious groups, and led them to emphasize their differences from the West.

In addition, Muslims have been united by Western actions that were interpreted as attacks on Islam. Although Saudi Arabia cooperated with the West in the 1991 Gulf War, in the eyes of the people it was an Islamic state, Iraq, that was attacked. The West seemed at first to do little to protect the Muslims in Bosnia. And, perhaps most importantly, the USA has continuously supported Israel in its dispute with the Palestinians and the surrounding Islamic countries. The attack on the World Trade Center, though in no way to be condoned, can be seen as yet another expression of this resentment.

The desire of Eastern countries to develop their industries, and the popularity enjoyed by many Western products such as jeans, hamburgers and Coca-Cola, can easily be understood as indicating that their inhabitants *want* to acquire Western standards of living, values and cultures. But that is a form of Western arrogance, perhaps inherited from a missionary past: it involves a confusion between *Western modernization,* which those in less industrialized countries desire, and *Western cultural values,* which often they do not.

It is easy for the inhabitants of any one country to think that the world would be a safer place if everybody shared their culture. It sometimes seems that tensions might be ameliorated if the cultural differences could be removed, or at least mutually understood. But in practice cultural values cannot easily be imposed or manipulated, and it is worth considering briefly why that is the case.

There is much evidence to suggest that a small number of basic principles guide the behaviour of individuals in all cultures and underlie their moral codes. These principles include propensities for individuals to behave positively and cooperatively to their own kin, and also to other members of their social group. Humans also have a basic tendency towards selfish assertiveness, to look after their own interests. Social living depends on the maintenance of a proper balance between these by encouraging a preponderance of prosociality, i.e. being kind, unselfish, cooperative, etc. Over the course of their histories, societies have elaborated moral precepts and sets of values that promote prosociality and the stability of relations between individuals. These precepts and values are based on the basic propensity for prosociality, but have been shaped by rulers, priests and others in positions of influence, sometimes as a result of their selfish assertiveness and in their own interests. They have also been

shaped over prehistorical and historical time according to the circumstances in which the society has been living, and the vicissitudes
to which it has been exposed. For instance, in some cultures a macho
male personality is esteemed much more than in others. In some
societies the balance has swung a little further towards emphasizing
that individuals should look after their own interests, towards individualism and competitiveness, than is the case in the UK; in others
it has swung towards prosociality and cooperation. The moral
precepts and values of the culture become deeply imbedded in each
individual's personality in the early years of life. They are thus
extremely difficult to change. For that reason there are limits to
which a shared culture can profitably be pursued.

Around 130 states have subscribed to the UN Universal Declaration
of Human Rights, and some apparently intransigent cases of conflict
have been resolved locally. For instance, ethnic overlap between
Hungary and Romania has caused ill-will going back for hundreds
of years. But the two nations have now signed a treaty that will
protect the cultural identity and civil liberties of national minorities.

Perhaps inevitably, the UN Declaration leaves some latitude in
how human rights are to be interpreted. In all cultures, outsiders
always tend to be seen as different. In time of war killing is legitimized
by perception of the enemy as non-persons. However, within the
group, societies differ in who is recognized as having full personhood,
as being a fully responsible member of the group and thus as meriting
prosocial behaviour. In many societies behaviour towards slaves,
members of a lower class, criminals, and even women, is such as
would be expected if they were lacking to a greater or lesser degree
the characteristics of personhood.

With China the situation is even more difficult than with Islam,
and cultural differences from the West may be even more difficult to
reconcile. The bases of the difficulty involve long stretches of cultural
history. In the West, the Christian religion has involved a deity which
can take human form, and all people are seen as individuals before
God. Christians believe that humans are so precious that God gave
his son to the world to save humankind. Indeed, some have argued
that humans possess characteristics of deities. It is thus basic that
humans are of high and equal value, and that that value should be
protected. This assumption pervades virtually all Western cultures,
though in the case of non-persons (see above) it is not respected.

Chinese culture stems from the Confucian emphasis on harmony
and from a correlative philosophy, formulated between the third and

first centuries BCE, and still today influencing the culture to some degree. According to this view of the universe, everything is part of a single system involving harmony between heaven, earth, and man, and there is no outside deity controlling it. Everything can be exhaustively listed, and people's position and condition are set by the correlations of the universe. You cannot change your condition. Actions perceived to be in harmony with the cosmos are seen as right, and actions that are not as wrong. The emphasis is on loyalty to the group rather than on individual fulfilment. Thus it is wrong to steal, and those who do so become to a degree non-persons. Dissenters occupy a dissenter's position and so attract the proper treatment for dissenters. If the government decides you are a dissenter, treatment proper for dissenters follows. Individuals can seek the assistance of deities, but whether or not the deities can help depends on the workings of the universe and not on the powers of the spirit.

Of course, these summaries grossly simplify reality, and it is not suggested that, either in the East or in the West, all individuals subscribe consciously to these ideas, but only that these ideas permeate their respective world-views. But the differences lead to marked differences in the views of human rights between societies, and simple-minded attempts to impose one on the other, or to reconcile the two, are prone to failure. Cultural values are incorporated early in life, and individuals are resistant to changing them.

It is probable that all cultures subscribe to some form of the so-called Golden Rule of 'Do-as-you-would-be-done-by.' But beyond that, there are many differences in practice, and rigidity in holding fast to cultural values is to be found in all cultures – for instance, members of all the world religions may reject the views of fundamentalist co-religionists, as well as those of other religions. Those who have acquired Western values are no different in this from those brought up in other ways, and both would find it impossible to accept some aspects of the values of the others' cultures. Thus, most inhabitants of the Western world would agree with the view that the values of Islamic fundamentalists concerning the position of women are unacceptable because they deny women full personhood. And virtually all Westerners agree that arranged marriages constitute an infringement of basic human rights, and (except for many in the USA) most that capital punishment is inhumane. Indeed, some individuals in Western countries find the values and beliefs even of their own fellow citizens totally unacceptable – for instance those of born-again Christians or Creationists. These issues have recently become politically important, for the policies of the present Bush administration are influenced by fundamentalist Christianity, and some fundamentalist Christians share the view of many Jews that the latter have a divine right to parts of Palestine.

But how far it is profitable for the members of one culture to impose their values on others is another issue. Certainly one is unlikely to be successful by using political or economic incentives to coerce members of another society into one's own way of thinking. The route to be followed is surely a different one. We must do everything we can to maintain our own basic values within our society, even though it is changing under the influence of capitalism and modernity, while at the same time we must make limited accommodation to those changes. What is best about our Western heritage is precious, and Westerners should do their best to preserve it in a world that they may cease to dominate. We must all recognize that there are difficulties in trying to impose a culture where at present it is not wanted. The missionary course of trying to convert others to one's own world-view is not always the best. The emphasis must be on the universals of human nature, the propensities for pro-sociality, often translated as 'Do-as-you-would-be-done-by', and the principles that follow from it, such as 'Thou shalt not kill.' We must try to understand how different cultural practices and religions can, in their different ways, satisfy common human needs. Above all we must show by example that the way of life we have developed brings dividends in human fulfilment and well-being.

This certainly does not mean that we need approve of cultural values or practices that contravene the basic principle of 'Do-as-you-would-be-done-by', but that, where they seem not to do so, example and discussion provide our best hope for changing the views of people from other cultures. Clearly, there are occasions when politico-cultural differences should properly inhibit dealings with another state: for instance, it is morally wrong for a Western country to sell arms to a country with a repressive regime. But, apart from such cases, it is of doubtful utility to make political agreements depend on whether 'they' accept 'our' values.

Seeking to understand the cultures of other societies is far from easy. A simple account of differences in cultural practices is unlikely to be sufficient to produce reconciliation and understanding. Here the answer must lie in the much larger questions of socialization and education, discussed in Chapter 13.

GLOBALIZATION

We are concerned here with changes in the structure of the world, which are having both positive and negative consequences on the potential for violence. As we saw in Chapter 9, 'Globalization' refers to the ways in which happenings in different parts of the world are becoming progressively more interconnected. We saw that this could contribute to some of the factors that make violent conflict more likely. But it has also some positive aspects.

Globalization is in part a consequence of the increasing efficiency of communications: information can now be transmitted to distant parts of the world almost instantaneously and at almost no cost. This has had some positive political implications. The 'hot line' between Washington and Moscow during the Cold War era was a forerunner of this. Now political leaders can more readily obtain information from other countries, and speak with their counterparts in other parts of the world. Communications technology has facilitated the growth of international organizations, including non-governmental ones such as Amnesty; and the greater integration of international networks, such as the community of scientists. Non-Governmental Organizations (see pp. 187–90) can act with greater efficiency in distant parts of the world.

Globalization has at least the potential for increasing international understanding. One can acquire greater knowledge about how other people live, the horrors of war can be made apparent to those not involved, and the plight of refugees, the homeless and the starving becomes more real.

Globalization has also had an enormous impact on the commercial and industrial world, for organizations can now establish branches, and operate more readily, in distant countries. Globalization has facilitated the exploitation of overseas markets, the growth of powerful transnational companies, and thus the spread of capitalism. As a result of their increasing power the commercial world is becoming increasingly dominated by companies with headquarters or satellites in many different countries. These companies can have such a powerful effect on the local economy that they are able to influence the governments of the countries in which they operate. While their influence is often detrimental (see Chapter 9) it is usually in a company's interests to foster peaceful relations between those countries in which their branches are situated. Furthermore, firms in countries exporting manufactured goods or technology to less industrially advanced ones have an interest in keeping their markets open and thus in discouraging conflict. The widespread effects of both the financial crash in the Far East, and the exposure of corruption in major firms in the USA in 2001, have demonstrated that the maintenance of stability over the whole world is in the interests of businesses everywhere.

Unfortunately, although it has this power for good, the business world has done little to prevent conflicts escalating into violence. And in parallel with its positive aspects, we have seen that globalization has many consequences that increase discontent in some parts of the world, and accentuate factors that make war more likely. Whether its beneficial consequences compensate the harm that results is dubious. But in any case, one cannot put the clock back: globalization is here to stay and is changing the world.

DETERRENCE

In the days of colonial wars, a show of strength may sometimes have been adequate to subdue an ill-armed opponent, or to deter rebellion. As a relatively recent but little-known example, the presence of British forces in Kenya, Aden and elsewhere in the Middle East deterred Iraq from invading Kuwait when it first gained independence.

However, a policy of deterrence can lead to escalation and to an arms race. In the past, countries that were approximately equal in military capabilities have been significantly more likely to allow their disputes to lead to war than were those with considerable inequality in strength. This is in accordance with expectation: if one country is much weaker than the other, it is likely to concede the issue in question rather than risk destruction by war, Saddam Hussein's Iraq being an exception here. But in a situation of near-equality, one side may perceive itself to be stronger than the other, and see war as involving an acceptable risk. And a side that feels itself to be slightly weaker than the other may seek to increase its strength to equal or surpass its rival. Such escalation is especially likely if information about the other's strength is ambiguous. Such an arms race occurred before the First World War and involved especially striving for parity or supremacy in naval power.

Another escalating arms race took place during the period of the Cold War, but then the situation was quite different. Nuclear weapons had become the crucial issue, and a pre-emptive strike by one side could have been devastating to the other's ability to respond. The aims of escalation were ostensibly to deter the other side from being the first to attack, by making sure that, if he did, you would survive with enough weapons to inflict unacceptable damage on him. Churchill, speaking about the development of the H-bomb in 1955, argued that its effect would be 'to spread almost indefinitely and at least to a vast extent the area of mortal danger ... Then it may well be that we shall by a process of sublime irony have reached a stage in this story where safety will be the sturdy child of terror, and survival the twin brother of annihilation.' As a consequence each side strove to achieve a 'credible deterrent'. Although the assumption was that these weapons would never be used, elaborate calculations were made as to what constituted a 'credible deterrent'. In 1968 Robert McNamara, the then US Defense Secretary, put this as the capability to destroy one-fifth to one-quarter of the Soviet Union's people and half her industry. For this it was calculated that about 200–400 one megaton explosions would have sufficed – about 1 per cent of the US nuclear arsenals at that time: this makes nonsense of the view that escalation was necessary. Later, as more accurate weapons were developed, the emphasis was put on destroying the other side's missiles.

It is worth noting that by no means everyone in a position of power was sure that deterrence would work. In 1980 a spokesman from the US Arms Control and Disarmament Agency wrote 'Military strategists can claim that an intelligent U.S. offensive strategy, wedded to homeland defenses, should reduce U.S. casualties to approximately 20 million ... a level compatible with national survival and recovery.' In the same year Vice-President George Bush is reported as saying 'You have survivability of industrial potential, protection of a percentage of your citizens, and you have a capability that inflicts more damage on the opposition than it can inflict on you. That's the way you can have a winner.' Apart from the callous ring, such statements do not indicate great faith in the effectiveness of deterrence in preventing war.

In the event, the Cold War did not lead to a nuclear exchange, though several times the two sides were on the brink of disaster. Whether it was this policy of deterrence that prevented war is doubtful. Certainly, nuclear deterrence is a policy that is basically unethical. In addition it is one of considerable danger, for a number of reasons. For one thing, it entails a constant risk of accidental nuclear war, especially when nuclear-armed rockets are kept on hair-trigger alert. During the Cold War there were also a number of serious accidents involving nuclear weapons – for instance, a nuclear bomber crashed in Greenland; a bomber carrying two nuclear weapon cores in their carrying cases was lost in the Mediterranean; and there was an accident to a nuclear store at a US base in the UK.

Furthermore, a policy of deterrence depends on the assumption that the enemy will act rationally, and that each side's rationality is comprehensible to the other. But countries do not act rationally over such matters. The problem of rationality of leaders goes back to the very beginning of the nuclear era. The rationale used by the British scientists, who started work on the atom bomb, soon after the outbreak of the Second World War, was that, if the bomb could be made, and if Hitler acquired it, the only way to prevent him from using it would be if the Western Allies too had the bomb and threatened to use it in retaliation; this was the first example of nuclear deterrence. But the flaw in this argument was the assumption that Hitler would respond in a rational way; all the evidence indicates that he was not a rational person and that his philosophy of *Götterdämmerung* would have made him use his atom bomb in a final gesture of defiance. A lack of rationality is to be seen in the escalation that took place during the Cold War: each side accumulated vastly more weapons than were necessary for deterrence. And at the heart of deterrence policy there is an insoluble dilemma, which in 1981 was described as follows: 'if you wish to deter war by the fear that nuclear weapons will be used, you have to appear to be prepared to use them in certain circumstances. But if you do so, and the enemy answers back … you are very much worse off than if you had not done so, if indeed you can be said to be there at all. To pose an unacceptable risk to the enemy automatically poses the same risk, or perhaps even a greater one, to yourself …'

There were some who saw the pragmatic issue quite clearly. In any case, the possession of nuclear weapons is unlikely to be an effective deterrent to attack by a non-nuclear power. Any nation that initiated the use of nuclear weapons would immediately be ostracized by the international community, with devastating economic and political consequences. It was probably for that reason that Argentina was not deterred from invading the Falkland Islands by the British nuclear-armed submarines. Furthermore, any democratic government that used nuclear weapons would be likely to be voted out by its electorate. It was probably for this reason that Richard Nixon did not employ nuclear weapons in Vietnam.

> *In the real world of real political leaders, a decision that would bring even one hydrogen bomb on one city of one's own country would be recognized in advance as a catastrophic blunder: ten bombs on ten cities would be a disaster beyond history; and a hundred bombs on ten cities are unthinkable.*
>
> McGeorge Bundy, 'To Cap the Volcano' (*Foreign Affairs*, October 1969)

The possession of nuclear weapons is most unlikely to provide protection against terrorists. The bases from which terrorists operate are likely to be dispersed, and attempted reprisal would involve the slaughter of innocent civilians – as has indeed been the case with so-called conventional weapons in Kosovo and Afghanistan. Neither is missile defence likely to be effective against terrorist attack, since biological, chemical and even nuclear weapons can be introduced to centres of dense population by means more subtle than long-distance missiles.

Even if they are not used deliberately, the possession of nuclear weapons by even a few states greatly enhances the dangers of widespread destruction. The danger of accidental release is always present. Wherever weapons-grade material is present, there is a danger that it will be stolen and used by terrorists or by other states. And the potential use of a nuclear weapon to force its will upon another is an incentive for the latter to acquire nuclear weapons so that it can threaten reprisal in kind. Thus China claims that its development of nuclear weapons stemmed from threats by the USA to use them in the Korean War and in the Taiwan Straits crises.

It is appropriate to emphasize again here that the very possession of nuclear weapons is immoral. Their enormous destructive power, inflicted on civilians even more than on the military, would make their use unforgiveable. The only solution is international agreement on the total abolition of nuclear weapons. Although the Non-Proliferation Treaty (Chapter 12) had that as its goal, the recalcitrance of those states in possession of nuclear weapons has prevented substantial progress. Even preliminary steps, such as an undertaking by each state not to be the first to use a nuclear weapon, have been impossible to achieve. And the stance of the US administration under G.W. Bush, involving a willingness to use nuclear weapons in a pre-emptive strike against any state to which they are opposed, is perilous to the whole world.

A less frequently discussed form of deterrence, and one that would perhaps be ethically more defensible if it involved only conventional weapons, is the formation of alliances between states. NATO, and the treaty between the USA and Japan, may be seen as not only preventing conflict between the countries concerned, but also as providing a more formidable opponent for any other state that would attempt belligerent action against any of the members of such an alliance. Against this is the worry that such alliances may take over from the United Nations its exclusive role in preserving peace in the world.

SANCTIONS

Few countries are totally self-sufficient: most depend on international trade for at least some of their needs. If a country were to be cut off from external contacts by internationally agreed sanctions, its internal economy would be liable to collapse. Sanctions, therefore, provide a possible course of action by the international community for the prevention of war.

Sanctions can take many forms. They may be limited to arms embargoes or the ending of military cooperation. They may involve isolating the country from its overseas markets, for instance by an oil embargo. They may involve restricting imports.

Sanctions have been used as a way of indicating international concern about the behaviour or policies of a particular state – for instance with South Africa during the Apartheid era. They may serve as a preliminary to possibly more extreme measures; or to punish a state for past actions. However, sanctions involving a wide range of goods may have deleterious consequences – namely, that they will hit the poorest and most needy section of the population without affecting the leaders. This happened with the sanctions imposed on Iraq after the 1991 Gulf War. In attempts to prevent war or to prevent preparations for war, the denial of supplies of weapons and ammunition, and restriction of access to hard currency, have been seen as most likely to remove the ability to wage war. Sometimes it seems appropriate and more practical to use sanctions targeted specifically on the leader or leaders – perhaps freezing their assets abroad or denying them access to hard currency. This was one of the few courses open in the attempt to restrict the activities of the al-Qaeda in the aftermath of the attack on the World Trade Center.

The effectiveness of sanctions is controversial. Because of globalization, they require wide cooperation between governments, commercial interests and NGOs: this is often hard to obtain. While sanctions have been widely used since the Second World War, for instance against North Korea, South Africa during Apartheid, in the Balkans, against Iraq, and against Zimbabwe, evidence of their efficacy is scarce. At best, they are a slow and clumsy method for producing results, and often they appear to be useless. They may cause suffering in the target country amongst just that section of the population that needs help. That has certainly been the case in Iraq, and probably in South Africa. The sanctions on Iraq were imposed in order to make the government allow UN inspectors into the country to check that there were no facilities for manufacturing weapons of mass destruction. In the case of South Africa, the economic effects on the country may have contributed in the long run to the abolition of Apartheid.

So far the use of carrots rather than a stick has been limited primarily to attempts to recruit allies: George W. Bush and Tony Blair used reward after the attack on the World Trade Center to recruit allies in the 'war on terrorism'. The combination of stick and carrot together seemed to be at least temporarily effective in preventing an alleged attempt by North Korea to manufacture nuclear weapons. The USA offered to provide technology for two light-water reactors, a supply of fuel oil, a reduction in military training in South Korea and other inducements, coupled with the threat of trade restrictions, UN sanctions, and other measures in the case of non-compliance. However, this approach failed in the longer term, in part because the US reneged on part of its undertakings: in 2003 North Korea admitted that it had renewed its nuclear weapons programme.

But, in general, sanctions seem an ineffective way to prevent war. This is in part because of the difficulty of obtaining the full international compliance necessary to make them effective, and the ubiquity of unscrupulous individuals, including arms dealers, able and willing to evade them.

INTERNATIONAL LAW

Adherence to and respect for international law provides a potentially powerful tool for minimizing the incidence of war and ameliorating its consequences.

In this context, international law has two prongs. First, it is concerned with the justifiability of resort to war (*jus ad bellum*). Under the United Nations Charter, military action is permitted only in self-defence unless agreed to by the United Nations. Military intervention to maintain or restore peace may be undertaken only on the authority of the Security Council. Unfortunately, these restrictions are constantly being flouted, the 2003 Gulf War being an example. Moreover, as discussed further below, according to its Charter the UN is concerned only with wars between sovereign states: most recent wars have involved parties within states, and it can be argued that they are beyond the jurisdiction of the UN. Only a more powerful, active and impartial UN can have the ability to tighten and enforce the restrictions embodied in its Charter (see p. 183).

Second, international law is concerned with the conduct of war (*jus in bello*). This is governed by the Geneva conventions concerned with the treatment of wounded or sick combatants and prisoners-of-war and the protection of non-combatants, and by the conventions prohibiting the development, production and stockpiling of biological and chemical weapons and landmines. After the Nuremberg trials in 1945–46 war crimes were defined as 'Violations of the laws or customs of war which include, but are not limited to, murder, ill-treatment of prisoners of war or persons on the seas, killing of hostages, plunder of public or private property, wanton destruction of cities, towns or villages, or devastation not justified by military necessity.'

The application of these principles in practice can run into difficulties. Without condoning such behaviour, the difficulty of taking prisoners in the heat of combat can seem insurmountable. The issue arose in the later stages of the war against Japan, and in the 2002 fighting in Afghanistan, where it is said that suicide bombers used 'surrender' as a means to carry out their self-sacrificial aim.

The International Court of Justice is supposed to be the supreme tribunal ruling on questions of international law. It has ruled against the threat or use of nuclear weapons except in self-defence when the survival of the state is at stake; on the latter issue the Court was divided. As we have seen, this ruling has been emasculated by the exception of self-defence and in Britain by a ruling that permits the possession of nuclear weapons in peacetime.

A second court, the International Criminal Court, was set up in 1998 and came into force in 2002. Its brief is to try crimes against humanity. The USA is unwilling to recognize this Court on the grounds that its own citizens might be seen as criminals, and at the time of writing the USA is refusing to participate in peace-keeping forces unless exception from the Court's jurisdiction is given unilaterally to its citizens. Ad hoc tribunals have also been set up by the Security Council to deal with crimes in the former Yugoslavia, including the Serbian leader Milosevic, and in Rwanda: convictions for genocide have been made in each case.

There is no need to point out that actions of warring states in the last half of the twentieth century have defied both the principle of *jus ad bellum* and that of *jus in bello*. At the time of writing neither Israel nor the Palestinians have respected human rights, and the USA is disregarding them in its treatment of prisoners taken in Afghanistan. The urgent need is for a more potent UN to enforce them.

Another serious problem arises when states disregard international treaties. A flagrant case, with very serious consequences, concerns the Nuclear Non-Proliferation Treaty (NPT).

The general abhorrence of nuclear weapons, following their use on Japan in 1945, resulted in a strong desire, expressed both in public opinion and in the United Nations, to abolish nuclear weapons. This led to the NPT, signed in 1968 and coming into force in 1970. Initially, it had a 25-year duration, but in 1995 it was extended indefinitely, after a reaffirmation of its goals by its signatories. By 2003 the NPT had an almost universal membership, although with the notable absence of three nuclear weapon states (India, Pakistan and Israel) and, following its withdrawal from the Treaty, North Korea. Under its terms, the 182 non-nuclear countries have undertaken not to acquire nuclear weapons, and the five overt nuclear states have undertaken to get rid of theirs.

NON-PROLIFERATION TREATY: ARTICLE VI

Each of the Parties to the Treaty undertakes to pursue negotiations in good faith on effective measures relating to cessation of the nuclear arms race at an early date and to nuclear disarmament, and on a Treaty on general and complete disarmament under strict and effective international control.

There was some ambiguity in the formulation of the relevant Article VI of the Treaty, which provided the hawks with an excuse for the retention of nuclear weapons until general and complete disarmament had been achieved. But this ambiguity was removed in 2000, in a statement issued after the Review Conference in that year. This statement, signed by all five nuclear weapon states, contains the following: ' ... an unequivocal undertaking by the nuclear weapon states to accomplish the total elimination of their arsenal leading to nuclear disarmament to which all State parties are committed under Article VI'. This made the situation crystal clear: the

United States, together with the other nuclear weapon states, is unambiguously committed to nuclear disarmament. But by the *de facto* policy of the United States, particularly after the 2002 Nuclear Posture Review and the more recently announced National Security Strategy of the USA, nuclear weapons have become part and parcel of the general military strategy, to be used, if need be, even pre-emptively, in any military dispute. Thus, we have a direct contradiction between an international commitment and a declared security policy.

CONCLUSION

In this chapter we have reviewed a number of factors that are believed to be effective in reducing the incidence of war. Democracy can act as a powerful force for peace, but it is to be regretted that the democracies have not always faced up to their responsibilities where their own interests did not seem to be concerned. Sharing a common culture or religion is by no means always effective in preventing war. Globalization has both positive and negative consequences, and it is by no means clear that the former predominate. The doctrine of deterrence in the nuclear age acts to increase, rather than decrease, the chances of conflict between nuclear powers. Sanctions are of dubious effectiveness. International Law may act as a brake, but the UN is at present too weak to enforce compliance. As discussed in the next chapter, international treaties must be accompanied by means both for verifying compliance and, if necessary, for enforcing them.

12 Preventing War: Arms Control

In the words of the Secretary General of the United Nations, 'Confronting the horrors of war and natural disasters, the United Nations has long argued that prevention is better than cure; that we must address root causes, not their symptoms.' In earlier chapters we have seen both that the causes of wars are never simple – wars break out as the result of networks of interacting causes – and, in the last chapter, that some factors believed to reduce the incidence of war are insufficient by themselves to bring this about. It is thus clear that action to prevent wars must address very diverse issues. And that in turn means that the abolition of war will not be accomplished overnight. The fact that a task is difficult is no reason for not embarking on it, particularly if the alternative is unacceptable. The suffering caused by wars and their aftermath is too great for *laissez faire* to be an option. But, until we are successful in abolishing war completely, action to ameliorate its effects is also necessary.

There is no need to spell out the humanitarian and moral issues here, but there are also financial ones. War imposes enormous costs both on those engaged in it and on the international community. Quite apart from the humanitarian and moral issues involved, there are thus hard pragmatic reasons why countries should not go to war and why the international community should prevent their doing so. Unfortunately, these reasons are too often disregarded.

World military expenditure per annum was estimated at \$852 billion in 1999, with an estimated expenditure of around \$500 per capita in the developed world and \$50 in developing nations. In 2003 the USA alone is set to spend \$382 billion on arms. This, representing 40–50 per cent of the world's total expenditure on arms, is seen by many as a tangible expression of the USA's long-standing ambition to gain world domination.

Although it is reasonable to presume that leaders are sometimes prevented from going to war by lack of funds, it seems that ways round this can often be found, and that leaders seldom take a long-term view. In recent wars in Africa, rulers have seen the gaining of their objectives as more important than the welfare of their people.

This seems to be the case, for instance, with Zimbabwe's intrusion into the Congo. Military rulers have been willing to prolong the war to gain resources to support its prosecution, or to spend a quite disproportionate slice of the nation's resources on military hardware.

For America, the chief geopolitical prize is Eurasia. Now a non-Eurasian power [the US] is pre-eminent in Eurasia – and America's global primacy is directly dependent on how long and how effectively its preponderance on the Eurasian continent is sustained.

To put it in a terminology that harkens back to the more brutal age of ancient empires, the three grand imperatives of imperial geostrategy are to prevent collusion and maintain security dependence among the vassals, to keep tributaries pliant and protected, and to keep the barbarians from coming together.

Zbigniew Brzezinski, *The Grand Chessboard: American Primacy and its Geostrategic Imperatives* (1997)

But the aftermath of war involves much more than the costs of soldiers and munitions. The financial consequences fall on the countries involved but, perhaps even more, also on the international community. Refugees and displaced persons must be cared for, disrupted businesses re-established, the foundations necessary for democratic governance established or re-established, and damage to the country's infrastructure repaired. And all this after the loss of much of the best of the country's talent and in the face of the ennui that war so often leaves behind. To quantify these issues is difficult, because estimates are inevitably inaccurate, but a few examples can give some feeling for the magnitude of the problem. Relief and reconstruction after the civil war in Rwanda is estimated to have cost over $2 billion. The total for the major wars in the 1990s (not including Kosovo) was estimated at $199 billion. Clearance of the landmines laid in past wars is likely to cost $33 billion – and in Africa alone landmines have been killing 12,000 people a year. Damage in Mozambique's civil war, which lasted 16 years, reduced post-war production to little more than a quarter of the pre-war capacity.

Although those who start a war may think little about what will happen after the war is over, and treat the clearing up as other people's business, such costs provide another reason why the international community as a whole should do all it can to abolish war.

The measures needed for the prevention of war fall into two overlapping groups – those aimed primarily at preventing conflict in the first instance, and those concerned with preventing conflicts escalating into violence and reducing suffering if they do. The distinctions are by no means absolute, but this chapter and the next deal with those primarily concerned with preventing conflict.

ARMS CONTROL

Although mostly primitive weapons were sufficient for the genocide in Rwanda, in general modern wars, whether within or between states, require modern arms. Attempts have, therefore, been made to prevent wars by control over the armaments that countries are allowed to possess or acquire. After the First World War German rearmament beyond a certain point was prohibited by the Treaty of Versailles. Some short-sighted Western politicians and their supporters subsequently came to regret this, as they saw in Hitler a possible means to defeat communism and the Soviet Union. In any case, the prohibition turned out to be useless because of the lack of will and the means to enforce it, and Germany's (in part clandestine) rearmament during the 1930s led to the Second World War.

In general, it is necessary to consider separately the control of weapons of mass destruction (nuclear, biological and chemical weapons), sophisticated conventional weapons, and light arms. For the control of weapons of mass destruction it is necessary for there to be general accountability of the stocks (if any) of such weapons, and for a supranational agency to be able to monitor their whereabouts. Accurate monitoring meets many obstacles, and is even less likely to be feasible after the 2002 Nuclear Posture Review.

Nuclear weapons

As described in Chapter 2, during the Cold War era the then superpowers, the USA and USSR, built up enormous arsenals of nuclear weapons, keeping large numbers in a state of instant readiness. The principal justification given for the accumulation of these weapons was that their possession would deter an attack by the other side. Russia still uses this argument, although its stocks have been much reduced. If one's stock of nuclear weapons were sufficient, it was argued, an enemy thinking of making a first strike could not hope to knock out all one's missiles, and a retaliatory strike would be possible. This would impose such heavy costs on the aggressor that it would be deterred from attacking in the first place. But had even one nuclear bomb been launched, whether deliberately or accidentally, it would probably have led to a calamitous exchange. And an accident was always a possibility, although elaborate precautions against premature launches were in place. An exchange of all nuclear weapons in the nuclear arsenals could have led to the elimination of civilization, and perhaps of the human species. It can, therefore, be said emphatically that the possession of nuclear weapons is basically immoral.

Unfortunately, that is not quite the same as saying that they are illegal. As discussed, in 1996 the International Court of Justice ruled that the threat or use of nuclear weapons was contrary to international law. This seems to put those states that possess nuclear weapons in the ridiculous position of having spent vast resources on weapons that they can never use. However, the Court left open whether it would be illegal to use them in self-defence, if the survival of the state were at stake. This has provided a basis for some countries to justify the retention of a nuclear arsenal. The argument here is that if they were the object of attack by conventional armed forces and were in danger of being overwhelmed, they would resort to the use of nuclear weapons. This has been the principal justification used by both Russia and NATO countries for not getting rid of all their weapons. It also provides an incentive for countries to conceal the precise circumstances in which they might resort to the use of nuclear weapons or, in the case of Israel, whether or not they possess them.

During the Cold War, there was a certain willingness to control the escalation of nuclear arms, though attempts to control the nuclear armouries met with only limited success. Their failure was due in part to the lack of trust between the two sides. This meant that it was essential to have procedures for verifying that the conditions imposed by any treaty were being met. Although satellite surveillance aided verification procedures, each side attempted to make such a method of verification unreliable by imposing strict security on all stages of the manufacture and deployment of its nuclear weapons.

Progress in restricting nuclear weapons has been incredibly slow, but over the years a variety of agreements have been reached – for instance, to eliminate nuclear testing in the open when it became evident that testing polluted the atmosphere, and so affected the health of people everywhere. Ironically, the very power of nuclear weapons, and the seismic shock waves created by an explosion, made it possible to detect an explosion thousands of kilometres away from the test site, even when it was conducted underground. This made international agreement to ban nuclear tests possible. Initially this agreement applied only to atmospheric testing (the Partial Test Ban Treaty of 1963), but it was later extended to all types of testing, including underground explosions. The Comprehensive Test Ban Treaty (CTBT) of 1997 has been signed by 165 states (May 2003), but it cannot officially come into force until ratified by the 44 states possessing nuclear reactors.

The change in nuclear doctrine by the Bush administration, contained in the 2002 Nuclear Posture Review and in the National Security Strategy, makes it very unlikely that the USA will ratify the CTBT. Indeed, with the decision to start the development of a new type (low yield but highly penetrating) of nuclear warhead it is very likely that the USA will resume nuclear testing. This could be followed by a resumption of testing by China, as well as by India and Pakistan, countries which, together with North Korea and Bangladesh, have not signed the CTBT in any case.

Table 8 lists the major multilateral and bilateral agreements on the nuclear issue. Several of these treaties deserve special mention.

One of them, the Nuclear Non-Proliferation Treaty (NPT) has been discussed earlier (pp. 141–5) in the context of the obligations on states to adhere to their legal commitments. But those states already possessing nuclear weapons have failed to meet their obligations to get rid of them, and this has acted as a disincentive for others not to acquire them. If the mightiest – militarily and economically – country in the world claims that it needs nuclear weapons for its security, how can one deny such claims by countries that really feel insecure? On these grounds, Israel, India and Pakistan have already built up nuclear arsenals.

A few other states, for example Iraq, Iran and North Korea, which have been named by President George W. Bush as an 'axis of evil', allegedly have, or have had, the capability to make nuclear weapons, or at least the intention to do so. The inevitable conclusion is that, if indefinite escalation is to be prevented, all states that possess them, including the original five, must get rid of them as soon as possible. So long as one state has nuclear weapons, others will see it as their right to have them too. As a shining example, the Republic of South Africa, which had possessed nuclear weapons, relinquished both the weapons and its capability to manufacture them.

A number of other states, for example Sweden, Brazil and Argentina, have, at one time or another, contemplated the acquisition of nuclear weapons. They decided against this action in the belief that a world without nuclear weapons would be a safer

Table 8   Principal nuclear arms control treaties

Treaty	Brief Description	Signatories (May 2003)
Limited Test Ban Treaty (1963)	prohibits nuclear explosions in the atmosphere, outer space & under water	108
Outer Space Treaty (1967)	prohibits placing of nuclear weapons or other weapons of mass destruction in orbit or on celestial bodies	129
Non-Proliferation Treaty (1968)	built around undertaking from non-nuclear weapon states not to acquire nuclear weapons, in return for promise of nuclear disarmament from nuclear weapon states	188
Anti-Ballistic MissileTreaty (1972, defunct 2002)	limits US/Soviet ABM defences to a maximum of 100 interceptors at each of two sites, its capital and one other site (later reduced to just one site)	US/USSR
Threshold Test Ban Treaty (1974)	prohibits underground testing of weapons with yields in excess of 150 kt	US/USSR
Intermediate-Range Nuclear Forces Treaty (1987)	eliminates ground-launched ballistic and cruise missiles with ranges 500–5,500 km	US/USSR
Strategic Arms Reduction Treaty (START) I (1991)	limits US/Russian Federation deployments to 1,600 strategic nuclear delivery vehicles and 6,000 accountable warheads	US, Russian Fed., Belarus, Ukraine, Kazakhstan
START II (1993, defunct 2002)	limits each side to 3,500 accountable strategic warheads	US/Russian Fed.
Comprehensive Test Ban Treaty (1996, not yet in force)	prohibits nuclear weapons test explosions of any yield	167
Strategic Offensive Reduction Treaty (2002)	commits US and Russia to reduce strategic deployed warheads to 1,700–2,200 by 2012 (when the treaty lapses)	US/Russian Federation

world than one with them. But, if the current nuclear weapon states continue to disregard the NPT, and maintain nuclear arsenals for their security, some of these states may revise their policies, and a breakdown of the non-proliferation regime will ensue.

While the NPT aims at the final goal, the total elimination of nuclear arsenals, other treaties, of much more limited scope, have been agreed to either by the nuclear weapon states or by the two superpowers, the USA and USSR.

Under the Intermediate-Range Nuclear Forces Treaty (INF), signed in 1987, the United States and the Soviet Union agreed to eliminate from their arsenals all ballistic and ground-launched cruise missiles, with ranges 1,000–5,500km (intermediate range) and 500–1,000km (shorter range). It was thought that the removal of an entire category of nuclear weapons (although the warheads themselves were not destroyed) which might have been used early and pre-emptively would ease the tense climate that was building up in Europe. The reduction in the number of the highly menacing long-range strategic nuclear weapons – either launched from stationary underground silos, the intercontinental ballistic missiles (ICBMs), or from mobile submarine-launched ballistic missiles (SLBMs) – was the subject of much discussion between the United States and the Soviet Union and resulted in agreement on a number of treaties, first, under the common name of SALT (Strategic Arms Limitation Talks), and subsequently under START (Strategic Arms Reduction Treaty). They resulted in decisions to eliminate certain types of missiles, such as MIRVs on ICBMs and the reduction of other strategic weapons, but the signing and ratification of the different stages of START became embroiled in political issues, such as the enlargement of NATO, and eventually came to a standstill (see Table 2 for the current status of strategic arsenals).

The latest stage in the efforts to reduce strategic nuclear arsenals was the Strategic Offensive Reductions Treaty (SORT), signed by Presidents Bush and Putin, in Moscow, in May 2002. Both sides undertook to reduce their inventories of nuclear warheads to a maximum of 1,700–2,200 warheads each by the end of 2012. On close examination, this treaty, which was hailed by the US administration as a historic breakthrough in arms control negotiations, is really nothing but a sham. There is no timetable for the removal of warheads during the duration of the Treaty; the warheads removed may not be destroyed but stored; and either side can withdraw from the treaty on three months' notice. And, of course, no mention is made of further reductions in the arsenals. A far cry from total nuclear disarmament envisaged under the NPT.

The Anti-Ballistic Missile (ABM) Treaty and Star Wars

In Chapter 2 we have shown how the application of discoveries in nuclear physics led to the development of weapons of ever greater destructive power. In parallel with this, progress in other branches of science and technology has provided greatly improved means for the delivery of these weapons. Little more than a decade after the end of the Second World War, the fantastic progress in rocket technology enabled a man to be put in orbit around the Earth, and – after another decade – to land on the moon. The same technology, applied to the nuclear arms race, has made it possible to transform the whole system of nuclear offensive capability, from having to use huge bombers, like the B2s, which take hours to reach a distant target (thus necessitating fleets of such bombers to be in flight all the time during the Cold War) to ballistic missiles, launched from ground-based silos or from submarines to reach any target in less than 30 minutes. (Incidentally, another application of fission technology, the compact reactor, made it possible for submarines to remain submerged, without the need for refuelling, for very long periods.)

If ballistic missile technology can be applied for offensive purposes, why not for defence? There are no known methods of protecting against the *effects* of nuclear weapons, like the gas mask against chemical weapons, or inoculations against biological weapons (except for the use of iodine pills against *one* radioactive element), and so the scientists who were mainly responsible for the dynamics of the nuclear arms race directed their attention to the development of anti-ballistic missiles, rockets that would intercept and destroy ballistic missiles carrying nuclear warheads or clusters of biological agents. 'There is nothing immoral in acquiring the means to prevent the destruction of one's own country', claimed the Soviet military, who began to develop anti-ballistic missile systems. But Pugwash scientists among others (see Chapter 14) presented a logical argument against this. Ballistic missile defence, like all other technologies, is not 100 per cent effective; a small proportion of the offensive missiles will always get through. And since the latter are much cheaper to manufacture than the anti-ballistic missiles, the consequence of developing defence systems would be a large increase in the offensive arsenals and greater instability. These arguments prevailed, and in 1972 the USA and USSR signed the ABM Treaty, under which both sides agreed not to develop, test, or deploy ABM systems for the defence of their countries (except for two sites, later reduced to one to defend the national capital).

Strangely enough, the ABM Treaty, which is based on the nuclear deterrence doctrine, came to be seen as the cornerstone of the nuclear arms control regime. Even those who were critical of the whole concept of nuclear deterrence, as inherently immoral, were strong defenders of the ABM Treaty. It was the hawks who systematically attacked it, until they finally succeeded in bringing about its demise.

Officially or unofficially, the US security programme always aimed at maintaining nuclear supremacy while at the same time protecting its territory from an outside attack. It always encouraged scientific research and exploited technological advances towards these aims, and there were always scientists who pursued these aims with enthusiasm. Thus, Edward Teller, who decades earlier initiated the hydrogen bomb project, managed to persuade President Reagan that the missile technology had reached the stage where it could produce a shield to protect the United States against a missile attack. In a famous speech, in March 1983, Reagan announced the Strategic Defense Initiative (SDI), which quickly became known as Star Wars, a programme of research and development of space-based weapons, such as lasers and beams of neutral particles, which would intercept and prevent any nuclear missile from reaching American soil.

It did not take other scientists long to prove that the projected shield from the United States was not technologically feasible. But, though Reagan's grandiose plan was abandoned, other more limited schemes for protection against enemy missiles were considered under the Clinton administration and promoted by the Republican majority in the Senate. They received a strong impetus under the George W. Bush administration – since they were in line with his unilateralist policy – and the project has been expanded and accelerated.

Since the Reagan days, when the Soviet Union was the enemy, things have changed both politically and technologically. The 'evil empire' has gone, and been replaced by the 'axis of evil': Iraq, Iran and North Korea, which were seen as attempting to acquire nuclear weapons, as well as ballistic missiles with which to deliver them. Indeed, progress in missile technology has made it possible for even relatively undeveloped countries, such as North Korea, to develop or acquire missiles of ever increasing range, so that some of them could reach the outposts of the United States.

> ... I call upon the scientific community in our country, those who gave us nuclear weapons, to turn their great talents now to the cause of mankind and world peace, to give us the means of rendering these nuclear weapons impotent and obsolete.
>
> Tonight ... I am taking an important first step. I am directing a comprehensive and intensive effort to define a long-term research and development program to begin to achieve our ultimate goal of eliminating the threat posed by strategic nuclear missiles. This could pave the way for arms control measures to eliminate the weapons themselves. We seek neither military superiority nor political advantage. Our only purpose – one all people share – is to search for ways to reduce the danger of nuclear war.
>
> My fellow Americans, tonight we're launching an effort which holds the promise of changing the course of human history. There will be risks, and results take time. But I believe we can do it. As we cross this threshold, I ask for your prayers and your support.
>
> Ronald Reagan, 1986

At the same time, the advances in missile technology have made it possible for the advocates of Star Wars to claim that the technical obstacles have been overcome and that interception of incoming enemy missiles has become feasible. To ensure the success of the project, Bush decided to develop in parallel three methods of interception: (1) in the *boost phase*: to develop an air-based or space-based laser weapon to intercept ballistic missiles shortly after launch; (2) in the *mid-course phase*, with a variety of projectiles to intercept and destroy a missile carrying a nuclear warhead while on its trajectory in outer space; (3) in the *terminal phase*, to achieve interception in the last few minutes after re-entry into the atmosphere.

The appropriated budget for 2002 was $8 billion (the total cost is estimated to be about $70 billion), and the project is running at full speed. One aspect, which became clear in the meantime, was that it is incompatible with the ABM Treaty. The implementation of the missile defence programme will also require the setting-up, or the use of, tracking stations, possibly located in other countries, such as the radar station at Fylingdales, Yorkshire.

And so, after giving the required six months' notice, President George W. Bush abrogated the Treaty in June 2002.

Weaponization of outer space

Will the demise of the ABM Treaty herald the birth of a new arms race in the 'last frontier', outer space?

At the beginning of the nuclear arms race, characterized by the increasing number of tests of nuclear weapons, some of these tests were carried out high in the atmosphere. When, later on, a limitation on tests, largely for health reasons, began to be considered, culminating in the Partial Test Ban Treaty of 1963 (p. 149), the ban included tests in outer space. Health reasons could be invoked here too: the destruction of ionization belts by the explosions would permit harmful ultraviolet and solar radiation to reach the earth. With the rapid increase in satellite technology, and its subsequent utilization, concern about the integrity of outer space led in 1967 to the Outer Space Treaty, which by the end of 2002 had 129 state parties. It prohibits the placing in earth orbit of objects carrying nuclear weapons or any other kind of weapon of mass destruction.

The treaty did not prohibit the military uses of outer space, hence the distinction between 'militarization' and 'weaponization'. Indeed, the military uses of outer space are already immense, particularly by the United States. By the end of 2001, the USA had 110 operational military-related satellites, while Russia had 40, and the rest of the world about 20. These satellites serve many purposes, i.e. communications, navigation, weather, early-warning, ocean surveillance, signals intelligence, imagery intelligence, and electronic intelligence. Some of these have important civilian uses. On the other hand, some may carry weapons designed to destroy other satellites. In this category are the anti-satellite systems, which are being developed under the Bush administration plans for the ballistic missile defence system discussed above.

There is growing international concern that the US quest for space dominance will give rise to a destabilizing arms race in space. A number of countries, led by Russia and China, have started a campaign for a new multilateral treaty prohibiting the deployment of weapons (mass destruction as well as conventional) in space, and restricting their use to peaceful purposes.

Apart from the threat of a new arms race, weaponization of space can have other harmful consequences. As an example, we will quote the problem of debris. Contrary to Star Wars movies, where things blow up in space and the fragments are quickly dispersed, in reality debris in high altitude orbits clears away very slowly, in decades or centuries. Travelling at great speed, even a tiny fragment could destroy a satellite. For example, a marble travelling at about 27,000 km per hour will hit with the energy of a one tonne object dropped from a three-storey building.

A test explosion of a nuclear weapon in space will enormously increase the amount of debris. With so much orbiting debris, pieces will begin to hit other pieces, fragmenting them into pieces, which will in turn hit more pieces, setting off a chain reaction. The communication satellites, including GPS satellites, on which we have become so dependent in our daily life, would become endangered.

Nuclear-weapon-free zones (NWFZs)

Nearly all non-nuclear weapon states have signed and ratified the NPT, under which they have agreed not to acquire nuclear weapons, but quite early in this saga it was suggested that the goal of nuclear disarmament would be accelerated if a number of states in a given geographical region would jointly agree to make the region nuclear-free in the sense that not only would its members undertake not to acquire nuclear weapons, but they would ensure that no nuclear weapons were allowed into that region.

The first idea (Rapacki Plan, 1958) of a nuclear-free zone in Central Europe came to nothing; it came too early, in a politically very sensitive area. But the idea itself was later accepted in other geographical regions.

NUCLEAR-WEAPON-FREE-ZONE TREATIES

The 1967 **Treaty of Tlatelolco** establishes an NWFZ in Latin America. All countries in the Latin American continent, as well as the Caribbean countries, are members of the Treaty.

The 1985 **Treaty of Rarotonga** embraces all the countries in the South Pacific, including Australia, New Zealand, and the smaller islands, and a few areas north of the equator.

The 1995 **Treaty of Bangkok** embraces all countries in South-East Asia, including Indonesia, Thailand and Vietnam.

The 1996 **Treaty of Pelindaba** covers the entire African continent.

If we add the 1959 Antarctic Treaty, the entire southern hemisphere (plus some of the northern hemisphere) is now a denuclearized zone. But the most populated countries (China, India) and the most industrialized ones are still outside. We still have a long way to go before the whole earth has become a nuclear-weapon-free zone.

Elimination of nuclear weapons

The destruction of Hiroshima and Nagasaki brought a wave of revulsion against nuclear weapons all over the world, which was expressed in the very first resolution of the General Assembly of the

United Nations to set up a commission with the task of eliminating these weapons. These early efforts came to nothing in the climate of the Cold War that began soon afterwards; nevertheless, they were kept going and are still going in the form of annual resolutions of the General Assembly calling for complete nuclear disarmament.

FIRST UN RESOLUTION

Established an Atomic Energy Commission mandated ' ... to deal with the problems raised by the discovery of atomic energy and other related matters'.

Its terms of reference called on it to:
' ... proceed with the utmost despatch and enquire into all phases of the problem, and ... make specific proposals: ... for the elimination from national armaments of atomic weapons and of all other major weapons adaptable to mass destruction'.

Various non-governmental organizations, national and international, have also been active with the same aim. Among the latter the Pugwash Movement (pp. 188–90) became prominent during the Cold War years as an important channel of communication between the two sides. Although the goal of Pugwash was, first, the elimination of weapons of mass destruction and, ultimately, the elimination of war itself, its immediate task was to prevent the Cold War turning into a hot war, by helping to facilitate the various partial measures that acted as a brake on the nuclear arms race.

As soon as the Cold War was over, efforts began towards the realization of the original aims. Pugwash was one of the earliest with its project towards a nuclear-weapon-free world (NWFW). It posed two questions: a NWFW: is it desirable? is it feasible? Its reasoned answer was yes to both questions: however, it acknowledged the great difficulties in ensuring that a treaty to abolish nuclear weapons would not be violated. The Pugwash study suggested that in order to safeguard this treaty, the usual technological verification system should be supplemented with a societal verification system, under which every citizen would be called upon to ensure that no violation of the treaty is taking place in their country. The treaty would have to include a clause under which the signatory states would be required to pass national laws that made it the right and duty of its citizens to report to the appropriate authority any knowledge acquired about attempts to violate the treaty. The spread of the Internet makes this task much easier.

One direct outcome of the publication of the Pugwash project was the decision by the Australian government to set up what became known as the Canberra Commission. It was the first time that a government of a country, Australia, allied to two nuclear weapon states, the UK and the USA, had taken an initiative in the field by sponsoring a comprehensive study on the elimination of nuclear weapons. The Canberra Commission consisted of 17 well-known personalities from a number of countries and a variety of disciplines: politicians, diplomats, military authorities and scientists (one of us, JR, was in that group, as was Robert McNamara). The Commission's Report, published in 1996, was a lucid, eloquent, reasoned but at times emotional, elucidation of the dangers arising from the existence of nuclear weapons and the need to get rid of them. It proposes a number of immediate steps that would significantly reduce the risk of nuclear war, and then outlines the long-term measures leading to the elimination of all nuclear weapons. When the Canberra Commission was set up, it was the intention of Australia's then Labour government to submit the report to the General Assembly of the United Nations and to press for action on it. However, in the meantime, the Labour Party lost the general election and the new government decided not to pursue the matter, and an important initiative was lost.

In the USA, several institutions (for example the Stimson Center, the Carnegie Foundation) carried out studies on an NWFW making more or less similar recommendations. The prestigious National Academy of Sciences has a Committee on International Security and Arms Control (CISAC) with a membership composed of experts in the nuclear field. Its recommendations on this issue included: 'the United States should announce that the only purpose of the U.S. nuclear weapons is to deter nuclear attacks on the United States and its

---

CANBERRA COMMISSION

Nuclear weapons pose an intolerable threat to all humanity and its habitat, yet tens of thousands remain in arsenals built up at an extraordinary time of deep antagonism. That time has passed, yet assertions of their utility continue.

Nuclear weapons are held by a handful of states which insist that these weapons provide unique security benefits, and yet reserve uniquely to themselves the right to own them. This situation is highly discriminatory and thus unstable; it cannot be sustained. The possession of nuclear weapons by any state is a constant stimulus to other states to acquire them.

allies ... ' The Committee found merit in the eventual 'prohibition' of nuclear weapons.

The period of lively discussion on an NWFW did not last long. In our opinion the main reason was the apathy of the general public in relation to nuclear issues. With the end of the Cold War, and the collapse of the Soviet Union, there was a general feeling that the nuclear threat was over altogether, and that the nuclear issue could be taken off the agenda of important world affairs. This lack of interest was exploited by the hawks in the United States who always viewed the possession of nuclear weapons by the USA as a way to ensure its dominance over the rest of the world. In particular, under the George W. Bush administration the whole doctrine of the nuclear issue has changed from deterrence to the treatment of nuclear weapons as part and parcel of ordinary military strategy, including the use of nuclear weapons in a pre-emptive strike. The danger of this policy is that it contains a real threat of a new arms race. The development of new types of warheads, announced by the US government, may result in its withdrawal from the Comprehensive Test Ban Treaty, likely followed by other states. China, in particular, may be eager to resume testing in order to update its nuclear arsenal to make up for the perceived threat to its security after the demise of the ABM Treaty and the increasing weaponization of space by the USA.

It is most important that the general public is kept informed about the increasing nuclear peril.

Biological weapons

Less is known about the effectiveness of biological weapons than about that of nuclear weapons, but it is clear that they could pose a major threat. Unforeseeable further dangers may arise from progress in genetic engineering (see Chapter 3). They could be especially dangerous in the hands of terrorists. This was evident recently in the near panic that ensued in the USA when letters containing anthrax spores were sent to a number of people, apparently by the action of one individual.

Unlike the case of nuclear weapons, there is a formal agreement to prohibit biological weapons. The 1972 Biological Weapons Convention (BWC) bans the development, production, stockpiling or acquisition of microbial or other biological agents or toxins. It came into force in 1993, and currently has 143 state members. It was the first worldwide treaty to prohibit an entire class of weapons. Its weakness is that – unlike the Chemical Weapons Convention (see below) – it has no organization, no budget, no inspection provision, and no built-in sanctions. A group of member states – including the USA – worked for seven years on a protocol to strengthen the Convention, including measures for verification. An agreement seemed to have been reached on a text for a Protocol to the Treaty, which would have provided for visits by an international inspectorate to factories with facilities that could be used for the production of biological weapons, and for procedures for the investigation of complaints. Unfortunately, almost at the last minute, the US government withdrew its assent. The reasons given were that the task might prove impossible, and that it would not be in the interests of its commercial firms manufacturing various drugs and other civilian products, as they often depend on secrecy for the competitive marketing of their products. Thus the implementation of the Biological Weapons Convention is at present in limbo.

Chemical weapons

The Chemical Weapons Convention (CWC) was signed in 1993 and came into force in 1997. It has 145 member states, the most conspicuous absentees being the group of Arab states in the Middle East. They view chemical weapons as 'the poor nation's atom bomb' as a counter to Israel's nuclear weapons, and will not accede to the CWC as long as the latter retains its nuclear weapons.

Under the terms of the CWC, each signatory undertakes not to develop, produce, otherwise acquire, stockpile or retain chemical weapons, or transfer, directly or indirectly, chemical weapons to anyone. Of course, they undertake also not to use chemical weapons, engage in military preparations to use chemical weapons, and not to assist, encourage or induce anyone to engage in any activities prohibited by the CWC.

Unlike the case with biological weapons, the CWC contains provisions to ensure that the Treaty is not violated. These include routine, as well as *ad hoc*, inspection of possibly relevant activities: suspect sites are subject to short-notice challenge inspections. For this purpose a special organization, the Organization for the Prohibition of Chemical Weapons, was set up in The Hague with a large staff of experts (and bureaucrats). A considerable number of routine inspections have already been carried out. It will, however, be extremely difficult to prevent terrorist groups acquiring, or countries manufacturing, the necessary small quantities of a chemical weapon, such as a nerve gas, in secret.

Conventional weapons and the arms trade

One must not forget that some of the heavy bomber raids during the Second World War, though using up to a thousand aircraft, resulted in casualties comparable to those produced by one of the nuclear bombs dropped on Japan. Since then, with modern technology, it has been possible for arms-manufacturing countries to produce conventional weapons of even greater destructive power. Thus, the control of conventional weapons is a task of great importance, but the problems involved are of a rather different nature from those facing efforts to eliminate weapons of mass destruction, since the diffusion of conventional weapons is closely linked to the international arms trade.

On the positive side, the Conventional Armed Forces in Europe Treaty, which came into force in 1992, places limits on various types of conventional weapons (e.g. tanks, military aircraft) and manpower held by most European countries. With provisions for verification and periodic revision, it has had considerable success in limiting European armed forces.

Whether this has had any effect on the incidence of war is another matter, for there has been little incentive for any of the countries involved to make war on one another.

Fortunately, the more sophisticated weapon systems are produced in any numbers by only a few countries: the five permanent members of the Security Council, and Germany. And the probability of war between any two of these countries is certainly very much smaller than it used to be, though not non-existent – a confrontation between China and the USA over Taiwan is quite possible. But the amounts spent on arms are still immense – especially the money spent by the USA on armaments of all sorts (see p. 145).

But sophisticated weapon systems are very expensive to produce. They take many years to pass through the stages of design, manufacture of prototypes, testing, refinement, production and deployment. The countries that produce them are, therefore, only too willing to defray some of these production costs by selling weapons to other countries (Table 9).

The morality of arms sales is extremely dubious. The arms may fuel conflicts in remote parts of the world, and they certainly divert the resources of the purchasing country from the more immediate needs of the population. Some Third World leaders have accumulated arms instead of using their resources for the well-being of their

Table 9a   Top ten exporters of conventional weapons

	Value of Exports 1996–2000 ($m constant 1990 prices)
United States	49,271
Russia	15,690
France	10,792
UK	7,026
Germany	5,647
Netherlands	2,014
Ukraine	1,956
Italy	1,720
China	1,506
Belarus	1,246

Table 9b   Top ten importers of conventional weapons

	Value of Imports 1996–2000 ($m constant 1990 prices)
Taiwan	12,281
Saudi Arabia	8,362
Turkey	5,664
South Korea	5,334
China	5,231
India	4,228
Greece	3,665
Egypt	3,619
Japan	3,558
UAE	2,983

Source: *SIPRI Yearbook 2001* (Oxford: Oxford University Press, 2001). Note that the figures, given in constant 1990 prices, should be seen as an indicator of the volume of international arms transfers and not of the actual financial values of such transfers.

people. As a result of arms sales, weapons have come into the possession of countries which subsequently used them for suppressing minorities and for other undesirable purposes. For instance, light tanks and Hawk aircraft sold to Indonesia may have been used to support the illegal occupation of East Timor. In addition, the sale of arms may rebound on the seller: Britain in the Falklands, and Britain and the USA in the Gulf War and in Afghanistan, have found themselves faced with enemies whom they have themselves helped to arm.

The UN and NATO have attempted to produce agreements that would limit the sale of arms by one country to another, and all states have a legal obligation to assess whether the arms and security equipment and training they export are likely to be used by the recipients to commit human rights abuses. In addition, most arms-producing countries claim that they are placing restrictions on the countries to which their weapons are exported, for instance, ruling out countries engaged in civil war, those with poor human rights records, and so on. Another restriction that should be included concerns whether the recipient country can afford the arms while taking adequate care of its own people. For instance, South Africa recently committed itself to spending £4 billion on arms from European companies. This is twice the country's housing budget and ten times the budget for dealing with HIV/AIDS.

However, such restrictions are difficult to enforce. In the UK export licenses for the sale of arms are not even open to scrutiny by Parliament before they are issued. British arms have in fact been sold to a number of countries whose relations both internally between individuals or with other states were in a highly unstable state – for instance, Israel, Pakistan, China and Sri Lanka. There has been no restriction on UK companies arranging for their products to be manufactured abroad and then exported to a third country. Unscrupulous arms dealers find ways of directing weapons to destinations other than those to which export has been permitted. Reliable information about the circuitous routes taken by arms shipments is, not surprisingly, difficult to obtain, but as one example, the UK supplied 300 shoulder-launched anti-aircraft missile systems which eventually reached Afghanistan in 1985. Manufactured by the then state-controlled Shorts Brothers, they were sent to the USA. From there they were transferred by CIA networks to Pakistan, and thence by Pakistan's Inter-Services Intelligence Agency to the Mujahideen-backed Afghan groups.

There is also difficulty in specifying whether the items in question are intended for use in conflict, internal control, or what. In October 2002 the UK Prime Minister devoted part of a brief interview with the Indian Prime Minister to lobbying for the sale of Hawk jets. These are ostensibly training aircraft, used to increase air safety, but as Indonesia has shown, can easily be converted for combat. It is noteworthy that the interview took place during a period of continuing tension between India and Pakistan.

Not surprisingly, much of the incentive for arms production comes from the arms-producing companies, whose turnovers surpass the imagination. For instance, the UK exports over £400 million of arms to Africa alone every year, and Tony Blair has made a promise that the Labour government would create conditions in which the arms industries would flourish. This is in apparent contradiction to the policy declared by Robin Cook, then UK Foreign Secretary, to include ethical considerations in the arms trade negotiations.

As a recent and more dramatic example, the USA recently chose Lockheed Martin to develop the Joint Strike Fighter aircraft. The deal involves building over 3,000 fighter aircraft for the USA and its allies. Beyond the sales to the USA, it is reported that the companies involved (which include Rolls Royce) expect to make over £140 billion from export orders. In many cases, arms producing companies receive from politicians or their parties support that is alleged to be a consequence of direct help provided to politicians or contributions to party funds.

The governments of arms-producing countries give financial support to the companies involved in more than one way. First, the companies receive subsidies for research and development. In the UK this is reckoned as being around £500 million a year. Second, in the UK a part of the Department of Trade and Industry insures the companies that export arms against the possibility that the recipient country will default on the loans that it has taken out to pay for the arms. If it does, the British taxpayer then pays indirectly to cover the deficit. The country's debts may then be transferred to the World Bank, and become part of its national debt. In addition, there is evidence that arms sales are often accompanied by bribes: these may involve promises of technological aid, credit, political concessions, and so on. For instance, aid given by Britain to Malaysia to finance the building of the Pergau dam was apparently conditional upon an arms sale.

While the arms companies no doubt profit from the deals, it is by no means clear that their governments do. Together with other items, the total UK government support is estimated at well over £900 million a year. It is claimed that this expenditure is justified by the preservation of jobs in the companies concerned. Not only is this claim extremely dubious, but the possibility of turning swords into ploughshares, much discussed twenty or thirty years ago, seems to have been forgotten.

Another cause of the dissemination of arms involves surplus stocks. Even the most sophisticated weapons become out of date – a process that is accentuated by competition between arms manufacturers to produce ever more effective weapons. Old weapons may be sold to other countries, or even given away. Between 1990 and 1997, the US government gave away more tham $8 billion-worth of surplus equipment, thereby increasing the potential for violence elsewhere in the world. In addition, disarmament involves the disposal of military hardware, and disposal does not always involve destruction.

Sometimes self-interest has got in the way of effective international agreement, and landmines provide an interesting example. As we have seen, landmines cause an enormous number of civilian casualties for years after hostilities have ceased. It is estimated that more than 110 million landmines are scattered in 73 countries, and that every month over 2,000 people are killed or injured by them. The mines can remain active for over 50 years. An important agreement to ban them, the Ottawa Convention, has been signed by 142 governments, but not by three of the biggest users, the USA, Russia and China. The USA is apparently delaying until alternatives can be developed that offer the US armed forces equivalent protection. It has been suggested that the special problem of the boundary between North and South Korea lies behind this reluctance. An alternative being considered in the USA would allow a soldier to watch a video display through which sensors would indicate the presence of an intruder: the explosives could then be detonated remotely. However, the design has been provided with an override switch that would allow the mines to explode on contact, and this would contravene the Ottawa Convention. Further development awaits clarification of the US attitude to that Convention. And this is not the only attempt that is being made to get round the ban. Anti-vehicle landmines, such as the German AT-2, requiring a stronger force for detonation, are being developed. But there is doubt whether even a 150kg force is a safe minimum, since the impact of a jumping child can produce a similar effect.

Light weapons, including hand-guns, rifles, automatic weapons, and some hand-held launchers, pose even more difficult problems. After the end of the Cold War the world became awash with small arms. In addition, there has been an increase in production, and extensive loopholes in export controls exist. In many parts of the world automatic rifles can be picked up for a few dollars – an AK 47 may cost as little as $6. And it is these small arms, rather than sophisticated weapons, that have made possible the recent wars in Africa, South America and Asia. Some attempts have been made to take these weapons out of circulation. El Salvador, where many weapons were acquired during the civil war, has offered to pay cash for weapons handed in, and in Mozambique a scheme to exchange them for commercially useful items, like sewing machines and farm tools, has been tried. In South Africa at least one 'gun-free zone' has been established by local initiative. But such schemes can make but a small impact on the vast numbers of these weapons left over from earlier wars. In the long run, perhaps the only solution will lie in national restrictions on both the manufacture and the ownership of weapons. In addition, the marking of weapons by the manufacturer could help police authorities to trace their source, and would make the illegal possession of weapons more difficult. However, there are powerful obstacles to the implementation of such measures.

Attempts to constrain the spread of small arms tend to meet with resistance from vested interests. On the opening day of a recent UN conference on small arms it was stated that the USA would reject proposals that would constrain legal trade and legal manufacture of small arms, thereby safeguarding American gun laws. The powerful 'gun lobby' in the USA resists any restrictions on the sale of guns on the grounds that citizens have a constitutional right to bear arms. And the UK is far from blameless. In 1999, $44 million-worth of light weapons were shipped abroad to countries which included Israel, Kuwait, Egypt and Indonesia, and adequate 'end use' controls have not been introduced. This means that arms ostensibly bound for Egypt or Jordan may have been sent through to Iraq. Furthermore, machine guns can still be made under UK licensed production abroad in the factories of Turkey, Pakistan and Iran.

It will be apparent that efforts to limit the manufacture and to control the sale of arms have so far met with only limited success. That does not mean that these efforts should not be pursued, but rather that they must be pursued more vigorously. Limitations on weapons can reduce the likelihood of war and limit the destruction that it brings. But ultimate success in controlling arms will depend on a new political and social climate in the world.

COMBATING TERRORISM

In recent decades the need to confront the dangers of terrorism has become as urgent as preventing war. Terrorism is sometimes the only means available to a minority group within a country to express its desire for independence. Countless examples exist – the Basques in Spain, the Palestinians in the Occupied Zones, and 'freedom fighters' in many other countries. That they have no other means in no way excuses the use of violence, but it does indicate that prevention should focus not only on suppression but also on providing other means for the expression of grievances and addressing those grievances. The problems differ between cases, and generalizations are of little value.

But terrorism has now become a matter of international concern. Too often it is linked to the drug trade, the illegal trade in weapons, or other outlawed activities. In such cases it crosses frontiers. And since the 11 September events it has become an important ideological issue, involving resentment at the attempts of Western nations to impose or to support unpopular regimes in order to further their own interests, and to impose their cultural ideals on others.

The prevention of terrorism now depends crucially on the international sharing of intelligence. Terrorist organizations, such as al-Qaeda, are often widely dispersed, and the preparations for an attack are likely to be made in a country remote from the target. The only individual so far charged by the USA for the 11 September attacks was identified in the French intelligence reports available to the Americans before the attacks occurred.

Of course, the perpetrators of such attacks must be caught and punished. But it is essential for governments to realize that violence breeds violence. A 'war on terrorism', to use a phrase coined by President George W. Bush in response to the 11 September attack, is surely a mistake. The use of violence to suppress terrorists is not only morally wrong, but ineffective, as the terrorist organization will simply go into hiding. In Afghanistan, the use of military force was effective in bringing to an end the undemocratic and oppressive rule of the Taliban, but did little to suppress al-Qaeda. Where military intervention is used to reduce the killing, as in Northern Ireland where two rival parties have used terrorist tactics in attempts to gain their ends, it may have reduced overt conflict but cannot provide a settlement. At most it may have contributed to building an environment where a settlement can be reached.

In the long run the causes of terrorism must be addressed. Powerful governments must not try to manipulate others, or to impose their will. As we have emphasized elsewhere in this book, the route towards ensuring good governance for the sake of the people is not an easy one. It must involve a degree of tolerance coupled with a willingness to admit that one's own system may not be wholly ideal for other people living with different traditions and in different conditions. And constructive change is most likely to be a consequence of good example, discussion and submission to international authority, not violence.

CONCLUSION

Effective arms control is clearly an essential aim. International agreements to prohibit weapons of mass destruction, and the means to verify adherence, are essential. The manufacture, dissemination and possession of arms must be regulated, with the ultimate intention of limiting their legitimate possession to UN forces and authorized intra-state police if that is necessary. The problems involved differ between the various types of weapons of mass destruction and of so-called conventional weapons. In all cases adequate means for verification and enforcement are essential for successful control.

Terrorism must be countered by attempts to understand and address the terrorists' grievances, as well as by the use of force to prevent attacks.

13 Preventing War: Promotion of International Well-Being and Peace Education

Any attempt to discuss ways of preventing war must address very basic issues, and in doing so lays itself open to accusations of mushy idealism. But although poverty and environmental degradation are seldom the direct cause of war, they provide a basis on which war is readily fomented (Chapters 8 and 9). Poverty and population pressure force people to live in places susceptible to natural disasters, and natural disasters are made more probable by unsustainable development practices, such as indiscriminate logging operations. These dangers, combined with poverty and crowding may either lead to aggressive self-assertiveness, or to passivity and susceptibility to manipulation by unscrupulous leaders.

Thus, although the intervening causal relations are complex, steps to remove poverty, and to achieve greater perceived equality of incomes, opportunities and freedoms, must be seen as essential elements in attempts to abolish war. Within any one state, there are bound to be frequent opportunities for those who are less well off to observe those who are richer or with more opportunities than themselves, and discontent easily arises. In a society of equals, mutual trust is more easily fostered, even when all depend on a common resource – for instance, water for irrigation or grazing land. But if people become suspicious of each other, the management of that resource breaks down. While globalization has been accompanied by a reduction in poverty over the world as a whole, and had some other beneficial effects, we have seen that it has increased the gap between the haves and the have nots (Chapter 9).

Reduction in poverty is no easy task. Poverty is related to over-population, and there is no single panacea for dealing with that. Analyses show that hope lies in the combination of a number of measures – family planning, the empowerment and education of women, the provision of potable water and fuel, changes in property rights, enhanced communication and civil liberties, as well as measures directly increasing the economic security of the poor. Of course, the relative importance of these varies with the characteristics of the community in question.

In the short term, there must be a large increase in international aid. This should be directed especially to the relief of populations whose need is already acute, but also towards encouraging sustainable development in poor countries. The effects of international aid have been most apparent so far in the very poorest countries: in those that are slightly better off its effectiveness depends on democratic governance and the efficiency with which the resources are directed to where they are needed. Too often, much is siphoned off by middlemen, and does not reach those for whom it is intended. Too often, it is spent on exports from the aid-giving countries, and not on what the people really need. But only about one-sixth of American aid is given to the 48 least developed countries, and sub-Saharan Africa receives about one-sixth of that going to the Middle East. Financial aid is often essential for alleviating the consequences of war, but by helping to fight poverty, disease and malnutrition it can also help to remove some of the factors that are conducive to war. The most basic reasons for the richer countries to help the poorer ones are moral ones, but politicians are more easily convinced by the knowledge that it is in the rich countries' interests. State failure can have worldwide repercussions involving not only financial issues but also increased drug-trafficking, terrorism, the spread of diseases, and influxes of refugees.

Food aid and financial aid relieve short-term suffering, but it is not a long-term solution. The society must be helped to rebuild itself so that it becomes self-sufficient. A new infrastructure may have to be built up. Technical assistance, geared appropriately to the country's needs, is essential.

An additional problem arises with financial loans intended to assist development. Many countries have been burdened with debts from loans, and the interest repayments have frustrated the purpose for which the loans were made. In only a few cases, where countries have committed themselves to sound macroeconomic policies and to poverty relief, have debts been cancelled or repayment been put off indefinitely.

In any case, the conditions for trade tend to be adverse for the poorer and less industrialized countries, enabling the West to increase its dominance even further. While the economic solution to this is inevitably complex, and it will always be difficult to persuade nations to accept an agreement to their own detriment, in the long run more equitable conditions throughout the world would be to the advantage of all.

EDUCATION FOR PEACE AND SOCIALIZATION

Wars are not possible without people willing to fight them, and we have seen how people's prejudices can be exacerbated and their attitudes manipulated by propaganda with religious, ethnic or political connotations, and by the military–industrial–scientific complex, so that war becomes an acceptable means for settling conflicts. What can be done to make people less susceptible to these influences? And what can be done to remove ethnic, cultural and religious prejudices?

Improvements in education can make a major contribution to decreasing violence both between and within countries, though many of its effects are indirect. For instance, the education of women contributes to a decrease in the birth rate, and this in due course to reductions in population density, environmental degradation and poverty. A certain level of education is necessary before the introduction of some technologies can improve living standards. One can distinguish two aspects of this problem, though they are closely inter-related. Education can help to create an environment in which people are less prone to see violence as an acceptable way of solving conflicts. And it can also encourage understanding of the cultures of other societies. Above all, education contributes to the prospects for better economy.

Ideally, we should start with adults. It is parents who have the greatest influence on the personality development of their children. How children are brought up affects the balance between the assertive/aggressive side of their natures and the prosocial/caring/cooperative side. Individuals brought up by parents who are sensitive to their needs, use appropriate control, and encourage responsible behaviour, tend to have less aggressive personalities. Upbringing also affects how easily individuals can be affected by propaganda.

However, as noted earlier (pp. 102–3) the behaviour of parents is affected both by their own upbringing, and more immediately by the circumstances in which they are living. It is understandable that parents who are living at the subsistence level, who have to compete with others to get enough to eat, who can see that others are unfairly much better off than they are, and whose life is a continuous struggle against impossible odds, may bring up their children to be assertive competitors in order to succeed.

There may also be a problem with the very rich, especially the newly rich, as they may bring up their children to emulate their own competitiveness. This is as yet undocumented and, because the rich are fewer in number than the poor, the problem is likely to be of less magnitude. However, it could have an importance of a different sort, for the poor may attempt to follow the example of the rich. In any case, raising living standards worldwide, and reducing the discrepancies between the rich and the poor, must be a major goal.

Parents tend to be set in their ways, and most educational efforts start with children. Between childhood and adulthood schools carry a heavy responsibility. Unfortunately, the need to assist children to make their way in the world, and the needs of the society, easily come into conflict. In a competitive world, training tends to be progressively oriented towards personal success, with an emphasis on work-related knowledge or skills. Training for citizenship gets neglected. Assertiveness is steered towards selfish ends, and not towards how to serve the community and how to resist pressures from peers, television and computer games that promote aggressiveness, status seeking and selfish ends.

Of course, the problems of education vary with the nature of the country concerned. As noted above, over much of the world the essential need is for basic literacy and for the education of women: these have been amongst the factors contributing both to a lower birth rate in over-populated countries and to greater prosperity – for instance, in parts of southern India. Prosperity and education are, of course, mutually supportive, the one making possible the other.

One of the most promising omens for a peaceful world is the increase in education at all levels, and the steady decrease in illiteracy, even among the poorest countries (see Figure 9).

The problems in industrialized countries, where subsistence levels are higher and there is relatively greater equality between the sexes, are rather different and more complex. However, in both developed and under-developed countries there is a need to increase understanding of other cultures. That, however, is far from easy. A simple account of differences in cultural practices is unlikely to be sufficient to produce reconciliation and understanding, and must be coupled with the encouragement of tolerance and respect for others.

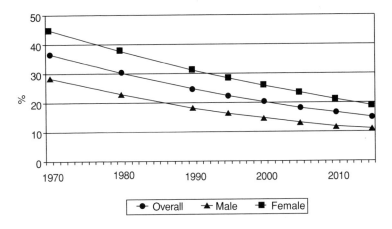

Figure 9   Estimated and projected world illiteracy rates.

Source: UNESCO Institute for Statistics

The UNESCO Recommendation of 1974 recommended that member states should strengthen the contribution of education to international understanding and cooperation, to the establishment of social justice, and to the eradication of the misconceptions and prejudices that hinder those aims. This was a carefully thought-out series of recommendations which was coupled with the suggestion that teachers should be trained to further those aims, and that the results should be monitored. But progress in implementing the UNESCO Recommendation has been disappointingly slow, and a sense of urgency has been lacking. The one honourable exception has been Finland, where education for peace has been actively encouraged. Other countries, such as Canada, have taken some steps in the same direction.

The case of Finland is in some ways surprising. Although it has continued to have national service, laws were passed in 1983 and 1985 requiring that day care and school education should support growth towards shared responsibility and peace, and peace education has continued to find a place in Finnish schools.

According to the Peace Education Network of the British National Peace Council, peace education should be based on respect for others regardless of race, gender, religion, ability and so on; a willingness to understand the views of others; a belief that individuals and groups can contribute to positive change; respect for diversity; acceptance

of the intrinsic value of oneself; commitment to social justice, equity
and non-violence; concern for the environment, and commitment
to equality. It will be apparent that implementation of these aims
poses many problems. How can one respect the views of others when
they disagree fundamentally with one's own? How can one be
committed to non-violence and respect societies that retain capital
punishment? How far should one expect immigrants to conform to
the culture of the host society? Nevertheless, while opinions will
certainly differ on the emphases to be placed on the points raised by
the Peace Council, they form a valuable background to the more
obvious aims of understanding the causes of violence and the means
for conflict resolution.

The Finnish example shows what can be accomplished, and there
is no reason why it should not be emulated elsewhere. There are of
course difficulties, and it is appropriate to spell out one of them.
While education should not aim at imposing one country's culture
on others, it should be such as to encourage pride in one's own
culture (patriotism) and understanding of others (see p. 112). This
does not mean devotion to one's country such that one is blind to
its faults, but rather realistic loyalty. And patriotism should be
cultivated without the denigration of other countries or other
cultures (nationalism). Rather it should contribute to the understanding of other cultures, and a degree of tolerance for the beliefs and
customs of other people. But how far should this tolerance go? Is it
possible for Westerners to understand another culture that
discourages the education of women? Or one that practices clitoridec-
tomy? Or, for that matter, for Muslims to understand Western
hedonism and materialism? Such problems have no easy answers
but, at the least, education for peace should introduce children to
such problems and help them to grapple with them.

Above all, education for peace should insist that all peoples, in
every part of the world, share a common humanity. Some needs,
desires, attributes, abilities, sensitivities and moral principles are
common to all individuals, no matter where they live and irrespec-
tive of the culture in which they were brought up. And everyone is
born with the capacity to be sensitive and caring towards others, as
well as to be selfishly assertive. Equitable relationships and group
living demand an environment in which our readiness to be kind to
our fellows predominates over our tendency always to assert our own
interests. This means both an environment in which parents can be

sensitive and loving to their children, as discussed above, and one in which competition between adults is not excessive.

But this immediately poses a problem: whom do we see as 'our fellows'? Humans tend to divide the world up into 'them' and 'us', but where the boundary comes depends on the context. Sometimes 'us' refers primarily to members of one's own family, sometimes to members of one's own football team: in a highly competitive business world it may refer to the members of one's own firm, but not those of others. But the danger of violence is most acute when we make a distinction between members of our own religious group, our own ethnic group, or our own nation, and those outside. Members of other groups are seen as in some way different. Happily today, for most people, the boundaries of the groups to which they see themselves as belonging are expanding. In Britain two centuries ago a pauper could obtain help only from his own parish; now we send aid to Ethiopia and Afghanistan. In France, Germany, and neighbouring countries, people are beginning to see themselves as Europeans as well as members of their own nation. In the face of global destruction by nuclear weapons and the threat of climate change, we must teach our children that mankind makes one community. And we must do this while retaining love of our own culture and traditions, and without denigrating cultures other than our own.

Obstacles to the promotion of global understanding abound, even to the most well-meaning enterprises. For example, during the Cold War efforts were made to reduce prejudice between East and West through arranging exchange visits, especially exchanges between individuals with common interests or between school children. Apart from the political difficulties involved, these efforts met with mixed success. In some cases, where there was an atmosphere of common interest and common purpose, greater understanding was achieved. But all too easily such visits confirmed stereotypes and exacerbated distaste for the other system – for life in a totalitarian regime amongst visitors to the Soviet Union, and distaste for materialism amongst many visitors to the West.

Probably more successful are organizations that provide young people with opportunities to travel for more protracted periods, so that they become enmeshed in the day-to-day life of another culture. Voluntary Service Overseas and the Peace Corps have done a great deal to widen the horizons of those who participated.

With an emphasis on common humanity, and an acknowledgement that we all share a few basic moral principles, even though

moral systems differ in many respects, education can help to reduce
and perhaps to eradicate religious, ethnic and national prejudices.
A practical requirement for this in Great Britain is the elimination of
faith-based schools: in our multi-cultural society such schools almost
inevitably exacerbate religious differences and the prejudices that go
with them. More emphasis on common humanity and basic moral
principles also requires that much thought be given to the details of
school curricula: although vast improvements in this respect have
been made in most industrialized countries, it is a matter that requires
constant vigilance.

Education can also help individuals to evaluate the news items
with which they are confronted, and to display a proper scepticism
to the propaganda to which they are subjected. It can help them to
see their way through the tortuous moral problems that are part of
everyday life. It can breed a state of mind that will make a peaceful
world possible. At the same time, it can lead individuals to distinguish
the proper limits of tolerance. A culture that legitimizes the assassination of those who do not share the majority's religious beliefs or
political ideology is surely to be condemned. And a government that
uses clandestine methods and even assassination to undermine the
governments of other countries seen as inimical to its own interests
is not to be tolerated.

Education should also be used to promote community organizations of many sorts. A society in which all individuals go their own
ways lacks a sense of community and individuals feel alienated.
Churches, local groups of all sorts, can correct this, giving people a
sense of common enterprises and fellow-feeling.

Education must also be extended to impart the characteristics of
good governance, and the nature of the national and international
institutions that try to provide it. The workings of NGOs, and even
more of the UN and its agencies, are remote to the man or woman
in the street – yet, in a democratic world, every individual should
have an opinion on how their business should be conducted.

CONCLUSION

The alleviation of poverty and the reduction of wealth differentials
must be pursued, not only for ethical reasons but also because they
are indirect causes of unrest and violence. Conflict is both
exacerbated by, and augments, differences in wealth. The costs of

war affect not only the countries involved, but may be global. Conflict anywhere has worldwide repercussions.

Education for peace must be promoted. This must involve education of adults as well as children, and inculcate understanding of other cultures and an appreciation that all people share a common humanity. It should involve methods for monitoring its success.

14 Organizations Involved in Prevention, Intervention and Conflict Resolution

In an ideal world, conflicts of interest would not occur, and if they did they would not escalate to violence. But we do not live in an ideal world, and conflicts do occur. Thus, the first priority must be to remove the causes of conflict. But when two states, or groups within a state, are in conflict, it may be difficult for them to find an acceptable solution. Emotions are involved, maximizing self-interest is likely to seem paramount, and the conflicting parties may be unable to cope with the problems of conflict resolution. Special problems arise in the increasingly frequent conflicts within states, where ideological issues are often seen to be central. Moderates tend to be seen as unpatriotic or self-centred and to be sidelined; and there is a grave danger that the situation will escalate towards violence. In such a situation, outside intervention can sometimes help.

Peace is in everybody's interests. This is not only for moral reasons, but also for more pragmatic ones arising from the interconnectedness of the world associated with globalization. Among other things, as we have stressed repeatedly, a conflict in one part of the world may disrupt life not only where it occurs, but also in countries that are far removed from it. Commercial enterprises and the industrial world are almost certain to be affected, and the financial markets thrown into chaos. After the conflict is over, international aid may be necessary to restore infrastructure, and reconstruction and humanitarian assistance may cost other countries very large sums. If there are losers, they may resort to terrorism which may spread to distant lands.

There are some very real dangers in conflict resolution. In discussing the role of intervention, it is easy to fall into an authoritarian, power-oriented mode, with intervention imposing solutions unacceptable to the local population. China claims to have prevented deadly conflict in Tibet, but this has involved suppressing the basic rights of the Tibetan people, and has led to long-term resentment and intermittent protests against the authoritarian regime. The Serbian authorities adopted a similar approach in

Kosovo, but it involved denying the basic rights of the 90 per cent of the population of Albanian origin. Imposed solutions seldom work well in the longer term. It is essential simultaneously to work towards the building of conditions for an acceptable form of democratic governance, security, justice and freedom that will make further conflict and violence less likely.

A more recent, and more ominous, example is the unilateralist policy of the G.W. Bush administration, a policy that has been referred to as twenty-first-century colonialism. By exploiting the most recent advances in science and technology, the United States has built up an enormous military strength, exceeding by many times the combined military strength of all other nations. And it attempts to use this superiority to impose its political will on other nations. It usurps to itself the role of the world's policeman, a role which rightly belongs to the United Nations.

Another danger arises from the question of who should intervene. We shall return to this later, but the general principle needs to be stated here. It is highly desirable that any intervention should be by, or at least authorized by, the United Nations. Otherwise, as noted in the preceding paragraph, the door is left open to a state to take on the role in its own interests. But this raises further problems. As we saw in Chapter 6, the UN Charter was drawn up in the post-Second World War world to deal with conflicts between nation-states. Sovereignty involves a recognition that the state is a member of the community of nations, and is a symbol of its dignity and unique identity. For this reason also, intervention is not to be taken lightly. Its Charter prevents the UN from intervening in 'matters which are essentially within the domestic jurisdiction of any state', although there is a possible exception to this in Articles 39–42 that require the UN to take action if there exists any threat to peace or breach of the peace. In recent decades, there has been a growing realization that, in the modern world, intervention in intra-state conflicts may be necessary both for the sake of those involved and also of the wider community. States are to be held accountable both for conflicts with other states and for conflicts within their borders if violence is likely to ensue or has already done so.

Unfortunately, as we shall see shortly, it may be difficult for the UN to muster adequate resources at short notice, and it is often a powerful neighbour who has most interest in solving the conflict. In addition, the UN operates under considerable, but remediable, handicaps. We return to these shortly.

Both in preventing war and in ameliorating its effects the UN may be greatly assisted by non-governmental organizations (NGOs) that operate across national borders. In addition, and especially in democratic countries, religious and grassroots organizations have a role in mobilizing public opinion against war itself, against the arms trade, against the manufacture and use of particular weapons, and in ameliorating the effects of violent conflict. This chapter is concerned with the nature of these types of organization.

THE UNITED NATIONS

Ultimately, peace in the world requires an organization for settling conflicts, if possible without the use of force. After the First World War, the League of Nations was set up in an attempt to eliminate future wars. It failed in part because some nations, including the USA, saw it as unduly restricting their own freedom of action, and refused to join, and others who did join failed to honour their commitment to refrain from military action. Furthermore, the collectivity of the League failed to take action when Japan invaded China and when Italy invaded Abyssinia (Ethiopia). Now we have the United Nations, and it is essential that it should have all the support that it needs.

The UN aims to provide a forum where countries can air their grievances and ask for assistance, and can learn where that assistance is to be obtained. It has already promoted greater security in the world, protected fundamental human rights, and fostered economic development, and it has played an important role in many situations of conflict. Most conspicuously, it authorized intervention that, for instance, prevented Iraq from taking over Kuwait, and helped to stop the killing in Bosnia. The UN Preventive Deployment Force was successful in Macedonia. Recently UK forces acting on behalf of the UN appear to have achieved a solution to the long-standing conflict in Sierra Leone. The UN's Department of Political Affairs (together with the Department of Peacekeeping Operations) is taking the lead in providing early warning of potential conflict and in the prevention of escalation. This involves preventive diplomacy, preventive deployment and humanitarian action, to which may be added preventive disarmament, development and peace-building.

Use of the collective strength of the UN is the most effective means we have for preventing conflicts of interest escalating into violence. It can authorize or organize intervention in conflict situations. But most of its work has been accomplished in part through diplomacy in the Security Council and the General Assembly, and in part through the agencies that it has generated. For instance, the UN High Commissioner for Refugees attempts to identify potential sources of conflict before violence breaks out, and is cooperating with the Organization for Security and Cooperation in Europe and the International Organization for Migration to discover the best means to prevent the forced movement of populations. To cite another example, among the aims of the Children's Fund have been the rehabilitation of child soldiers, the protection of women and children, and the establishment of humanitarian zones in areas of conflict. In addition, the UN has been instrumental in setting up international criminal tribunals for crimes committed in the former Yugoslavia and Rwanda. The International Criminal Court is now operating although the USA has failed to ratify its statute. The United Nations Educational, Scientific and Cultural Organization (UNESCO) seeks to promote cross-cultural understanding, and the World Health Organization (WHO) to cope with problems of disease and nutrition. There is a welcome trend for such organizations to work together and to expand their perceived spheres of responsibility, so that many are concerned with the prevention of war or the amelioration of its consequences.

During the Cold War the effectiveness of the United Nations was greatly diminished by disagreements between the two superpowers, but that seemed to have become somewhat less of a problem until the debate over the Resolutions concerning Iraq in 2002/03. There is now fairly general agreement about how nations should conduct themselves. The UN has had many successes, but also many failures, and the present state of the world shows that its aims are far from being achieved. The principal obstacle has been the desire of national governments to preserve their autonomy and to seek after their own goals. They resent intrusions into their national sovereignty. One consequence of this is the danger, now becoming much more than a cloud on the horizon, that rivalry between two superpowers will be succeeded by the hegemony and unilateralism of one.

The problems of the UN arise in part from its internal structure, and in part from the inadequacy of the support given by the member states.

With respect to the structure, the greatest problem has been the constitution of the Security Council. This was devised for the immediate post-Second World War situation, and the world has changed in the intervening decades. The UN itself has grown from 51 member states to 192. As at present constituted, the Security Council is clearly unrepresentative, as countries such as India and Japan, which play an important role in world affairs, are excluded from permanent membership. Moreover, the decision to give the five permanent members (who happen to be the five overt nuclear weapon states) the power of veto proved disastrous in the Cold War era: each of the opposing powers could block the suggestions of the other. Even since the Cold War, full effectiveness has been prevented because one or another of the veto-wielding members has striven to protect its interests, or those of its allies or ideological colleagues. The urgent needs are to abolish or amend the right to veto repeatedly majority decisions, and to make the Security Council more representative.

Changing the composition of the Security Council, however, involves overcoming many obstacles. So long as the five permanent members have the power of veto, they can veto any change that would abolish that right. They can also veto a move towards making the Council more representative of the countries of the world. At the very least, there must be agreement between the five permanent members to limit the use of the veto.

While there is widespread agreement that the Security Council should be expanded, how representativeness could be achieved itself poses major problems. An increase in the number of permanent members might merely continue the present anomalies, so there is much to be said for an increase in the number of rotating members' seats. But if countries had voting powers in proportion to their populations, the more powerful states would still effectively have the power. On the other hand, if votes were distributed equally between countries, issues might be dominated by those whose collective populations were small. Several formulae have been suggested, including breaking the world into blocs, perhaps on a regional basis, with each represented on the Council. Or the use of an index based on a number of factors, such as population, gross national product, and the level of contribution to international efforts.

In an ideal world the members would seek for the good of all peoples rather than those of their own countries: indeed, in the long run, it may well turn out that it would be in their interests to do so. Regrettably, however, it seems that hope for a more genuinely altruistic climate in the UN must be a matter for the long-term future. The same problem, the priority given to narrow national interests, is partly responsible for the inadequacy of the support given by the member states.

To be maximally effective in preventing war, the UN must attempt mediation or act in some other way very early on in the genesis of conflict. This means that it must have both good intelligence, and the ready means to take effective action. In practice, the facilities available are such that attention is focused only when matters are somewhat urgent. And having identified a potential danger to peace, the UN must have the resources to act. The UN's failure in Rwanda was largely due to the unwillingness of those nations who might have contributed to an adequately trained force to be involved. Similarly, the protection of a number of cities in the former Yugoslavia collapsed in part because resources adequate for the task were not available. It is always likely to be difficult for the UN to recruit adequate support at short notice. The recruitment of a UN force requires cumbersome procedures, and any that is assembled may suffer from a lack of joint training and compatible weapon systems. Therefore, the UN should have a rapid reaction force for such occasions: delay may be fatal and will inevitably make the task more difficult. It will always be preferable to solve disputes without violence, but a display of force, and even the use of military power, is likely to continue to be sometimes necessary for the foreseeable future.

For such purposes the UN needs more financial resources. Although the UN has come under criticism for the proportion of its budget spent on bureaucracy, that situation has now been addressed and the fact remains that, in relation to the enormity of the problems with which it has to grapple, the UN is chronically underfunded, particularly so if it should acquire a standing military force. At times it has been severely handicapped by the refusal of member nations, including the USA, to pay their dues. But even when all dues at current rates are paid, the sums available are not fully adequate and the level of dues should be higher. According to the report of the Carnegie Commission on Preventing Deadly Conflict, US citizens spent over four times as much on the cinema as the UN's budget for core functions, and considerably more on spectator sports than the UN and its specialized agencies spend on economic and social development. The UN and its specialized agencies employ fewer people than the Disney organization employs in Disney World, Disneyland, and Euro Disney, and only one-third of the number of McDonald's employees.

One possible solution to the UN's financial problems would be the institution of a 'Tobin Tax'. The suggestion is that a levy, amounting to a fraction of 1 per cent, should be levied on all international financial transactions. This could produce more than enough to meet the UN's needs. While this possibility is much discussed, there are difficulties in getting international agreement, and the practical difficulties in its implementation would be far from trivial.

But these are not the only problems that dog the UN. There has been a growing tendency for powerful countries to act without UN approval, when that should have been a prerequisite. Britain was culpable in this way when Margaret Thatcher launched the Falklands war. The USA and UK, convinced of their own rectitude, proceeded in this way in Iraq in 2003 and, as noted later, the legitimacy of the bombing of Kosovo is still a matter for dispute (p. 201). Any such action undermines the authority of the United Nations. Of course, it is far from easy for a country to subordinate its own interests to those of the rest of the world, but the progressively more unilateralist policies of the USA have been especially conspicuous. Repeatedly it has pursued its own interests without regard for the world as a whole. For example, it has failed to cooperate over the Kyoto agreement to alleviate the effects of global warming; it refused to ratify the Comprehensive Test Ban Treaty; it has refused to endorse the Protocol to the Biological Weapons Convention; it is pushing ahead with a ballistic missile defence system against the wishes of nearly all other countries (see pp. 152–4); it refused to sign the landmines treaty and has posed difficulties for any agreement on the control of small arms. It has refused to subscribe to the International Criminal Court unless its own nationals are exempt. The failure of the League of Nations was due in part to lack of support from the USA, and there is a very real danger that its present stance will again contribute to plunging the world into conflict.

Even some of the UN associated agencies have been too prone to act without adequate local consultation. The World Bank, though it has contributed substantially to building up the economic base in war-torn countries and to expansion of the global economy, has often failed to take into account the full range of local opinion. Thus, in concentrating on providing infrastructure, such as dams, in a manner that may have the approval of local politicians, it has tended to neglect the interests of the local people. The World Bank has also been prone to make loans that the country concerned was unable to repay, with the result that many Third World countries have been denied progress by the need to use their resources to repay their debts.

As mentioned earlier, another very important issue concerns the degree of responsibility that the UN should have for interfering in the affairs of individual states. When it was set up, its main goal was the prevention of war between states, and it was deemed important to protect smaller states from unwarranted interference by a more powerful entity. In recent years, the main problem has become wars within states. In addition to the humanitarian problems that such conflicts bring, they may have widespread repercussions in neighbouring states, and even throughout the world. Yet, as we have seen, the United Nations Charter can inhibit it from intervening in affairs that are within the jurisdiction of its member states (though see pp. 63, 179). A rewriting of its Charter could clear this up – though this would have to include safeguards to ensure that interference in the internal affairs of states is not a form of imperialism.

ARTICLE 52 OF THE UN CHARTER

1. Nothing in the present Charter precludes the existence of regional arrangements or agencies for dealing with such matters relating to the maintenance of international peace and security as are appropriate for regional action provided that such arrangements or agencies and their activities are consistent with the Purposes and Principles of the United Nations.
2. The Members of the United Nations entering into such arrangements or constituting such agencies shall make every effort to achieve pacific settlement of local disputes through such regional arrangements or by such regional agencies before referring them to the Security Council.
3. The Security Council shall encourage the development of pacific settlement of local disputes through such regional arrangements or by such regional agencies either on the initiative of the states concerned or by reference from the Security Council.

Article 52 of the UN Charter can be interpreted as giving regional organizations the flexibility to act to curtail violence amongst its members. Such action should have the approval of the Security Council, though on occasion this has been sought after the event. Their right to intervene in states not within their own membership is more dubious – as occurred with the NATO intervention in Kosovo (p. 201).

After a special meeting of the Security Council in 1992, involving heads of state, the Secretary-General produced an 'Agenda for Peace' with a number of recommendations for broadening the role of the

UN, emphasizing preventive diplomacy, preventive deployment of UN forces before fighting starts, and post-conflict peace-building. Most importantly, perhaps, he emphasized the importance of changing the concept of sovereignty, arguing that it is necessary to find a balance between the needs for good governance and the requirements of an ever more interdependent world. Such a balance will require states to restrain self-interest, and to work together for the common good.

REGIONAL AND INTER-GOVERNMENTAL ORGANIZATIONS

In part from self-interest, and in part to remedy the deficiencies of the UN, a number of regional organizations have been set up (Table 10). Of these, perhaps the best known are the North Atlantic Treaty Organization (NATO) and the European Union. Such organizations

Table 10   Regional, sub-regional and inter-regional organizations and arrangements cooperating with the UN in peacekeeping and peace-related activities

	Region
African Union	Africa
Central African Customs & Economic Union	
Economic Community of West African States	
Inter-governmental Authority on Development	
South African Development Commission	
Association of South-East Asian Nations	Asia-Pacific
Black Sea Economic Cooperation	Europe
Commonwealth of Independent States	
European Union	
Organization for Security and Cooperation in Europe	
Western European Union	
North Atlantic Treaty Organization	(Euro-Atlantic)
Organization of American States	Americas
Caribbean Community	
Asian-African Legal Consultative Commission	Inter-regional
Commonwealth Secretariat	
League of Arab States	
Organization of the Islamic Conference	

Source: *Cooperation Between the United Nations and Regional Organizations/Arrangements in a Peacekeeping Environment: Suggested Principles and Mechanisms* (Lessons Learned Unit, UN Department of Peacekeeping Operations, March 1999).

have had a considerable number of successes in preventing or terminating conflicts – though it remains important that they should not act without UN authority.

The Organization for Security and Cooperation in Europe (OSCE) is a large non-military intergovernmental organization comprising 55 states plus the USA. It has sent missions to help manage conflict in a number of areas and has helped to rebuild society after the conflicts in the former Yugoslavia. It has a special role in providing early warning of potential conflicts and terrorism.

Not surprisingly, a major problem for regional organizations, as for the UN itself, is that of finance. The UN spends about $2.8 billion on peacekeeping each year. The UK has done better than many other national governments, allocating £120 million for conflict prevention and management, and £440 million for peacekeeping, for the year 2002–03. This, however, is but a tiny proportion of the budget for the Ministry of Defence. The USA has a new office for Conflict Management and Mitigation: while its defence budget is much larger than that of the UK, that for conflict prevention is even less.

THE ROLES OF NON-GOVERNMENTAL ORGANIZATIONS

Many UN agencies and non-governmental organizations operate internationally. They contribute information and warnings of crisis situations, and humanitarian aid during violent conflicts and in the aftermath of war. The term 'non-governmental organization' covers a wide range of bodies which number in the tens of thousands. Some are virtually global organizations, such as OXFAM, while others operate only within their countries of origin. Perhaps the oldest and most effective NGO is the International Red Cross, but since the Second World War the Red Cross (and Red Crescent) has been joined by many others. These include CARE International, *Médicins sans Frontières* and many religious organizations. NGOs may operate at near-governmental level, or at the grassroots.

Some NGOs, such as the International Crisis Group, have the specific aim of giving early warning of conflict, others of conflict resolution. Perhaps the most prominent example of the latter is the Carter Center, which attempts to bring conflicting parties together at the head-of-state level. It tries to include business and religious organizations in the negotiations. The Carter Center played a crucial part in averting war in Haiti and between North and South Korea, and has been involved in conflict prevention in several other areas. It also has an ongoing role in monitoring the situations in other countries. Another example is the Project on Ethnic Relations, which sees its role as the reduction in ethnic tensions in Eastern Europe and the former Soviet Union.

NGOs are often in a position to provide information about the internal conditions in a country that is not available through governmental channels – for instance in Cambodia in the 1980s. Sometimes they can act as honest brokers: a Norwegian group facilitated the Oslo agreement which offered hope for peace in the Middle East. It operated outside the focus of the media, organizing a series of confidence-building measures and 'academic contacts' that led to a joint declaration of principles.

NGOs are often in a position to spread ideas and to distribute technical assistance: many of them have extended their aims to include functions other than those for which they were originally founded. They often have special advantages in local knowledge and, where they are international, the absence of political allegiance can give them access that would be denied to political organizations. But while they must remain independent, their value can be even greater if integration between their efforts and those of governments can be achieved. Considerable progress in cooperation between government, NGOs and the general population has been made in Norway.

There are two important effects of both international NGOs and grassroot organizations (see below) which, because they are intangible, are often forgotten. Where their operations and impact are international they contribute to an appreciation of humanity as a unity that transcends national boundaries. For that reason alone, their very existence is important. Second, many of them make a contribution to the abolition of war that is indirect and thus seldom noticed in this context. For instance, Greenpeace and other similar organizations are primarily concerned with environmental conservation, but they may thereby be instrumental in removing causes of conflict that could lead to violence.

In Chapter 10 we discussed the special duties of scientists in the nuclear age, when advances in science may result in catastrophe for the human society. One group, an international NGO, which took up this challenge, is the Pugwash Conferences on Science and World Affairs.

Immediately after Hiroshima and Nagasaki a number of scientists, mainly those who worked on the Manhattan Project, set up national organizations (Federation of American Scientists in the USA, Atomic

Scientists' Association in the UK) with the aim of influencing the policies of their governments on the military and peaceful applications of nuclear energy. Their main objective was to prevent a nuclear war, but such efforts were limited during the early post-war years, when it was practically impossible to talk to Soviet scientists. The situation changed after Stalin's death.

RUSSELL–EINSTEIN MANIFESTO (1955)

We are speaking on this occasion, not as members of this or that nation, continent or creed, but as human beings, members of the species Man, whose continued existence is in doubt.

We appeal, as human beings, to human beings: Remember your humanity, and forget the rest. If you can do so the way lies open to a new Paradise; if you cannot, there lies before you the risk of universal death.

The initiative for international action was taken by the British philosopher Bertrand Russell and the physicist Albert Einstein. Together with nine other scientists, mostly Nobel Laureates, they issued a Manifesto calling on scientists from both sides of the Iron Curtain, to assemble in conference to seek to avert the dangers that had arisen from the development of the H-bomb.

As a consequence of the Manifesto, a group of scientists from ten countries met in 1957 in the Canadian village of Pugwash (the birthplace of Cyrus Eaton, who financed the meeting). This was a historic meeting, the first time that eminent scientists, influential with their governments, met to discuss the most sensitive security issues of the day.

This was the start of the Pugwash Movement, an organization that brings together, from around the world, scientists and scholars concerned with reducing the danger of armed conflict and seeking cooperative solutions to global problems. Meeting in private, as individuals, not as representatives of governments or institutions, Pugwash participants seek ways to prevent the harmful application

---

PUGWASH CONFERENCES ON SCIENCE AND WORLD AFFAIRS

The Pugwash Movement is an expression of the awareness of the social and moral duty of scientists to help to prevent and overcome the actual and potential harmful effects of scientific and technological innovations, and to promote the use of science and technology for the purpose of peace.

---

of science and technology, and, in particular, produce original ideas for reducing the nuclear peril and leading to the elimination of nuclear weapons, and, ultimately, of war itself.

During the Cold War years, the main effort of Pugwash was directed to the prevention of a nuclear war. These efforts were recognized in the award of the Nobel Peace Prize (shared with Joseph Rotblat) for 1995. Over the years it has also worked on the control of other weapons of mass destruction and on the elimination of war itself.

RELIGIOUS GROUPS AND RECONCILIATION COMMISSIONS

Although religious differences are often seen as a cause of war, and the brotherhood inherent in sharing a religious faith is no bar to war between two countries, religious groups sometimes help to secure or maintain peace, both within and between states. For instance, religious groups played a leading role in the reconciliation between the Czechs and the Germans in the years after the Second World War. This was a particularly noteworthy achievement because the atrocities committed by the Germans in the occupation of Czechoslovakia, and the bitter reprisals enacted by the Czechs, had left an exceptionally harsh residue of ill-will. In East Germany the Protestant churches fostered the turnaround to a democratic regime in 1989–90.

The Community of Sant'Egidio, a private Catholic organization, has been effective in a number of contexts, including Mozambique, Kosovo and Burundi. In Mozambique the Community established a series of relationships over many years which led to its assuming a mediating role. In due course, the UN became involved, as the peace agreement included a UN peacekeeping force. As further examples, the World Council of Churches helped to bring peace to Sudan in 1972, and the All Africa Conference of Churches has been active in the Democratic Republic of the Congo and elsewhere. It is clear, however, that the full effectiveness of religious bodies in working for a peaceful world depends on their ability to put doctrinal differences aside.

Success in Czechoslovakia depended on a joint rewriting of history that merged the viewpoints of both sides. A related principle has operated in the Truth and Reconciliation Commissions that have been successful in healing wounds after bitter internal conflicts. While these do not bring justice for those who have suffered, they do open the way for acceptance of the peace that has been achieved.

For instance, in Chile outside forces made a number of attempts to destabilize the government of President Allende, which led eventually to his assassination. This was followed by 16 years of government by General Pinochet accompanied by widespread abuses of human rights. When Pinochet was finally evicted by popular vote, a commission was set up with the initial goal of establishing the truth about the history of those 16 years. This paved the way for a gradual healing of the breach between those who had, and those who had not, supported the Pinochet regime.

The success of a process of Truth and Reconciliation in South Africa after the ending of Apartheid is well known. After years of Apartheid, involving segregation and oppression of the non-white populations and intermittent reactive violence by non-whites, principally against the white police, a Truth and Reconciliation Commission was set up. Immunity from prosecution was promised to those who gave truthful evidence about past actions. While the Commission probably only scratched the surface of the total violations committed, an important principle was established.

GRASSROOTS ORGANIZATIONS

It is too easy to give the impression that the abolition of war must depend on the work of international bodies, national groups, or large non-governmental organizations. It must never be forgotten that leaders cannot go to war without followers. The citizens of a country can do much to prevent violence by bringing pressure on governments to produce civil conditions that are not conducive to conflict or unrest; by campaigning against involvement in foreign wars; and by bringing pressure on their government to ameliorate conditions in other countries that might be conducive to violence. These goals, and especially the last, may require restraint on self-interest, at least in the short term, but such restraint is essential if wars are to be abolished.

And it must not be thought that the ordinary citizen is powerless to influence government. Gandhi's advocacy of non-violent protest against British rule, and Martin Luther King's against racism in the USA, are classic examples of successful protest. In Britain, the suffragettes were successful in bringing pressure for votes for women – though there still is a long way to go before equality between the sexes is achieved in all aspects of community life. In East Germany, the evident desire of many citizens to escape to the West was associated with popular demonstrations against the authoritarian communist regime. And in Poland, workers' committees, leading to the formation of the Solidarity movement, played a central role in the transition to democracy. Although Solidarity was forced underground for a while, the government eventually had to enter into discussions with it. Women's groups have played an important role in establishing peace in a number of instances – for example in Argentina and, to some degree, in Somalia.

Indeed, in some cases it may be fruitful for ordinary citizens to lead the way towards peaceful conflict resolution. As mentioned already, the dispute between Greeks and Turks on Cyprus has dragged on for many decades, and has been fostered by misunderstandings and propaganda. Although it now seems that political negotiations have good prospects for making progress, the process might have been accelerated by an attempt at gradual integration. At the Hague Peace Conference in 2000, three Turkish and three Greek citizens produced a plan to that end. They suggested a number of small steps, including a bi-communal zone where the two communities could buy and sell and thereby meet; a bi-communal school or youth club; a hospital offering specialized services to both communities; and optional courses in the other language in schools. This could lead to a form of Federation, a larger joint zone, bilingualism, and so on. Such suggestions may seem impractical and idealistic, but deserve serious consideration.

CONCLUSION

Preventing war requires a supranational forum where grievances can be aired and disputes settled, and which can authorize intervention where necessary. The United Nations was set up to that end. The UN (and its agencies) has been successful in many contexts, but its activities have been handicapped by its internal structure, including the right of some countries to veto majority decisions, lack of adequate resources for forceful intervention where necessary, and an inadequate budget. Its work may be supplemented by regional organizations.

In preventing and ameliorating conflict, non-governmental agencies and religious organizations have been playing an increasingly important role. Grassroots organizations can be very important in influencing governmental policies.

15 Intervention and Conflict Resolution

When a conflict is escalating, intervention may be the best course. Because it involves infringement of sovereignty, and involves many hazards, it must be undertaken only after very careful consideration. It should in any case be initiated by, or have the approval of, the United Nations, have clear objectives, and have a reasonable chance of success. It should not involve the use of force unless that is felt to be the only feasible option, when major harm to civilians is occurring or is likely to occur, and internal control is either incapable of or is not being used to terminate the violence.

THE IMPORTANCE OF EARLY WARNING AND EARLY ACTION

If the UN or members of the international community acting under its auspices are to intervene, the importance of the international community becoming aware of danger spots well in advance of their degenerating into violence cannot be overestimated. The massacres in Cambodia caught the world unawares: it is likely that prior warning of the impending tragedy could have saved many lives. It is necessary for the UN to monitor carefully totalitarian regimes that lack popular support, especially those in which the rulers belong to a different ethnic group from the majority of the population. Marked economic disparities and long-term grievances may also be signs of internal conflict within states, or of potential interference by other states.

Most countries have their own intelligence agencies. Monitoring of communications, surveillance from satellites, and the gathering of information by individuals on the ground all play their part. In the USA nearly a dozen different agencies are involved, and cooperation between them is not always all that it should be. In the UK the same has been true of its intelligence agencies.

UN agencies, like the Office of the UN High Commissioner for Refugees, have been active in warning of such potential dangers. Other UN or international organizations, as well as non-governmental organizations, other relief agencies, and individuals may also be important here. There is, however, still a need for a more effective collection and assessment of data at UN Headquarters.

Whatever its source, the information should be shared freely in the community of nations. Governments collect information to further their own interests. While one expects that the foreign embassies in unstable countries will be active in warning their governments about potential problems, there is an urgent need for such information to be passed beyond individual governments to central agencies that have some responsibility for action. To be fully effective, it should include information on the precise nature of the danger, indication of whether or not intervention is likely to be helpful, and the form it should take.

Information about impending trouble is of no use if outsiders are not prepared to take action. Hitler made his intentions clear in *Mein Kampf* and in his speeches, and his intentions were reported to their home governments by ambassadors in Berlin, but no action was taken – perhaps because Hitler had some influential supporters outside Germany. The dangers in the Rwandan situation were known well beforehand, but no one was prepared to act. In 1987 the disintegration of Yugoslavia was foreseen by some politicians, but no action was taken. Unfortunately, while the willingness of states to commit forces for intervention should be governed by humanitarian considerations, in practice it is usually governed by self-interest. It is no coincidence that it was the USA that intervened in Haiti, or Russia in Tajikistan. There have been, of course, many honourable exceptions. Canada, Norway, and many other countries have contributed to the solution of conflicts in parts of the world where their interests were minimal. The successful UN/UK intervention in Sierra Leone is another example: a number of different UK government departments collaborated in establishing security. It is to be hoped that one consequence of increasing globalization will be that all states will look further into the future and recognize that war anywhere may have global repercussions.

The importance of immediate action is amply demonstrated by the civil war in Rwanda, and this deserves a digression. Formerly a Belgian colony, its borders were drawn to include two ethnically distinct groups, the Hutu and the Tutsi, with a long history of mutual animosity. As one of the poorest and most over-populated countries in Africa, it had been economically dependent on producing coffee and the insect deterrent pyrethrum. The pyrethrum market disappeared when pesticides came into general use, and the coffee market crashed in 1987. In 1990 the Rwandan Patriotic National Front, led by Tutsis and supported by Uganda, invaded the country. In 1993 it was known that the Hutu extremist leaders had drawn up a list of Tutsi individuals who were to be killed, and there were other warnings that genocide was imminent. But the international community failed to act.

In 1994 a plane crash killed the presidents of both Rwanda and Burundi, and this triggered the genocide. At the time, the UN Assistance Mission for Rwanda, with 2,500 troops, was present in the country on a peacekeeping mission. But when the massacres started, the UN shirked its responsibility and withdrew practically the whole force. Up to 800,000 Rwandans were slaughtered, mostly from the Tutsi minority but also from the Hutu opposition. Many Tutsis fled to neighbouring countries. Four months later the UN decided to send a force of 5,000 troops to protect civilians and make humanitarian assistance possible, but member states failed to implement this by sending adequate troops. As a result, a force of Tutsi-led exiles invaded Rwanda from Uganda. This ended the genocide, but many Hutus fled across the borders as refugees, retaining their arms. They disrupted the refugee camps and commenced a guerrilla campaign against the new Rwandan government. The violence spread across Zaire, and its aftermath is still to be felt in the countries in the region.

Careful post hoc analysis of the situation, sponsored in part by the Carnegie Commission and including the Commander of the UN Mission, concluded that intervention by 5,000 well-trained troops in early April 1994 could have largely prevented the slaughter. Unfortunately, the Organization for African Unity was unable to provide such a force, NATO was unwilling, Britain and France were participating in the UN Force in Bosnia, and the USA was feeling that it had had its fingers burned in Somalia.

The lesson here is clear. Early warning, coupled with timely intervention as appropriate, is essential.

IS INTERVENTION NECESSARILY DESIRABLE?

We do not wish to imply that intervention is always the right course: the maintenance of peace and good governance within any society is primarily its own business, and there are occasions when intervention can make things worse. Intervention in Iraq in the 2003 Gulf War resulted in large numbers of civilian casualties as well as bringing down a tyrannical regime. Where the problem involves former colonies, there is a special danger if the initiative for intervention is taken by the former colonial power, as its action may be seen as that of a former master trying to reassert his will.

But in many cases intervention is the proper course, though intervention does not necessarily mean the use of force. As mentioned already, every state has a moral duty to prevent human suffering if it is in its power to do so, no matter where the violence threatens. And, with increasing globalization, an effort to prevent an outbreak of violence is pragmatically the right course. This is not only a matter of the inevitable disruption of trade and of the financial markets that violence anywhere is liable to bring, for the cost of prevention is likely to be less than the costs of relief and rebuilding after the conflict is over.

When war between states threatens, there is usually a flurry of diplomatic activity. A common first step involves the breaking off of diplomatic relations between the countries concerned. This is usually intended as a warning of sterner measures to follow, but may increase the probability of violence because channels of direct communication are cut just when they are most needed. Diplomacy is more likely to be effective in preventing violence if discourse continues, and can be greatly helped by outsiders provided they are seen not to have an axe to grind. In inter-state conflicts, this should be the special role of the United Nations or, given UN authorization, groups of neighbouring states. In intra-state disputes it may be valuable where possible also to include in the conciliatory process respected individuals who are seen to be independent of the conflicting issues, such as former Presidents Jimmy Carter and Nelson Mandela, and Senator George Mitchell.

CONDITIONS FOR INTERVENTION

Fruitful intervention, whether by preventive diplomacy or by use of force, is most likely to be successful if certain conditions are fulfilled.

In the first place, we have seen that the UN Charter forbids it to interfere in the affairs of a sovereign state. This is beside the point if the dispute is between sovereign states, or if both sides in the conflict accept intervention.

Second, attempts to intervene in violent conflict must be tempered by the need to maintain justice and human rights. There have been some regrettable, though heterogeneous, counter-examples. For instance, interventions by the USA or the USSR in disputes within

African and South American states proved disastrous in the long run, and in some cases led to persisting civil war. Though arguably not involving intervention in another state, Slobodan Milosevic attempted to suppress conflict in Kosovo by force, but his efforts were without success and led to immense suffering, and in turn to NATO intervention. China's longer-running suppression of freedoms in Tibet has merely forced the conflict underground.

Third, there is a danger that any intervention will be seen as partisan or imperialist interference. Intervention must take into account the legitimate interests of both sides, even though mere compromise may not be the best solution. It is also essential that any intervention, unless fully accepted by both sides, should be seen to be authorized by a respected and non-partisan body – preferably the UN or, in exceptional cases, a regional organization of states.

Fourth, intervention is most likely to be successful if it is not coercive. Establishing effective communication between the two sides must be a first priority though, if the means used are diplomatic, a degree of confidentiality is also essential. A conflict between any two states is likely to involve many others, so the use of diplomacy may be a complicated task. Diplomatic intervention involves many dangers, and should be undertaken only after careful consideration of the consequences. For instance, if the dispute is intra-national, intervention on supposedly ideological grounds may be fatal, especially if it goes against popular opinion in the country concerned.

Fifth, in the case of military intervention especially, it is essential that the goals of those who are sent to intervene should be clear and appropriate. The UN troops sent to Bosnia-Herzegovina to protect civilians were handicapped because a sharp distinction between peacekeeping and war-fighting had not been drawn. But the main problem at that stage was not fighting between sides but violence against civilians. The UN was afraid that any use of force would involve, or be seen as, taking sides and would escalate both the violence and UN involvement. They were thus sometimes unable to protect safe havens or aid convoys, and could only watch from the sidelines.

Sixth, for conflict resolution and conciliation, the conditions must be right for discourse between the groups in conflict. Most important are efforts to reduce mutual suspicion, and to convince both parties that resolution is in their own best interests. Sometimes the media, whose influence is used too often to inflame passions, could help by presenting both sides of the case, pointing out the disastrous consequences of conflict, and emphasizing the common humanity of those involved. For example, in Cambodia broadcasts of the UN Transitional Authority provided an unbiased source of information that helped to undermine the Khmer Rouge.

Finally, it is essential that any intervention be overt, and does not involve clandestine operations, such as those undertaken by the CIA in South and Central America, for covert operations imply that the third party is motivated by self-interest. CIA involvement has in fact had unfortunate consequences and has occasionally led to the destruction of democracy, for instance in Chile. The Watergate scandal revealed that the CIA had been involved in a number of illegal acts of repression (see pp. 84–5).

WHO SHOULD INTERVENE AND HOW?

In the previous chapter we referred to the categories of bodies that may be involved in preventing conflict. In doing so we were certainly not attempting a comprehensive review, but rather pointing to the important roles that they can play.

In some cases at least, temporarily successful mediation has been achieved by prominent politicians – for instance President Carter in the dispute between Israel and Egypt following meetings at Camp David, and President Kosygin in that between India and Pakistan in 1966.

Special Representatives of the Secretary-General of the UN have played a successful role in some cases: for instance, in 1998 a special envoy of the Secretary-General of the UN prevented tensions between Iran and Afghanistan erupting into war. Often the success of such efforts may be unknown to the wider world just because the criterion of success is simply that nothing happens.

The United Nations itself has had some successes in this respect. In 1960 the UN intervened in the Congo; a peace initiative in Cambodia in the early 1990s was led by the UN; the UN intervened successfully in Mozambique; it authorized international efforts to defeat Iraq's attempt to annex Kuwait in 1991; and the UN sent a peacekeeping force to Bosnia (though see above); and a Protection Force to Macedonia in 2001. The UK/UN intervention has brought peace to Sierra Leone. (See Table 11 for a list of current UN peace-keeping operations.)

However, intervention by the UN may encounter some problems. As we have seen, since the United Nations is based on the concept of sovereign states, its Charter prevents interference in the affairs of sovereign states and thus in disputes within them. Furthermore, its approach to the resolution of conflict between sovereign states seems often to be inherently conflictual – in a dispute it becomes a question of weighing up the rights of this state versus those of another. In addition, the UN often takes time to act, partly because its component states lack the political will to contribute forces. Intervention may be a matter of urgency: regional groups may be able to act more quickly and with more adequate local knowledge. They may be less likely to bear the stigma of representing former colonialism.

For such reasons, regional groups sometimes have a number of advantages. *Provided they have UN approval*, regional organizations may sometimes be more appropriate, more willing, or more able to intervene than the UN, especially in cases of civil war. Because democracies have experience in handling conflicts within their own borders, and share common values, regional groups of democratic states are most likely to be effective in preventing conflict.

An interesting example is provided by the trained civilian monitors dispersed in Kosovo by the Organization for Security and Cooperation in Europe. Their mission was to report on outbreaks of ethnic violence or intimidation. The evidence indicates that the appearance of one of their orange landrovers was effective in curbing violence. But they were withdrawn when bombing started, and it was then that the killing intensified.

However, there are arguments for and against intervention by regional organizations. Some of the arguments against are historical. China has memories of its exploitation by Western powers in the nineteenth century. African states, having freed themselves from colonialism, are deeply suspicious of Western interference. Russia remembers Western support for the White Russians after the Revolution, and sees the 1941–45 war as a struggle against Nazi interventionists. And those in the non-Western world can legitimately ask, is intervention by a group of Western states, such as NATO, a pretext for imposing Western materialistic values on the rest of the world? However, such anti-interventionist attitudes are slowly changing, especially when it is a question of preventing genocide or major suffering in the population. And intervention by a local organization can be successful at least temporarily – as recently seen in the Ivory Coast.

Table 11   UN peacekeeping operations in 2003

	Date Begun	Military troops (31 March 2003)
United Nations Truce Supervision Organization (Middle East)	1948	113
United Nations Military Observer Group in India and Pakistan	1949	44
United Nations Peacekeeping Force in Cyprus	1964	1,373
United Nations Disengagement Observer Force (Golan Heights)	1974	1,042
United Nations Interim Force in Lebanon	1978	1,998
United Nations Iraq–Kuwait Observation Mission	1991	suspended (see notes, below)
United Nations Mission for the Referendum in Western Sahara	1991	27
United Nations Observer Mission in Georgia	1993	116
United Nations Interim Administration Mission in Kosovo	1999	see notes, below
United Nations Mission in Sierra Leone	1999	14,549
United Nations Organization Mission in the Democratic Republic of Congo	1999	3,805
United Nations Mission in Ethiopia and Eritrea	2000	3,863
United Nations Mission of Support in East Timor	2002	3,598

Source: United Nations Department of Peacekeeping Operations website. The UN Iraq–Kuwait Observation Mission was withdrawn from its area of operations, and its mandate suspended, in advance of the 2003 military campaign against Iraq. The UN Interim Administration in Kosovo has a wide (and unprecedented) remit to establish an interim civilian administration led by the United Nations, involving far more than military troops.

In addition, regional organizations may not have the resources necessary for effective intervention, and may have the same difficulties that have plagued the UN in obtaining the necessary agreement between the constituent states.

Whoever intervenes, its actions must be fully justified. Intervention by regional organizations or alliances of states, without prior approval by the UN, is very much open to question: every such intervention undermines the authority of the United Nations. Military intervention is justified only by the occurrence or imminence of large-scale loss of life or genocide.

However, there is always the question, at what point does the infringement of human rights, or the killing and displacement of civilians, justify the infringement of sovereignty by outside military intervention? The NATO air strikes on Kosovo provide an interesting example, because the legality of the air strikes by the USA and UK is still a matter of dispute. It was undertaken to prevent the Serbs forcing the Albanian section of the population to leave their homes, persecuting and killing them in the process. On the one hand, it is estimated that 1.5 million Albanians were forced to leave their homes, and 11,334 were reported missing believed killed. On the other, the bombing resulted in the deaths of 600 Yugoslav military and 500 civilian deaths, as well as immense damage to the country's infrastructure. Although it led to the withdrawal of the Serb forces, the bombing was undertaken without the agreement of the Security Council. Two days after the bombing started, a Security Council resolution calling for cessation of violence, sponsored by Russia, had been defeated by twelve votes to three – China, India and Namibia voting in favour. The NATO decision to use bombing was supported by 19 democratic nations. And it was successful. Whether the end result could have been achieved without so much loss of life and damage to the infrastructure is a matter for debate.

When they do intervene, it is important that such regional organizations, or the UN itself, should not lack the muscle, or the uniformity in policy, to intervene effectively. Even more importantly, they should not lack the will to do so. An opportunity to prevent or minimize the genocide in Rwanda was lost because of the lack of will to intervene. But, at the same time, only such force as is necessary should be used.

PEACEKEEPING AND PEACE-ENFORCEMENT

As noted above, intervention often involves the use of military force. A distinction is often made between peacekeeping and peace-enforcement. Peacekeeping implies that an agreement between the two sides has already been reached, but there is a need to ensure that the agreement is being and continues to be implemented. The preventive deployment of military forces must involve complete impartiality and implies that there will be no use of force except in the case of infringements. The UN successfully used preventive deployment between 1992 and 1999 to prevent hostility within the former Yugoslavia.

Peace-enforcement, by contrast, means intervening on one side to check activities by the other side contrary to an agreement that has been made. It implies the use of force. In practice, the distinction is far from clear, and both are referred to by the catch-all phrase 'peace support'. Sometimes peacekeepers are required to ensure the safe delivery of humanitarian aid or to protect a safe haven. They may then have to resort to force, or fail in their task, as happened when the safe haven of Srebrenica was shelled and finally overrun by Bosnian-Serb soldiers in spite of the presence of a UN force. In practice it is essential, before any peace support mission is launched, that clear and achievable goals be defined in advance, and that the resources be adequate to achieve the goals.

As we have seen, if military intervention is to be effective, it is best that it is set into operation quickly. That means that intervention is much more likely to be successful if the force is ready beforehand, and the forces properly trained and equipped to fight if necessary. If the intervention is to be in the hands of a coalition, it must be a stable one and time must not be lost in its formation. On the occasions when a UN or regional force has had to be assembled, it has led to considerable delay. Furthermore, lack of common training, and of standardized munitions, can handicap such a force. Funds for the establishment and maintenance of a continuously available peacekeeping force should be made available to the UN as a matter of urgency.

Peacekeeping and peace-enforcement inevitably involve many problems, and some attempts have been unsuccessful. When internal violence between rival clans threatened to lead to mass starvation in Somalia in 1972, the UN attempted to achieve a peace agreement. Unfortunately, UN member governments managed to assemble a peacekeeping force of only 500. However, the USA offered to send a force of over 30,000 men to ensure the delivery of humanitarian aid, which probably saved the lives of a quarter of a million people. But later a smaller multilateral UN force took over, and was given the additional task of peace enforcement. A number of UN personnel were killed or wounded, including a number of Americans, and the USA gave notice that it would withdraw all its troops. The failure of this enterprise seems to have been due to the intractability of local conflicts and the lack of a local government willing to work with the UN.

Another example of intervention with only partial success occurred in 1993 when the Organization of African Unity tried to intervene in the Congo. That some efforts have brought only temporary peace to the country in question provides no grounds for supposing that comparable efforts will not be successful in the future, though perhaps it implies that such efforts need to be sustained.

A little-known but thought-provoking example of intervention is the entry, in 1998, of South African troops, as part of a Southern African Development Community Task Force, into the neighbouring state of Lesotho in order to prevent a military coup. This succeeded in preventing an unconstitutional change of government, restoring law and order, and creating a stable environment in which the political parties could resume their dialogue. Nevertheless, the first 48 hours of the operation resulted in a considerable number of casualties on both sides, and was nearly disastrous. Subsequent analysis blamed this on lack of clarity concerning the authorization for the intrusion, leading to the attribution of self-interested motives to South Africa; and to the perception that the force was not truly multinational. The secrecy surrounding the intervention also militated against its success. It is also argued that such missions should be civilian-led and should employ the minimum of necessary force.

In the so-called 'war against terrorism' the USA minimized American casualties in Afghanistan by organizing Afghan warlords against the Taliban, but after the Taliban were defeated, made rather meagre efforts to stabilize the country. The USA and its allies, with a mandate from the UN, kept a stabilization force in Kabul – the International Security Assistance Force. The interim government seems to be functioning there, and schools and universities are being re-established. It remains to be seen how successful it will be in the long term. However, the situation outside the capital seems to be far from stable and the Force has little influence.

It is evident that successful intervention depends not only on its timeliness, but also on the ready availability of adequate forces, the willingness to commit them, precise specification of the goals of intervention, careful assessment of the local situation, and knowledge of the probable attitudes of local leaders to the operation.

ESTABLISHING PEACE

Too often, efforts for the resolution of conflicting issues come too late to prevent the outbreak of violent conflict. But, both in attempts to prevent violence and in efforts to maintain a stable situation when violence has ceased, an agreement between the parties concerned must be sought. A considerable body of research on conflict resolution, built on past experience, is ready to be used. Far from demonstrating a simple solution, it shows the necessity of fitting the approach to the particular circumstances: recognizing the precise difficulties goes some way towards solving the problem.

Reconciliation between the previously warring parties is, sooner or later, essential. The difficulties that have been experienced in peacekeeping and in peace-enforcement, especially in intra-state wars, indicate the need for an approach that does not rely on merely patching up the differences between the two sides. Sometimes, the intervention of outside bodies is essential. This seems to be the case in Northern Ireland, and the British government carries a heavy responsibility. But overcoming the deeply entrenched prejudices on both sides may seem an almost insuperable problem: power-sharing may seem the most hopeful alternative.

In every case, to restore a peaceful society it is essential to restore legitimate governance. Often, the conflict has involved warlords or religio-ethnic groups who have been operating outside the bounds of legitimacy, attempting to impose their rule on others by violence. In such cases, negotiations and compromises between the two sides are almost bound to fail. A solution based on the aspirations of the two opponents is unlikely to be seen as just or legitimate, either by those directly affected or by the outside world. Apart from anything else, compromise between two groups led by individuals, who perhaps should be regarded as international criminals, does not necessarily give them and their aims any sort of legitimacy. And territorial divisions or power-sharing rarely seem to succeed – as is too painfully apparent in Northern Ireland, Cyprus and Kashmir. Furthermore, the opposing parties may have based their power on fear and on inculcating a sense of insecurity. That is no base on which to build either trust or legitimacy.

None of this means that military intervention will not sometimes be necessary to restore order, but it must be used to build a new political approach involving civility, democracy and tolerance. The transfer of power to a new government can take time, and the intervening force may have to assist in reconstruction, perhaps acting temporarily as a police force. While negotiations between the leaders may be necessary to stop the violence, it is necessary to create a climate in which an alternative political approach can be fostered. This should embrace contributions from local advocates of less particularist policies, civilians who have stood outside the war, local elders, religious representatives, and/or others as appropriate to the circumstances. Local areas of peace often exist. In Northern Ireland, for instance, ecumenical schools have been established, and there are islands of peace where Protestants and Catholics live together in harmony. In the conflict between Inkatha and the African National Congress (ANC) there were instances of local leaders joining with residents in efforts to control the violence. If such groups have sufficient support, they can be used as nuclei for building legitimacy, or as a source of wisdom in any negotiations.

Sometimes military intervention may be necessary to protect 'safe havens' where new political approaches can be fostered – and even to facilitate their expansion. Soldiers may be necessary for a number of other purposes – restoring order, guarding refugees, or capturing war criminals – but a degree of consent from the local population must be obtained and their work must be seen to be impartial. Conditions must be created for the construction of the country's political system along democratic lines, and a rebuilding of its infrastructure and economy. This does not mean that free elections are necessarily an adequate goal. The aim must be to build a free society in which political growth can occur so that elections do not merely legitimize the warring parties.

Disarming the combatants, and destroying their weapons, will not only avert an immediate return to violence, but also prevent the use of those weapons elsewhere. This has been accomplished with at least partial success in a number of cases, including Mozambique and El Salvador. Specialist teams may be necessary to work with local NGOs in such tasks as mine-clearance, emergency relief measures, creating an impartial police force, overseeing elections, replacing damaged infrastructure and facilitating development. Internal security is necessary for development, and vice versa.

THE AFTERMATH OF WAR

War, or the threat of war, nearly always implies refugees, food shortages, damage to infrastructure, and other problems. Thus, humanitarian assistance must accompany military intervention. There are, however, many problems in delivering assistance in a war, or immediately post-war, situation. For example, authorization for the intervention by a multinational force in East Timor prevented much bloodshed, but bringing peace and stability posed very many further problems.

The security of citizens from the former combatants, from criminals, or from over-officious police, and from threats of famine or other disaster, must be a primary consideration as has been so painfully demonstrated in Iraq in 2003. No peace agreement can be secure for long if the citizens do not feel safe. In the very short term, this may require the use, or at any rate the display, of force: peacekeepers can not only keep the former combatants apart, but also prevent looting and take other measures to restore order. But that can be only a short-term solution. Minimum standards of security are a precondition for development, but measures must be taken to build a harmonious community.

Ideally, humanitarian agencies should be strictly neutral, and operate with the consent of both parties. But, especially where the removal or elimination of a population has been a war aim of one or both sides, the combatants may intervene, often covertly by disrupting or delaying convoys carrying humanitarian aid, or overtly, attacking convoys and appropriating the provisions. Personnel of aid agencies have often been in danger and have themselves suffered casualties.

If interference by one of the two rival groups, perhaps motivated by revenge, makes it necessary for the UN agency or agencies to work alongside peacekeeping forces, difficulties may arise from their differing goals and styles of operation, and the peacekeeping forces can easily be seen as no longer neutral. The task of peacekeepers in protecting human rights, supervising elections and protecting humanitarian efforts easily becomes confused with those of the agencies themselves, and perhaps also with the attempts of the UN Development Programme to co-ordinate the rebuilding of society. The necessity for the establishment of basic values may be neglected. And where different agencies are operating in the same area there may be great difficulties in co-ordinating their efforts, deciding where food is most needed and so on. The UN Office for the Coordination of Humanitarian Affairs was set up in an attempt to deal with such problems, but it operates under great difficulties and with inadequate resources.

By caring for refugees, outside agencies can reduce chaos and simplify the military situation, but even this task is open to abuse. For instance, Hutu genocide leaders sheltered in refugee camps in Zaire exploited the aid intended for refugees, and subsequently launched attacks from the safety of the camps.

In outlining some of the difficulties that may arise in peacekeeping, peace-enforcement, and the establishment of peaceful conditions on a long-term basis, we do not mean to imply that such attempts are not worthwhile. But they are more likely to be successful if lessons from the past are not disregarded.

THE PROMOTION OF DEMOCRACY

We have seen that wars between democratic states are at most rare, and that democratic governance can lessen tensions within states. At present over 120 countries out of 192 could be called democracies, though not all countries that call themselves democracies have truly democratic governments. Should Zimbabwe, Iran, or China be called democracies? Be that as it may, it would clearly be desirable if the number of democratic countries could be increased. However, opportunities to achieve this occur all too rarely, and when an opportunity does arise, the transition from non-democratic to democratic governance is likely to be a matter of great difficulty. The issues here apply especially in the aftermath of civil wars. The country may lack the necessary political and civic infrastructure, and educational, financial and technical resources.

A major obstacle lies in the need to create an adequate infrastructure. There may be a lack of trained administrators capable of taking on the construction and maintenance of a democratic regime. Corruption, which becomes traditional and almost invariably accompanies authoritarianism, may be extremely difficult to eradicate, and it becomes essential to nurture the personnel, attitudes and bureaucracy necessary for the transition. This may be a slow process, but democracy can rarely be imposed.

The measures required inevitably differ with the local circumstances. In general, a free press and an educated opposition must be encouraged when elections are held, for a fair result can be obtained only if the public understand the issues. A large number of abstentions can lead to an unrepresentative result, so access to voting stations must be made easy and voting secret. In Australia, voting is compulsory. Ethnic and religious tensions may present a substantial obstacle, for it is important that a reasonable distribution of power and moderation should be encouraged. Prejudices may bias voting, and what is fair for individuals may clash with what is fair for constituent ethnic or religious groups. A situation must be built in which there is not only equality of opportunity, but opportunity is seen to be equal. Economic and social development must be fostered as an essential element in the rebuilding of normal life. Development must be such as not to increase wealth differentials.

In many cases, the military pose a special problem in the transition to democracy. Demobilized soldiers, suffering from the trauma of war, may need special care. Formerly holding high status under an authoritarian ruler, they must come to terms with living under ultimately civilian control, while retaining their self-image of belonging to a valued group on which the security of the country may depend.

When two or more ethnic or religious groups are present and the political parties are aligned with them, individuals will tend to vote not according to the issues or the acceptability of candidates, but along religious or party lines. Therefore, the majority party will always win, and may pay little attention to the needs of others. Some form of institutionalized power-sharing is then essential. It has been argued that this requires that all the significant groups have a considerable degree of autonomy, that they all participate in government, and that there is a possibility of limited minority veto over issues of special importance to the minority group. These requirements are best met with some system of proportional representation within parliamentary government. An alternative to power-sharing involves both incentives for inter-group cooperation, and finding ways to ensure that individuals do not necessarily vote along group lines. This is often difficult to achieve, but people can be encouraged to think of themselves as more than one thing at once – Muslim and Indian, Black and American. But the word 'and' is important here: labels such as Black American could have the effect of encouraging sectarianism.

In any case, something must be done to remove the anger and hurt that caused the conflict in the first place. Where the conflict involved retribution for the pain inflicted on preceding generations, this is an extremely difficult task. But, as we have seen, the success of South Africa's transition to democracy after years of struggle has been due largely to its gradual nature, and to the openness and admission of guilt consequent upon the Truth and Reconciliation process (see p. 190).

SOME OUTSTANDING ISSUES

A few points deserve further emphasis. One concerns the willingness of states, either alone or in a wider alliance, organizations, or the UN itself, to become involved in conflict prevention or resolution, or in building peaceful democracies. There is likely always to be consider-able difficulty in obtaining international consensus on any particular intervention: the major powers have not only their own agendas, but also their own allegiances.

Too often the decision as to whether to intervene or help is made on the basis of self-interest. The tragedy of Rwanda was due in part to the feeling that it was a far-away country, and that happenings there were not so important to the West. From some perspectives, this is a matter that may have grown worse since the end of the Cold War because, while the international political climate was still a major determinant of international politics, wars were mostly proxy wars for the two major power blocs. With the end of the Cold War, the major powers have simply lost interest.

There also is controversy as to whether forceful intervention should always be subject to international law. While the legitimacy of the intervention in Kosovo is controversial, many would argue that international law as at present constituted should not be the final arbiter of human actions (see p. 201). For instance, interven-tion may be justified on humanitarian grounds if ethnic cleansing or mass killing is in progress or deemed to be imminent. But difficult judgements are involved in assessing the merits or the probable effec-tiveness of intervention in ending a catastrophic situation, and the damage that the use of force inevitably involves, including the damage to civilians. And, since the UN should be the final arbiter, every intervention without UN approval reduces the authority it can wield on future occasions.

Although in some cases the former colonial powers have continued to feel some responsibility for, as well as interest in, their former colonies, that is not enough. As one stage beyond that, the growing interdependence of nations requires a more extended view of self-interest, for conflict anywhere on the globe may have widespread repercussions. But even beyond that, it is necessary to establish an ethos in which the alleviation of suffering anywhere in the world is the responsibility of all. That this is an idealistic goal is no reason for us to turn our backs on it. In the words of the Secretary General of the United Nations, 'Humanity, after all, is indivisible.'

CONCLUSION

When other measures for preserving peace have failed, intervention may be necessary. The issues involved are complex. For intervention to be successful, early knowledge of the possibility of violent conflict is essential. Such knowledge is much more likely to be useful if it is shared with international organizations. Early interventionist diplomacy is the preferred course, but military intervention may be necessary: information of impending disaster may be of no use without the will and the means to act on it. Military intervention is more likely to be successful if resources are ready in advance.

Implementing preventive or ameliorative strategies may require extensive cooperation between states, and between NGOs and other organizations. Peacemaking involving mere compromises between the parties in conflict is often unsuccessful: it must be seen to be non-partisan. Intervention measures may have to continue after the conflict is resolved or violence has ceased, when peace-building measures will be necessary. Finally, the rebuilding of a stable state, or states, poses further problems that must be addressed.

Preventing war requires a supranational forum where grievances can be aired and disputes settled, and which can authorize intervention where necessary. The United Nations was set up to that end. The UN and its agencies have been successful in many contexts, but its activities have been handicapped by its internal structure, including the right of some countries to veto majority decisions, lack of adequate resources for forceful intervention where necessary, and an inadequate budget.

Eventually, a more effective body will have to be established to reflect the growing interdependence between nations and closer contacts between people all over the world. Some form of world governance will have to take over from the present United Nations Organization, with the military forces of individual states being replaced by an international police force.

16 Epilogue: Eliminating Conflict in the Nuclear Age

In this concluding chapter we go back to the issue that we raised in the Introduction: the creation of a war-free world. In this respect there has, in recent years, been a deterioration of the situation, with the prospects for ending the institution of war appearing less promising than a decade ago.

At the time of writing, in 2003, the general world situation is far from being a happy one; indeed, as far as the nuclear peril is concerned it is much worse than would have been expected 14 years after the end of the nuclear arms race. With the end of the Cold War, and the termination of the ideological divide between East and West, the imminent danger of a nuclear holocaust has diminished, but it has not gone away; and now it is on the rise again.

To a large extent this is a result of the policies of the only remaining superpower, the United States of America, particularly those of the George W. Bush administration. Since the end of the Cold War, there has been an awesome increase in the military strength of the USA. Making use of the latest advances in science and achievements in technology, and supported by astronomical budgets, the United States has become the greatest military power that ever existed, exceeding in military potential all other nations combined. And it shows every sign of intending to use this power to impose its policies on the rest of the world. Many see those policies as threatening the basic guidelines of a civilized society: morality in the conduct of world affairs and adherence to the rules of international law.

The Iraq war of 2003 was an illustration of these developments and a portent of the shape of things to come.

Soon after the end of the 1991 Gulf War, a group of hardliners began to advocate policies aimed at giving the USA political, economic, and military control of the Middle East. The overthrow of Saddam Hussein was part of that policy. After the controversial election of George W. Bush to the Presidency, these same people became the chief policy-makers, and immediately proceeded to implement their policies. The events of September 11 provided an

211

excuse for putting them into practice. The decision was made to invade Iraq, with or without approval by the Security Council, and it was pursued relentlessly. It was executed as soon as the necessary military force was assembled. Within a few weeks the objective was achieved: the Saddam Hussein regime collapsed with hardly any resistance.

The chief official reason for the invasion, the threat that the regime was said to present to the security of the world, including the United States, has proved to be unfounded. No weapons of mass destruction have been found in Iraq, by the time of writing. And no link with al-Qaeda terrorists, another alleged reason for the military action, has been established.

All the same, it would be hypocritical for those of us who were against the war, not to rejoice over the downfall of a tyrannical regime and not to admit that this would not have come so quickly without military intervention. But the price that has been paid is far too high: the reinstatement in world affairs of the old maxim that the ends justify the means.

For the time being the rule seems to be: might is right. Whatever the real feelings of the people may be, the governments of many countries may feel obliged to adopt a 'pragmatic' policy, acknowledge that there is now a single superpower, and accept the role of the United States as the world's policeman. But such a situation is intolerable.

Apart from weakening the basic guidelines of civilized society (morality and respect for international rules of law), with the United Nations being the immediate victim, a real danger to world security has arisen in relation to the nuclear issue, which has undergone a radical change (see Chapters 2 and 12).

In a reversal of the previous doctrine, whereby nuclear weapons have been viewed as weapons of last resort, the new Nuclear Posture Review spells out a strategy that incorporates nuclear capability into conventional war planning. Nuclear weapons have now become a standard part of military strategy, to be used in a conflict just like any other high explosive. It is a major and dangerous shift in the whole rationale for nuclear weapons.

The implementation of this policy has already begun. As we have described in the text, the United States is developing a new nuclear warhead of low yield, but with a shape that would give it a very high penetrating power into concrete. It is intended to destroy bunkers with thick concrete walls in which public enemies may seek shelter.

To give the military authorities confidence in the performance of the new weapon it will have to be tested. At present there is a treaty prohibiting the testing of nuclear weapons (except in sub-critical assemblies), the Comprehensive Test Ban Treaty, which the United States has signed but not ratified. Given the contempt that President Bush has shown for international treaties, he would need little excuse to authorize the testing of the new weapon.

If the USA resumed testing, this would be a signal to other nuclear weapon states to do the same. China would be almost certain to resume testing. After the US decision to develop ballistic missile defences, China feels vulnerable, and is likely to attempt to reduce its vulnerability by a modernization and build-up of its nuclear arsenal. Other states with nuclear weapons, such as India or Pakistan, might use the window of opportunity opened by the USA to update their arsenals. The danger of a new nuclear arms race is real.

The situation has become even more dangerous under the new National Security Strategy introduced by Bush in September 2002. 'To forestall or prevent ... hostile acts by our adversaries, the United States will, if necessary, act pre-emptively.' The new planning does not specifically refer to nuclear weapons, but in the light of the Nuclear Posture Review we have to conclude that the statement includes pre-emptive military strikes with nuclear weapons.

The danger of this policy can hardly be over-emphasized. If the militarily mightiest country declares its readiness to carry out a pre-emptive use of nuclear weapons, others may soon follow. The Kashmir crisis, in May 2002, is a stark warning of the reality of the nuclear peril.

India's declared policy is not to be the first to use nuclear weapons. But if the United States, whose nuclear policies are largely followed by India, makes the pre-emptive use of nuclear weapons a part of its doctrine, this would give India the legitimacy to carry out a pre-emptive strike against Pakistan. More likely is that Pakistan would strike first.

Taiwan presents another potential scenario for a pre-emptive nuclear strike by the United States. Should the Taiwan authorities decide to declare independence, this would inevitably result in an attempted military invasion by mainland China. The USA, which is committed to the defence of the integrity of Taiwan, may then opt for a pre-emptive strike.

Finally, we have the problem of North Korea, described by Bush as one of the 'axis of evil'. Under the Bush policy not to allow the

214 War No More

possession of weapons of mass destruction by any state considered to be hostile, North Korea will be called upon to close down the Yongbyon reprocessing facility and all other work on nuclear weapons. It is by no means certain that Kim Jong Il will submit to these demands and a critical situation may arise in that part of the world.

Altogether, the aggressive policy of the United States under the Bush administration has created a precarious situation in world affairs with a greatly increased danger of nuclear weapons being used in combat.

The only way to avert this danger is to eliminate nuclear weapons, in accordance with Article VI of the NPT – a treaty signed and ratified by the USA and to which it is thus legally bound.

The elimination of nuclear weapons is necessary to prevent an immediate danger, but in the long term it will not be sufficient to ensure the security of the human race. As we said in the Introduction, nuclear weapons cannot be disinvented.

Moreover, future advances in science may result in the invention of new means of mass destruction, perhaps even more powerful, perhaps more readily available. We already know about advances in biological warfare whereby gene manipulation could change some pathogens into terrifyingly virulent agents. But entirely different mechanisms might be developed. Just as we cannot predict the outcome of scientific research, we cannot predict the destructive potential of its military applications. All we can say is that the danger is real.

The threat of the extinction of the human race hangs over our heads like the Sword of Damocles. We cannot allow the miraculous products of billions of years of evolution to come to an end. We are beholden to our ancestors, to all the previous generations, for bequeathing to us the enormous cultural riches that we enjoy. It is our sacred duty to pass them on to future generations. The continuation of the human species must be ensured. We owe an allegiance to humanity.

As we said in the Introduction, to most people, the concept of a war-free world is a fanciful idea, a far-fetched, unrealizable vision.

The Cold War exposed us to graver risks than most would knowingly have accepted. The danger of nuclear devastation still looms, but threats stemming from new science are even more intractable.

Martin Rees, *Our Final Century* (2003)

Even those who have come to accept the concept of a world without nuclear weapons still reject the notion of a world without national armaments as unworkable.

Nevertheless, we *are* moving towards a war-free world, even if we do not do so consciously. We are learning the lessons of history. In the two world wars of the twentieth century, France and Germany were mortal enemies. Citizens of these (and many other) countries were slaughtered by the millions. But now a war between France and Germany seems inconceivable. The same applies to the other members of the European Union. There are still many disputes between them over a variety of issues, but these are being settled by negotiations, by mutual give-and-take. The members of the European Union have learned to solve their problems by means other than military confrontation.

The same is beginning to take place in other continents. As we have shown, military regimes are on the decline; more and more countries are becoming democracies. We gradually comprehend the futility of war, the utter waste in killing one another.

All the same, for the concept of a war-free world to become universally accepted, and for war to be made illegal, a process of education will be required at all levels: education for peace, education for world citizenship. We have to eradicate the culture in which we were brought up, the teaching that war is an inherent element of human society. We have to change the mind-set that seeks security for one's own nation in terms that spell insecurity to others.

This will require efforts in two directions: firstly, a new approach to security, in terms of global security; secondly, developing and nurturing of a new loyalty, a loyalty to humankind.

With regard to world security, the main problem will be preventing conventional wars between nations and the use of military arms by governments in settling internal disputes. This will require a limitation on the sovereignty of nations and a modification of the Charter of the United Nations, which is based on the notion of sovereign nation-states.

Surrender of sovereign rights is going on all the time, brought about by the ever increasing interdependence of nations in the modern world. Each international treaty we sign, every agreement on tariffs or other economic measures, is a surrender of sovereignty in the general interests of the world community. To this equation we must now add the protection of humankind.

It is a thorny problem but it has to be addressed. One of the main functions of the nation-state is to ensure the security of its citizens against threats from other states, which is taken to mean possessing the ability to wage war. A change will be called for in this respect: sovereignty will need to be separated from, and replaced by, autonomy. In particular, the ability of states to make war will have to be curtailed. This means no national military forces. The only legal coercive power on the world scale will have to be vested in some kind of police force responsible to a global authority. Some form of world governance, which respects local culture, seems a necessary step in the evolution of the United Nations.

As a way towards this we have to acquire a loyalty to humankind. As members of the human community, each of us has developed loyalties to the groups in which we live. In the course of history we have gradually extended our loyalty to ever larger groups – from our family, to our neighbourhood, to our village, to our city, to our nation. (We should emphasize that loyalty to a larger group is an addition to, not a replacement of, loyalties to the smaller groups.) At present the largest group is our nation. This is where our loyalty ends now. We submit that the time has come for a loyalty to another, still larger group: we have to develop and nurture a loyalty to humanity.

The prospects for developing a loyalty to humankind are becoming brighter due to the growing interdependence between nations, an interdependence not only in the realm of economics, but also in social and cultural areas. The interdependence is being brought about by the advances in science and technology, in particular, the progress in communications technology: the fantastic advances in transportation, communication and information that have occurred in the twentieth century.

Progress made in information technology is much slower in some countries than it is in others but it is still progress. Education – true education, as distinct from propaganda or indoctrination – is an irreversible process and can go in only one direction, towards a better world. This is why we see information technology as a beneficial factor for all, even if its advantages reach some nations faster than others.

Where is this going to lead us? A likely outcome of the widespread use of information technology will be the breaking down of national boundaries: communicating with one another anywhere in the world, people will begin to ignore geographic frontiers and divisions based on ethnicity or ideology. The role of the nation-state will gradually diminish. People will cease to see themselves primarily as subjects of a state; instead, their status as individuals will come to the fore; they will become world citizens, members of the species Man.

Such moves will no doubt be opposed by nationalistic rulers who will try to retain a hold on their subjects by restrictive legislation or oppressive measures; or by the multinationals, or the pan-technocrats, trying to maintain their strangleholds. But these attempts must be defeated. Notwithstanding current US policies, the trends over the past few decades have been towards strengthening democratic values and compliance with international laws. We see it in the setting up of international courts, such as the International Criminal Court, with jurisdiction taking precedence over national laws. We see it also in the ever increasing respect for the rights of the individual, in accordance with the Universal Declaration of Human Rights.

Eventually, this may lead to some form of world governance and the delegitimization of the institution of war. In the era of science and technology in which we now live, this is the only way to ensure the continuing existence of the human species and the enhancement of civilization.

In summary, the applications of science and technology, both the negative and the positive, have created the need and the opportunity to foster world citizenship. There is the need for a new educational process that teaches loyalty to humankind; the need to preserve the human species and the continuation of our civilization.

In the course of many thousands of years, the human species has established a great civilization; it has developed rich and multifarious cultures; it has accumulated enormous treasures in arts and literature; and it has created the magnificent edifice of science. It is indeed the supreme irony that the very intellectual achievements of humankind have provided the tools of self-destruction, in a social system ready to contemplate such destruction.

Surely, we must not allow this to happen. As human beings it is our paramount duty to preserve human life, to ensure the continuity of the human race.

As we said, a nuclear holocaust does not appear imminent. Having come close on several occasions during the Cold War, we are now somewhat more cautious. But war is still a recognized social institution and every war carries with it the potential of escalation with fatal consequences for our species. In a world armed with weapons of mass destruction, the use of which might bring the whole of civilization to an end, we cannot afford a polarized community, with its inherent threat of military confrontations. In this nuclear age, an equitable global community, to which we all belong as world citizens, has become a vital necessity.

Abbreviations and Acronyms

ABM	Anti-Ballistic Missile (Treaty)
ANC	African National Congress
BCE	Before the Christian Era
BWC	Biological Weapons Convention
CARE	Cooperative for Assistance and Relief Everywhere
CE	Christian Era
CIA	Central Intelligence Agency
CISAC	Committee on International Security and Arms Control
CTBT	Comprehensive Test Ban Treaty
CWC	Chemical Weapons Convention
EU	European Union
GPS	Global Positioning System
GW	gigawatt
ICBM	inter-continental ballistic missile
INF	Intermediate-Range Nuclear Forces (Treaty)
IRA	Irish Republican Army
MIRV	Multiple Independently-Targetable Re-entry Vehicles
NATO	North Atlantic Treaty Organization
NGO	Non-Governmental Organization
NPR	Nuclear Posture Review
NPT	Nuclear Non-Proliferation Treaty
NWFW	nuclear-weapon-free world
NWFZ	nuclear-weapon-free zone
OPCW	Organization for the Prohibition of Chemical Weapons
OSCE	Organization for Security and Cooperation in Europe
PTBT	Partial Test Ban Treaty
SALT	Strategic Arms Limitation Talks
SDI	Strategic Defense Initiative
SIPRI	Stockholm International Peace Research Institute
SLBM	submarine-launched ballistic missile
SORT	Strategic Offensive Reductions Treaty
START	Strategic Arms Reduction Treaty
UNESCO	United Nations Educational, Scientific and Cultural Organization
UNICEF	United Nations Children's Fund
WHO	World Health Organization
WMD	weapons of mass destruction

Suggested Further Reading

This list contains titles that may be of interest to the reader. Their inclusion does not indicate that we agree with all that is in them.

Bird, K. and Lifschultz L. (eds), *Hiroshima's Shadow* (Connecticut: Pamphleteer's Press. 1998)

Boutwell, J. (ed.), 'Intervention, Sovereignty and International Security', *Pugwash Occasional Papers, 1:1* (Cambridge, MA: Pugwash, 2000)

Boutwell, J., Hinde, R.A. and Rotblat, J. (eds), 'Eliminating the Causes of War', *Pugwash Occasional Papers, 2:3* (Cambridge, MA: Pugwash, 2001)

Bruce, M. and Milne T. (eds), *Ending War: The Force of Reason* (London: Macmillan, 1999)

Canberra Commission on the Elimination of Nuclear Weapons, *Report of the Canberra Commission* (Canberra: Department of Foreign Affairs and Trade, August 1996)

Carnegie Commission on Preventing Deadly Conflict, *Preventing Deadly Conflict: Final Report* (Washington DC: Carnegie Commission on Preventing Deadly Conflict, 1997)

Cooley, J.K., *Unholy Wars: Afghanistan, America and International Terrorism* (London: Pluto Press, 2000)

Elworthy, S. and Ingram, P. (eds), 'International Control of the Arms Trade', *Current Decisions Report, 8* (Oxford: Oxford Research Group, 1992)

Evangelista, M., *Unarmed Forces* (Ithaca, NY: Cornell University Press, 1999)

Fussell, P., *The Great War and Modern Memory* (London: Oxford University Press, 1975)

Garwin, R.L. and Charpak, G., *Megawatts and Megatons* (New York: Knopf, 2001)

Grisolia, J.S., *et al.* (ed.), *Violence: From Biology to Society* (Amsterdam: Elsevier, 1996)

Guibernau, M., *Nationalisms: The Nation-State and Nationalism in the Twentieth Century* (Cambridge: Polity, 1996)

Hinde, R.A. (ed.), *The Institution of War* (Basingstoke: Macmillan Academic, 1991)

Hinde, R.A. and Parry, D. (eds), *Education for Peace* (Nottingham: Spokesman, 1989)

Hinde, R.A. and Watson H. (eds), *War: A Cruel Necessity?* (London: Tauris, 1995)

Howard, M., *The Causes of Wars* (London: Temple Smith, 1983)

Keegan, J., *A History of Warfare* (London: Hutchinson, 1993)

Laqueur, W., *The New Terrorism: Fanaticism and the Arms of Mass Destruction* (London: Phoenix Press, 1999).

Marshall, S.L.A., *Men Against Fire* (New York: Morrow, 1947)

Mosse, G.L., *Fallen Soldiers* (New York: Oxford University Press, 1990)

Rees, M., *Our Final Century* (London: Heinemann, 2003)

Rhodes, R., *The Making of the Atomic Bomb* (New York: Simon & Schuster, 1986)

Rhodes, R., *Dark Sun: The Making of the Hydrogen Bomb* (New York, Simon & Schuster, 1995)

Rotblat, J., Steinberger, J. and Udgaonkar B. (eds), *A Nuclear-Weapon-Free World: Desirable? Feasible?* (Boulder: Westview Press, 1993)

Royal Society, *Measures for Controlling the Threat from Biological Weapons* (London: Royal Society, 2000)

Sherif, M., *Group Conflict and Cooperation* (London: Routledge, 1966)

Solomon, H. and Turton, A. (eds), *Water Wars: Enduring Myth or Impending Reality?* (Pretoria: Accord, 2000)

Taipale, Ilkka (ed.) *War or Health* (Capetown: NAE, 2002)

Tetlock, P.E., Husbands, J.L., Jervis, R., Stern, P.C. and Tilly, C. (eds), *Behavior, Society, and International Conflict* (New York: Oxford University Press, 1989, 1991, 1993)

Thompson, H.O., *World Religions in War and Peace* (London: McFarland, 1988)

Turner, J.C. *et al.*, *Rediscovering the Social Group: A Self-Categorisation Theory* (Oxford: Blackwell, 1987)

Wright, Q., *A Study of War* (Chicago: Chicago University Press, 1966)

Index

Organization for the Prohibition of
Chemical Weapons, 160
Oslo Agreement, 188
OXFAM, 187
Ottawa Convention, 165

Pacifism, 42–3, 76
Pakistan, 16, 78, 163
see also India *vs* Pakistan;
Kashmir
Patriotism and Nationalism, 76, 80,
111–12, 113–14
Peace Corps, 175
Peaceful Societies, 68–9
Phillipines, 85
Pinochet, Augusto, 191
Poland, 53
Political leaders, 56–61
Dependence on population
support, 59
Financial interests, 60
Group influences on 57–9
Industrial influences on, 60
Outside influences on, 60
Personal concerns, 58
see also individual leaders
Population growth, 83, 86–7, 169
Portugal, 87
Poverty, 86, 94–100, 169–71
Propaganda, 73–4, 77–8, 111–14
Protestant *vs* Catholic, 73, 76–7, 98
Pugwash, 157–8, 188–90
Putin, Vladimir, 151

Radiological warfare (dirty bombs),
35
Reagan, Ronald, 29, 127, 153–4
Religion, 75–9
Regional groups, 86–7; 199
see also NATO
Religious groups, 190–1
Republic of South Africa, 61, 71, 87,
140–1, 203
and Nuclear weapons, 149
Gun-free zone, 160
Resources, as a cause of war, 83–8
see also Environment
Retribution (Revenge), 80–1
Romania, 132

Romero, Archbishop Oscar, 11
Russell–Einstein Manifesto, 189
Russia, 62, 147, 155, 199
see also USSR
Rwanda, 13, 39, 72, 74, 104, 143,
146
Failed intervention, 183, 194–5,
209
Rwandan Patriotic National Front,
195

Sadam Hussein, 50, 114, 136,
211–12
Sakharov, Andrei, 25
Saudi Arabia, 50, 84, 131
Saxony, 65
Secession, *see* Autonomy
September the 11th, 11, 17, 36, 39,
41, 78–9, 81–2, 98–9, 131, 167,
211
Sierra Leone, 85, 180, 194, 198
Sikh, 65
Solidarity Movement, 191
Somalia, 64, 195, 202
South Africa, *see* Republic of South
Africa
Southern Africa Development
Community Task Force, 203
Sovereignty, *see* Nation-state
Spain, 87
Sri Lanka, 64, 72, 88, 163
Stalin, 55
Star Wars; *see* Treaty, Anti-ballistic
Missile
Stimson Center, 158
Strategic Defense Initiative (Star
Wars), 29, 153
Sudan, 87, 190
Suez, 78
Suicide bombers, 41, 66, 77, 106,
142
Sweden, 111, 149
Switzerland, 65
Syria, 87

Taiwan, 213
Tajikistan, 194
Taliban; *see* Afghanistan
Teller, Edward, 23, 25, 153